REFUGEES SOUTH OF THE SAHARA
AN AFRICAN DILEMMA

CONTRIBUTIONS IN AFRO-AMERICAN
AND AFRICAN STUDIES

REFUGEES
SOUTH
OF THE
SAHARA

AN AFRICAN DILEMMA

EDITORS:

HUGH C. BROOKS
St. John's University, New York
YASSIN EL-AYOUTY
St. John's University, New York

NEGRO UNIVERSITIES PRESS
WESTPORT, CONNECTICUT

2-14-95

Copyright © 1970 by Negro Universities Press

Library of Congress Catalog Card Number: 71-105994

SBN: 8371-3324-6

Negro Universities Press
51 Riverside Avenue, Westport, Conn. 06880

Printed in the United States of America

Designed by Verne Bowman of Publishers Graphics

CONTENTS

PART III

ASPECTS OF NATIONAL AND
INTERNATIONAL AID

APPENDIXES

FOREWORD

I should like to pay tribute to St. John's University and to the two editors, Dr. Brooks and Dr. El-Ayouty, for their initiative in highlighting the plight of refugees in Africa through the publication of this book. It will acquaint not only academic circles but also the general public with a problem which deserves to be more widely known.

The problems of African refugees can be looked at not only from the historical and political point of view, but also in their economic, social, legal and humanitarian aspects. It is these aspects alone which are of concern to the High Commissioner for Refugees. According to the statute of his office, it is not his task to ascertain the fundamental reasons for the troubles or conflicts which bring about refugee situations, but, rather, to seek a remedy for the problems to which these situations give rise. These remedies should be of a durable nature and should enable refugees, in cases where they are unwilling or unable to return to their homes, to take an active part in the economic and social development of the country which has accepted them. The remedies should also continue to the point where they decide to cease to be refugees by acquiring a new nationality.

It is to this eminently constructive and humanitarian task that my office devotes itself. Experience has proved that by so doing, it also contributes to the areas involved an element of stability and of peace which is undoubtedly in keeping with the present needs and desires of the African people. Such an objective is one to which the youth of today, in their search for humanity and justice in a better world, can certainly subscribe.

SADRUDDIN AGA KHAN
United Nations High Commissioner for Refugees
Geneva, 16 July 1969

ix

INTRODUCTION

Most of us are continually inundated by statistics—hundreds flee; thousands made homeless; two hundred thousand forced to move. Numbers mount on numbers until the mind can no longer comprehend the human tragedy behind them.

Africa now has more than one million refugees out of a population of 325 million, a statistic most people read and quickly pass over. What they do not realize is that it means that one of every two hundred and fifty Africans is a refugee. What does this statistic represent in terms of broken homes, human suffering, anxieties, and fears? It is an entirely new dilemma for the new continent of Africa. Every man is born in one certain country where he is at home with the smell of the soil and the feel of the wind. There his soul is free; there he will live and die unless forced to move. Most continents have their share of refugees—they have existed as long as mankind. But the vast numbers of refugees that Africa must deal with today is a relatively recent phenomenon. Intranational cooperative efforts to deal with this problem are certainly of recent development. The Office of the United Nations High Commissioner for Refugees (HCR), for example, began its African operations in the Congo in 1960 and then in Algeria in 1961.

Refugees are usually defined as those who seek shelter or protection from danger or disease. What compels a man to leave his birthplace? Men are often forced from their homes for political or social reasons, and refugees have symbolized this human dispossession from man's beginnings when Adam and Eve were driven from the Garden of Eden. The Jews have suffered one diaspora after another throughout their long history. In fact, in the tumultuous history of mankind, movement appears as the one constant. Generally, man's movement would appear to be governed by the prospect of economic improvement rather than the need for space. Witness the crowded conditions of cities all over the world and the attraction of people from the country to urban centers. Today, in nearly every country in the world, man feels he will fare better in the cities, which is not to say that he will actually live better. He often finds less freedom than in the country as living costs, including rent and food, place a greater burden on his time and energies. By their very nature, cities force men into new and different forms of livelihood. In the city few men are truly economically free. Whether in the slums of an African city or in Shaker Heights, Ohio, most men must work for a living.

This group of papers examines various aspects of the modern refugee problem, particularly those of African countries whose refugee numbers have swelled since independence was granted after World War II. It is not the intention of the author to more than touch on the history of traditional intratribal warfare. These conflicts drove weaker groups from their customary areas; those groups in turn often displaced still other groups. So it continued until the even more poorly organized people, like the Pygmy and the Bushman, were pushed into some of the world's most uninhabitable areas.

These papers, presented at a St. John's University symposium held in November 1967, deal with this new phenomenon brought into being by a multitude of factors including nationalism, economic transformations, the problems of nation-building, and tribal and frontier issues. The topics discussed in these papers include not only the economic and social aspects, but also the political, constitutional, and juridical issues related to the dilemma of the African refugee.

These newly independent countries, now in the process of building a nation, are trying to teach their people to think as a national unit instead of the traditional family, clan, or tribe. Nowhere in Africa is this process or goal near completion.

Egypt, that most ancient of civilizations, had a national government. Afterwards within Africa, there came a long line of empires, kingdoms, and regional governments from Kush to Ghana and Mali, from the Buganda to the Ashanti. Yet, today most of these nations are not the outgrowth of these ancient indigenous units but, instead, of the colonial period.

Before 1885 there was no Nigeria, no Congo, no Zambia. The borders of these nations are to large extent the results of inter-European rivalries and agreements made in Europe. Britain dreamed of a "Cape-to-Cairo" network of countries, while France struggled for trans-Sahara control. The result was a series of arbitrary borders, often straight lines, plotted from a T-square in the meeting rooms of Europe with no correlation to physical geography. Since World War II these nations have become independent and they have had to be content to try to develop within these borders. Because they were created by European powers, a great amount of data has become available to African politicians, and even to Europeans, showing the mistakes of these borders; but today it is nearly impossible to change them.

With independence, a nation will strive to institute citizenship and passports. Borders created by the European powers—most of them after 1965—and still today not completely defined, may suddenly take on meaning to a new government. It has often been said that one of Africa's greatest attributes is its ability to adjust; for years borders established after the Treaty of Berlin were completely ignored by Africans living near them. Not so today. If necessary, nationals are hired to police the borders to enfore strict conformity to the new rules. The borders of Ghana, Tanzania or Lesotho, for example, abruptly become sacrosanct. Foreigners must be kept out to protect the employment of the local work force; taxes must be collected to ensure the provision of governmental and social services.

By further definition, refugees are those who cross one of these borders to seek safety and asylum in another region. They generally look for areas where they can follow, as closely as possible, the way of life they have always known. Those who are actually fleeing a given way of life are a distinct minority in Africa and are not within the scope of this book.

There are many types of refugees. But, for the most part, African refugees are considered to be the products of political, insurrectional, or military action. They have fled because of insecurity in an area or because a government at some point in the many stages of nation-building has forced them to flee. In 1945 there were but two independent African nations; today there are forty-two independent nations with only five or six still under direct or indirect European or colonial rule (which in the eyes of world opinion means "not free").

Politicians have become aware that natural geographic regions were arbitrarily divided; that clans and tribes were split; that, in short, the African nations inherited absurd borders—so absurd that they resist changing them for fear of opening Pandora's box. Periodically, a national unit is tempted to enlarge itself at the expense of its neighbors—an age-old practice everywhere in the world. The border lines that appear on a map delineating a nation's territory are, in many parts of the continent, simply nonexistent. During past colonial rule, the African has shown almost complete disregard for political borders, but the newly independent African states feel obliged to change this. Borders must be protected. Algeria and Morocco have fought pitched battles over their ill-defined border; Kenya and Somalia have only recently agreed to stop fighting over an ill-defined and, to the local inhabitants, nonexistent border. The Ethiopian-Somali border is another area of continual strife. People living in these areas of conflict want for the most part only to be left to continue their own way of life; grazing, oasis farming, or whatever. There is no conflict between them and their neighbors who also follow a traditional way of life. Nevertheless, central governments may choose such an area as the focal point of an argument, with the result that the inhabitants are forced to flee, and thus become refugees.

Political instability is another factor contributing to the growing numbers of refugees. New nations striving for national unity are beset by insecurities. The trend toward military rule in so many of the countries is one evidence of this instability. Sometimes, almost all vestiges of the old colonial form of control disappear, but new patterns take time to become effective. The most spectacular example in postwar Africa was the almost total collapse of the Congolese government immediately after independence in 1960. What could be called a civil war broke out in several parts of the country and, in spite of massive U.N. help and international assistance, the country has still not totally regained its economic strength. During this crisis, people naturally fled to the surrounding countryside.

To clans and family units who have disregarded vague, ill-defined borders for the past seventy-five years, economic development can suddenly become a hardship. They are often forced to cut all ties with people of their own blood, as new economic considerations come into play. For example, since the development of the copper industry in Zambia, Africans from Angola and Malawi as well as Rhodesia frequently migrate to these regions to seek employment. Well-trained businessmen from the Cameroons, Dahomey, and Nigeria, to mention only a few, often seek employment outside their own countries when there are not enough jobs available. For centuries, fishermen from Ghana have lived in various west coast regions, returning to their homeland only after a period of years. With the postwar attempts at creating a national identity, this mobility and these activities are often curtailed.

Borders have been reinforced and patrols and customs officials added to border crossings, with the net result that farmers may be forced to choose between one political-economic system and another. People have moved to another country only for the sake of better economic conditions. They are not refugees in the political sense, but that is their very real condition in terms of the cutting of old ties and the building of new.

To most of us in the developed world, it is simply the lure of economic opportunity elsewhere that prompts us to move. Every developed country suffers *and* benefits from man's internal migrations. In the United States, young men from the South or West move into the New York area; in Sweden young men move from the north to Stockholm or the more developed south; in the United Kingdom, Scotch, Welsh, and Irish move to the industrial cities of England. In an underdeveloped nation where the vast majority of the people are subsistence farmers, the economic motivation is not nearly so strong. Yet, in many cases, economics outweigh political motivation. For example, in South Africa, when we speak of a refugee, we generally refer to a man fleeing the political system's apartheid—despite reasonable economic conditions—to seek asylum in a neighboring country where his economic prospects are bleak. There are, however, for each refugee that flees, probably a thousand Africans who are recruited to enter the republic legally or illegally to work in the mines or to avail themselves of higher wages.

Excluding the economic refugee, the majority of people termed refugees today, are those who have left because of political frustration, discontent, or specific acts of a government in the process of what is now broadly called nation-building.

Most of us assume that men want to be free. Yet, in many cases, freedom seems to be a *negative* word. It may be easier to find freedom "from" certain oppressive conditions than to find freedom "for" a good life. Roosevelt and Churchill declaimed the Four Freedoms in the Atlantic Charter in the early 1940s: Freedom of Speech, Freedom of Religion, Freedom from Fear, and Freedom from Want. This, of course, was during the Allies' darkest period of World War II and served as a very stirring proclamation in place of news from the battlefront. As the fortunes of war changed, so did the Allies' concept of freedom.

Freedom, as its terms were understood by the Europeans, was not really meant to include the colonies. Freedom was not meant to apply to the Nigerian or Kenyan. The Allied leaders probably did not expect freedom to encompass the common man in Africa. But a great number of people in the world took this charter to heart—they worked for it and they used it to help achieve their goals.

In the postwar period the Charter was held up as a goal for the developing world. Since 1945, the majority of the peoples in this world have gained their freedom (at least politically) from colonial powers. Yet, during this time, we have witnessed a rapid growth of the "unfree"—the refugees.

The growth of nationalism and various ideologies has created a whole group of people who are no longer free to live where they please or to act as they want.

Today's world opinion favors independent nations and the freedom of *all* citizens; at least that is what is professed. To aid those people who are not at present free, many international, national, and social organizations have been set up. Most African states adhere to the 1951 Convention on Refugees. This Convention limited the freedom of the refugee, the host country, and the country of origin as to the future actions each might take. While it was designed for European refugees after World War II, its basic philosophy is valid in the 1960s in Africa, and is dealt with in several of these chapters.

A man does not have to be formally educated to know that he wants to live with his family; to decide where he wants to live—which may not be where an official tells him to live, to move about freely and not require a pass; to earn a decent wage; to be free to work for the employer of his choice for as long as he wants;

and, finally, to be ruled by those he wants to be ruled by and not by those who rule him because they have more guns than he has.[1] It is a hazardous gamble for the refugee fleeing from one country to another in search of the "Four Freedoms." He is often willing to give up the freedom of a familiar way of life for what he hopes will be greater freedom. At best he will achieve his goal of political freedom, in exchange for self-exile. At the worst, he gives up his homeland and gains nothing.

To study this African dilemma, the St. John's University Symposium of 1967 brought together a group of people from around the world to contribute their knowledge on the subject. Scholars from all continents with the exception of Asia were involved in these discussions. As is generally the case in such conferences, few specific answers to the problems were reached. It is hoped, however, that through further discussion and study, specific answers to specific problems may be achieved.

One positive omen is that the U.N. General Assembly decided in 1968 to extend the Office of the United Nations High Commissioner for Refugees for five years, beginning January 1969. This expression of the great need for an agency functioning on a global basis for the protection of the refugee and his eventual settlement stressed the two aspects of "protection" and "assistance." In practice the High Commissioner's Office carries out its mandate in various directions. It facilitates repatriation, local integration, and resettlement on a voluntary basis for the refugees who come within its jurisdiction. The renewal of this HCR mandate is all the more significant in view of the ever-increasing number of refugees in Africa.

It is indeed with appreciation that we welcome the foreword written for this book by His Highness, Prince Sadruddin Aga Khan, the U.N. High Commissioner for Refugees, who has also contributed a chapter on the work of his organization.

Moreover, the U.N. General Assembly in 1968 urged all States to lend their support to the humanitarian task of HCR and invited them to accede to the 1951 Convention Relating to the Status of Refugees and to the 1967 Protocol to the Convention. These important documents, reflective of the deep concern of the international community for the plight of the refugee, whether in Africa or elsewhere, are reproduced in the Appendixes to this book.

It is the editors' and contributors' hope that this book will not only stimulate the interest of scholars and policy makers alike in the plight of refugees in Africa, but will also help to provide insights into the factors giving rise to refugee situations elsewhere. If our world is to be one of conflict and consequently one which is liable to continually create refugee situations, we must evolve better approaches and mechanisms for meeting the problems of the uprooted.

HUGH C. BROOKS
YASSIN EL-AYOUTY
New York
July 1969

NOTES

1. From Toivo Hermann ja Toivo's statement delivered at the trial of thirty-seven South West Africans in a Pretoria, South Africa, courtroom.

PART I

HISTORICAL, POLITICAL, LEGAL, AND HUMANITARIAN PERSPECTIVES

HISTORICAL BACKGROUND OF THE AFRICAN REFUGEE PROBLEM   1

JOHN HATCH, The New Statesman, London

I am sure you are all aware of the many benefits which have been brought by refugees to their various countries of asylum. This applies throughout the world, not least to your own country. In the United States you have, of course, some distinguished African refugees—people like A. C. Jordan, whom I first knew in Capetown University seventeen years ago, and who has now been in your country for some years introducing African languages. I would also recall Leslie Rubin, who is now at Howard University, and whom I also knew in South Africa many years ago when he was a senator in that country. In most of your African programs over here you have been accustomed to welcoming refugees from various African states. We in Britain also have a long heritage of receiving refugees who have made a distinguished contribution to our national life. I should mention that the two chief economic advisors to Harold Wilson are both refugees from central Europe.

The President of this University opened this session by urging us to seek solutions for this great problem. I am sure that this is the central purpose of the present symposium; but it is not my function at this moment. I am not looking for solutions. The contribution I offer you is an attempt to paint the back cloth which I hope will supply you with an understanding before which you can seek your solutions. I believe that in a symposium of this nature it is important first to understand the character of those societies out of which the refugee problems have arisen. Being principally a historian, I conceive it to be my function to provide some understanding of the development of African societies so that the refugee problem can be considered in its context, rather than as an isolated phenomenon of the present age.

What I shall try to do, therefore, is to evaluate the European impact on Africa during the last four or five centuries, leading to a situation in which, today, hundreds of thousands of refugees present a great human problem to those of us who feel responsible in that continent.

I want to begin by suggesting that it will be convenient to divide the refugee problem into two broad categories. The first applies to those refugees from African-governed countries, from the newly independent states of Africa. The second includes refugees from the white-governed states, mainly of southern Africa. This is convenient, not only because it allows us to divide this vast problem into two parts, but also because the circumstances which create the refugee problem in these two separate situations are somewhat different.

Some of us, I suppose, can ourselves claim to be refugees from countries which have declared us prohibited immigrants. There is, however, a difference in the circumstances which create the problem of refugees from countries like Rwanda and Burundi and the Congo, and now from West Africa, from conditions which have created the refugee problems, over a longer period, in South Africa, South West Africa, Angola, Mozambique, Portugese Guinea, and Rhodesia.

Let us look first at the causes of the refugee problem in the African-governed states. These can be divided into three groups. First, for some years and as an outgrowth of political conflict, we have seen a trickle from countries like Ghana, Nigeria, the French-speaking states of west and central Africa. This trickle of refugees, including some of the best minds, has been directed towards Europe, America or to other African states. It was composed of people not prepared to accept the political conditions of a specific regime. There have been political conflicts which have led some members of these states to leave the country and go into voluntary exile or, on rare occasions, to be expelled by such regimes. Second, there have been various economic and social tensions within the new African states, inevitable in the early years of independence, inevitable perhaps to the character of the modern world. These economic and social tensions have led to various forms of discontent, to the inability of some people to find the kind of work, the kind of social life, or the kind of status at which they were aiming. Such people have, therefore, moved to other countries, either in Africa or overseas. Third, and, unfortunately, not least important to the contemporary scene, there have been tribal hostilities. Such hostilities have arisen between communities which, for want of a better word, we can call "tribes". Although it is a much abused noun, it is perhaps less clumsy than constantly referring to "communities". These are conflicts between sets of people who feel that they have a particular allegiance, a special form of security, common traditions, and a home within the structure of a particular society. On occasion, hostilities develop between such a community and its neighbors. We have seen this clearly in the unhappy history of Nigeria, not just over the past few years, but over a period of many years. It has erupted into tragic loss of life, property and security since the beginning of 1966. We have seen similar tragedies in the Congo. It is, I think, a common characteristic of mankind that, when an individual or a family is threatened, when society becomes unstable and insecure, a natural reaction is to return to where security subconsciously appears most certain. In Africa, that is normally to be found in the tribal community. Thus, since the troubles, violence, and disturbances in the Congo have grown since 1960, there has been a widespread return to the tribe. From that return, increased hostility between tribal communities has developed. This, in turn, has led to the growth of the refugee problem, some people leaving the area of hostility, some fleeing to other countries like Congo Brazzaville, Burundi, Rwanda, Zambia, and so on.

These then seem to me to be the three main categories with which we should deal in looking at the causes of the refugee problem in so far as African-governed states are concerned.

Next, let us seek the main roots of the refugee problem in those countries in the southern tip of the continent, where white minorities control the governments. Again, the causes can be conveniently divided into three categories. First, there are those who reject the ideology sometimes callel "apartheid," sometimes "separate development," and often "white supremacy." This ideology is rejected by many Africans, Asians, Coloreds, and by some Europeans. Consequently, one finds in America, in Europe, and in various parts of Africa, refugees from South Africa. Many of them have been forced to make the choice between becoming permanent refugees by leaving their country for good, or remaining at home under various forms of disability laid down by the state.

The case of Helen Joseph is a typical example. She had been restricted to her own house under a form of house arrest for five years. The instant that this five-year ban expired, it was cruelly extended for yet another five years. Here is a woman over sixty years of age who has spent the last five years in virtual isolation, unable to meet her friends, prevented from leaving her home area, prohibited from leaving her house at all after dark. She is now condemned to another such period of five years, with no reason to suppose that this restricted existence will not be indefinitely maintained. Then, there are those who are in detention, a detention again that can be indefinitely extended. The only option which those who refuse to accept the ideology of apartheid can take, is to leave the country permanently, despite the fact that it is their country. If they leave it without the permission of the government, they know that they will not be allowed back. One finds many such people, often some of the best brains of the country, of all colored skins, now residing outside their unhappy homeland. Contributing to our program here is one of the best known Africans, one of the best South African minds, irrespective of color. He is Professor Matthews who has been in voluntary exile for many years.

Second, there are those who actively escaped, who were not given the choice of becoming voluntary refugees, but who fled through one of the various escape routes that some of us have been trying to keep open for many years. From South Africa, Rhodesia, South West Africa and the Portugese territories, fugitives have been finding their way to various other African countries, to Europe, here to the United States. Dar-es-Salaam is full of them; Lusaka has many of them; they are found in the cities of West Africa, in Cairo, Paris, London, and in American cities. Here are men and women who, because of their protest, because of their criticism of white minority regimes, have come under the lash of white supremacist laws and have escaped rather than submit themselves to incarceration for five years, ten years, or, in some cases, for life. They have managed to get out ahead of their police pursuers and find other means of employing their talents outside of South Africa.

Third, and by no means least important, there are those unable to reconcile their concept of life with the atmosphere of racial discrimination which is an essential part of all white supremacist regimes. Those teachers, artists, writers, doctors, lawyers, artisans and craftsmen who cannot reconcile their view of the way in which their individual lives should be lived with the environment of racial discrimination, leave their country voluntarily, without deliberate coercion, to seek a different environment. They are not the least important refugees who have left the southern states of the African continent.

Having outlined what seems to me the basic roots from which the refugee problem arises, I want to address myself to an examination of the degree to which the colonial legacy has created circumstances in which the refugee problem has grown to such magnitude. First, we must examine the major consequences of the European impact on African life.

I do not think that enough attention has yet been paid to the effect within African society itself of the influence of contact with the European world. This goes right back to the days of the 15th century when the first of the Europeans, the Portugese, came into serious contact with Africans. We are accustomed to reading in modern history about the activities of the Portugese explorers, of Henry the Navigator and his followers, and the manner in which Europeans made contact with the West African coast as far south as the River Congo. We are also told something about the activities of other European explorers, travelers, and merchants. What we have not yet been told—and it is time that some of us concerned with African history seriously examined this—is the effect which this contact with the European economy had within African society. I propose to make a few generalizations, at least in order to stimulate argument about the subject, because it seems to me that one cannot begin to understand the character of modern African life without examining the influences which have produced these particular forms of society. For it is within these societies, and from the historical influences which have affected them, that the tensions and conflicts producing the refugee problems have grown.

Much attention has been paid—and rightly so—to the effect of the slave trade on African life. But, usually this examination has been superficial, dwelling mainly on the depopulation of African society as a result of the removal of many millions of their people. The estimates of numbers vary from as little as 15 million to as many as 50 million during the 300 years in which the slave trade flourished. It seems to me that the effects of depopulation were of less significance to African society than other aspects of European economic influence. Let me elaborate on this conclusion.

At first, the effect of European legitimate trading with the West Africans produced the normal kind of impact seen when Europeans traded with each other around the Mediterranean basin, the Middle East or anywhere else. Within a short period, trade was stimulated, thought provoked, production expanded. The unique impact of European economy on West Africa came with the change from legitimate trading to slave trading, from the effect of using the human being as a commodity and exchanging that human being for the commodities of Europe.

At the time that the Europeans first made contact with the peoples of West Africa, it is a fairly reasonable generalization to suggest that the development of some parts of African society were roughly parallel to those of Europe. There were certain areas in Africa like Timbuktu, Sofala on the east coast and a number of similar socioeconomic centers which could be compared as being in the same league with Venice and Genoa. There were many other areas which could be roughly compared with the more backward parts of medieval Europe. Some societies in Africa were less developed than parts of Europe. Others were at a higher stage of development. We know something, at least from the time of the first millenium onwards, from the years of the great Ghanan empire, of clothes manufactured in Ghana, Mali, Songhai, in the Hausa states, around the Congo delta, and in Benin. We are able to read firsthand accounts of flourishing textile industries, metal craft, mining, and tropical agriculture—techniques, incidentally, contributed by slaves on this side of the Atlantic. We can trace the rise of crafts and arts of the Nok culture back from days before the period of Christ, and an artistic continuity from Nok to Benin and Ife.

At the first stage, therefore, two parallel and comparable cultures came into contact with each other. Now what happened? Here I return to the paramount and crucial effect of the slave trade. Because, for three-hundred years African society right down the west coast concentrated on collecting and delivering human beings as its major commodity, and receiving in exchange firearms and manufactured goods, metalware, hardware and cloth from Europe, the whole of the social and economic development of African society was stunted. It was retarded because just at the time that Europeans were growing out of their similar handicrafts into cottage industries, leading to the great industrial complexes of the nineteenth century, African society became obsessed with warfare for the purpose of capturing prisoners. It was beset by the insecurity created by war, with the growing habit of expelling members from societies to be picked up as slaves, and with a concentration on the use of the human commodity as a major source of wealth. One may presume that, left in peace, African society might well have progressed in parallel, if not identical, lines, based on specific African needs with Europe. It would seem natural for it to have developed from its earlier foundation of crafts and skills to more effective productive methods. But, at the same time that the demand for slaves undermined the economic life of African society, the European slave traders were bringing to the continent precisely those products—like cloth and metalware—which effectively stunted the growth of African manufacturers and the development of African industry.

This seems to me to be the major impact of the initial European contact on African society. Yet, it goes deeper than this, into the whole field of African political and social structures. In a period of warfare, insecurity, obsession with the human commodity, the power of authority was greatly increased. What had been a rough means of checks and balances between authority, bureaucracy, and the mass of people within each African society, was perceptively channelled into increasing degrees of authoritarianism. At the same time, a wide variety of the smaller and weaker African societies were broken up before the rapid expansion in the more powerful Oyo, Benin, and Hausa states, with, later, the Fulani taking over control of the Hausa states. The whole of this process saw a shift of power towards those commercial routes supplying the slave trade. It ignored the constructive social, viable aspects of production. This afforded a watershed, in the development of African society, of its economic and political growth. If there were time, we could trace a similar course during this period in both east and central Africa.

The period of the slave trade, of the stunting of economic and social growth, and the distortion of political development, was immediately followed by a short period of frank commercialism. Palm oil now took the place of slaves as the main commodity. The Niger delta became something like another Barbary Coast. Feuding and warring spread between small merchant groups for the sale of palm oil or the illegal continuation of slaving. Following this short period came the final coup de grace of the European impact when the whole continent of Africa was partitioned during the last quarter of the nineteenth century.

The partition of a continent, which had already seen its progress slowed and often distorted over the past 300 to 400 years, was the final blow to any possibility that African society might develop in what we may term "the natural growth from African traditions". The partition of Africa led, by the beginning of World War II, to a division of the entire continent—with the exception of Ethiopa and Liberia—between European rulers. These new frontiers were drawn in Europe by the Europeans according to the European balance of power, often dependent on whose army arrived in an area first. There was no reference to anything African, to the geographic, economic, social or political elements of African life. This was surely an insuperable barrier to the development of any form of healthy social growth within the African continent. This partition made it virtually impossible for African communities ever to follow the path of similar medieval European societies by developing into nations. The frontiers of the African continent, if you were to see them superimposed on a map over the tribal communities, would illustrate my point. Every frontier is drawn across at least one, and often several, tribal communities. The great Dakongo tribe, for instance, is divided into four by the frontiers drawn between the various states at the mouth of the Congo River.

Africa was thus Balkanized, fragmented, before its people had had any opportunity to develop that kind of nationalism which we saw in the European world, in areas, for example, like that of the Austro-Hungarian Empire. There might have been some possibility that Africa, perhaps after a period of conflict, would draw its own frontiers around something resembling nations. This was impossible after 1885.

Moreover, the partition was followed by a period of European colonial rule which had various consequences according to the policies followed by different European colonial powers. Perhaps too little attention has been paid to the differences rather than to the similarities of the various colonial policies. There were certain similarities of course. The first was another tremendous increase in the whole spirit and practice of authoritarianism. Whatever else colonial rule may be, it is inevitably authoritarian. It must always teach the principles and practices of authoritarianism right up to the time when colonial rule is removed. It should be remembered that much of the original imposition of colonial rule involved the use of physical force against resisting Africans. One has only to remember the history of the Congo. No one who knows anything about the character of Belgian rule in the Congo can have been surprised at what has happened in that unhappy country during the past seven years. One has only to read the revelations of the Belgian government's own commissions on the rule of Leopold and his agents, without having to accept the more passionate testimony of people like E. D. Morel and those who set out to expose to the world the conditions of European rule in the Congo over the last twenty years of the nineteenth century and the first years of this century. Here is to be found indisputable proof of the brutal methods that were used—the cutting off of hands, the deliberate mutilations and killings for the sole purpose of forcibly collecting more rubber—and this during the lifetime of people who are still living in the Congo who have told their children and grandchildren what was done to their forefathers. Brutality was the common practice of European rule of the Congo from its inception under the personal administration of King Leopold.

To describe the type of coercion used in the French territories during the same period and right up to the years after World War II would provide further evidence that violence and brutality are two of the characteristics of colonial rule. In the case of British administration, we come down to even more recent times. It is only a few years since fifty Nyasas were killed in British Nyasaland because of their revolt against what they saw as the permanent imposition of white settler rule on the South African pattern.

One should not exaggerate unnecessarily the extent of force and violence in the African continent. At the same time, we must recognize that these are characteristics of colonial rule and have been pursued at all stages of European colonial government in the African continent. Within the imperial policies of every European colonial power, much more subtly and profoundly damaging to the social structure of African society under colonialism, have been various methods used through ignorance. We should recognize that ignorance, for example, of social anthropology in the nineteenth and early twentieth centuries was not a crime. There had been virtually no work done in this field. Consequently the knowledge was not available and colonial administration was inevitably based on ignorance.

Tragically enough, this early ignorance did considerable damage to African society. I have in mind, as an example, the fact that it was commonly accepted by British administrators right down to the Second World War that all African societies were ruled by chiefs. Today we know that this is not true. But, in the meantime, British administrators, in their way, and the French, in another, had given power to people whom they designated as chiefs. If they could not find an indigenous chief, they simply appointed one. As a consequence, much of the fabric of African society came to be based once more on various types of authoritarianism, in this case, underpinned by the power of colonial administrations.

Second, under colonialism, the administrator, sometimes in conjunction with local white residents, sometimes on his own, tends to set the social standards; inevitably these have been based on the values of Europe, despite the totally different environment of a colonial society. I believe this to be a very profound question and here must content myself with simply referring you to what I think is the clearest and simplest statement of the issue. You will find this in a little pamphlet written by Dunduza Chisiza entitled "Africa—What Lies Ahead," which was published sometime before his tragic death four or five years ago. As an African, at that time fitting himself for service to his new country, Malawi, he recognized the tremendous importance of social values to the younger generations of Africans. Yet, often these had been conditioned to accept European values in wealth, status, social practices, artifically imported from European environments, contributing little constructive to the alien societies of Africa. The fact is that, under colonial rule, the colonial administrator, from the local district commissioner up to the governor, in East and Central Africa, in conjunction with the white settlers, set the whole social pattern. They provided the ladder of social values. We have seen the consequences since independence. Today, we have only to read the reports of commissions set up to investigate the manner in which these social values were put into practice by those who inherited power from the colonial rulers, to see the effects of the social patterns on African life. Every day brings new revelations of the economic temptations into which men and women have fallen in Sierra Leone, Ghana, and Nigeria, which are only the three current examples of a much wider spread malaise. Here we see demonstrated how the social values of Europeans have become such a part of African life that corruption and bribery have been used by African public figures in order to sustain them in the post-independence world.

Third, one must recognize that the general rule of colonial administration and the central objectives of imperialism is to obtain wealth for the metropolitan country according to the needs of its economy. Consequently, again referring to the African map, one can see how the whole pattern of communications, the routes, railroads, telegraph systems, the location of and, indeed, the whole direction of economic life is organized to facilitate the movement of goods from productive areas to the coast, and from the coast to Europe. Until only a few years ago if one wished to telephone from Accra in Ghana to Abijan in the neighboring Ivory Coast, the call had to be routed through Paris. Intercommunication between the African states was almost entirely neglected and remains difficult to the present day. This concentration of colonial rule on the needs of Europe inevitably stunted the growth of those economic activities essential to the diversification of African economy. It, therefore, handicapped any increase in national income or per capita standard of living, basing itself on the production of those materials, particularly in minerals, which supplemented the growth of the imperial economy, providing additional wealth for the rich worlds of London, Paris, Brussels, Lisbon, Madrid, Berlin, and Rome.

During the period approaching the time of independence, a

number of conflicting issues arose which I want to summarize briefly. Again, there was a European impact on African society which was conditioned on the one hand by preparations for independence and, on the other, by the opposition to it. Britain was preparing its West African colonies for self-government from the time of the Second World War onwards. The French tried to consolidate their concept of a Greater France—black and white France —and to some extent they succeeded in doing so. Certainly they secured an acceptance and assimilation of Africans into French society to a greater degree than the Anglo-Saxons have ever done. The Belgians believed that they had at least a century, perhaps several centuries, ahead, and until as late as 1957 they based their policies on this supposition. In that year they completely reversed their former policy.

In each of these cases, though, there were balancing factors. When one refers to preparations for independence in the colonial context, one is inevitably referring to the independence of a European political unit which has been devised for the administrative convenience of the European colonial power. It is not anything which is indigenously African. The case of Nigeria is an obvious example. There was no Nigeria before 1914. Nigeria was a British creation. There had been many states and empires within the frontiers of what is today Nigeria. But there had been no Nigerian unit or community. Britain established two protectorates, northern and southern. These were brought together in 1914 as one administrative unit in order to make administration easier for the British and cheaper for the British taxpayer. So Nigeria was created; but there was no Nigerian tradition, no common Nigerian culture, no single Nigerian religion or even language.

Consequently, when independence came into view over the horizon, preparations were being made—and often quite genuinely made—for Africans to take over the structure which was still that of alien Europe. It was based on the concept of the nation-state which, after all, has no long history, but is the product of modern Europe. Thus, the African leaders were left with the alternative of either accepting the structure which they knew had no national roots within it, or of trying to accomplish the virtually impossible task of redrawing the frontiers of Africa in order to coincide with what might be identified as tribal, communal or ethnic nationalism.

During this period there was also some degree of opposition to the progress of independence within each of the imperial states. In Britain, there was always hostility from some conservative sections of political opinion to the idea that independence based on majority rule should be conceded to those territories where there were considerable white settled communities. Indeed, there were some people in the British political world who aimed at allowing such countries to attain a situation roughly parallel to that of South Africa at the time she gained her virtual independence in 1910. Until very recently, such political figures and groups were hoping that countries like Kenya, the three Central African territories and, perhaps for a short period, even Tanganyika and Uganda, would attain a kind of modified South African model. They believed that in this way the European settlers could promote the rise of a small African middle class, and that then the two communities would be able to create a form of efficient government so as to avoid the demand for adult suffrage and popular government which would inevitably leave the white community stranded politically as a small minority. The Central African Federation provided the strongest focus for this policy, which only broke down in the federal context as recently as 1963. For ten years, politicians in Britain had virtually promised people like Roy Welensky and his supporters that they could count on this attitude. It was only when African movements in Malawi and Zambia, at that time Nyasaland and Northern Rhodesia, had proved their strength, that the policy was defeated. It left behind, of course, the intransigent problem of Rhodesia.

There was, thus, considerable opposition within the imperial powers to the concept of popular independence. Similar opposition was found in French political circles towards any concept of autonomy within the French African colonies. We should remember again that it was as late as 1957 before Belgians were persuaded to reverse their policy which had been to deny Africans any kind of political rights and any experience in the higher forms of administration, political representation or education.

Nor should it ever be forgotten, because it is of paramount significance in Africa today, that to many Africans it appears that the ex-colonial powers are still supporting the white minority regimes of Southern Africa. In the case of South Africa much of the effect of British colonial policy during the nineteenth century was to drive the white Afrikanen nation, which has a three-hundred-year history, into an ever-increasing sense of insecurity and persecution. This undoubtedly played some part in the exaggerated myopia and fanaticism which have become characteristics of Afrikanendom. British policy culminated at the end of the century in a war against the Afrikaners, largely promoted by the desire to defend British investment in South African minerals. The bitterness engendered by this war and the methods employed in it remain a significant political factor in the Republic.

But, the most important impact of British policy on South Africa was the grant of self-government in 1910. The self-governing powers handed over by Westminister to the South Africans in that year were given solely to the white community. Indeed, one of the paper rights held by non-Europeans before 1910 was actually removed. It was this grant of self-government to the South African minority white community which made possible the eventual implementation of apartheid. Thus, Africans today see Britian as partially responsible for the conditions in South Africa which lead to the flow of refugees from that country.

Yet, responsibility is held to be both more direct and wider. Africans are constantly aware that the major investment in South Africa is British and American; that much of South Africa's trade, on which the strength of her economy depends, is directed to the same two countries; that the armaments which sustain the apartheid regime are derived from Europe or from local armament industries financed and equipped by Europe. Moreover, the Africans know that Portugal is a member of NATO and can obtain through that organization arms which she may then use against her colonial subjects in Angola, Mozambique and Portugese Guinea. Above all, the fact that when the small white community in Rhodesia rebelled against British authority in 1965 it was not met with the force which Britain has been accustomed to use against rebellious colored subjects, seems to many Africans to have unquestionably established British commitment to the white supremacist regimes. The difficulties in Rhodesia, the unique character of the British colonial position there, are ignored. To Africans, the simple fact remains that Britain has allowed 220,000 Europeans to seize power over 4 million other Africans.

This involvement of Europeans and Americans in the maintenance of the white southern African *laagar* is only one part of the interference of the outside world in post-independence Africa. Africans feel, with some justification, that all the great powers—the United States, Britain, France, Belgium, the Soviet Union and China—have appeared since independence in various guises, usually promoting their own national interests at the expense of healthy developments in African society. This may be done by financial maneuver, by deliberate political meddling, by the use of bribery, by the operations of the various spy systems or by pressure on different sections of the new African elites. The consequences are always the same; further division, greater strengthening of the centrifugal forces of African society, increased hostilities, and reduced opportunities for developing stable, planned futures for societies of modern Africa.

One must not exaggerate the extent of this interference, nor must we take the patronizing attitude of suggesting that all the evils and troubles of Africa today are to be placed at the door of Europeans, Americans, Russians, Chinese, Asians or any other people. Africans are just as capable as the rest of us of making mistakes, entertaining feelings of jealousy, envy, greed, and it is patronizing to suggest otherwise. What I am trying to do is to analyze the historical factors, the social forces, the political elements, rather than the character or motivation of the men and women involved. So, one should also include within such an analysis the fact that African traditional societies in their contact with the modern world produced a set of tensions which contributed their own part to the problems we are facing, those which have some bearing on the refugee problem. The general absence of state bureaucracies, of the tradition of the nation-state or national organization, create weaknesses in organizing national cohesion. The distortion of social and economic objectives, to which I have already referred, influenced by, conditioned by, but by no means wholly the responsibility of the European impact, has handicapped the effort to meet the needs of the African peoples. The easy transition from the social custom of the "dash" in West Africa to corruption, bribery and nepotism, a transition from a traditional habit to modern forms of corruption, provides one example of this phenomenon. The fact that often tribal feeling remains stronger, deeper, more all-pervading than loyalty to the modern nation is a constant obstacle to the efforts of African leaders. It is obvious, too, that some African leaders and elites, like public figures in any other country, have been playing the power game because they like power, have used it for their own ends and often retained it against the will and interests of the masses.

These are some instances illustrating the indigenous sector of those forces leading to violence, disruption, hostility, fragmentation and instability in the African life we have observed over the past ten years. Nevertheless, despite these indigenous elements contributing to the centrifugal trends of African life, there is one factor in the converse equation which is specifically and uniquely African. We have seen the history of divided Africa and divided African communities. We have seen the creation of authoritarian governments and oppressive forms of minority rule. We have seen racialist governments set up over Africans, both before and after independence. We have seen divisive forces undermining African society. Yet, when we consider the continent as a whole, there is one remarkable achievement of greater significance than all the elements of disintegration. Within a few years of the great surge towards independence, which began in 1957, Africa managed to create a continental organization, an ambition which has escaped the efforts of every other continent over many centuries. Africans have indeed created something which Europeans are still arguing and quarreling about, which Americans are still hesitating over, and which Asians have not even approached. Although the Organization of African Unity has been beset by many problems, strains, and stresses, while it has not, and probably cannot, realize the idealistic dreams of four years ago, nevertheless it exists. This seems to me to have considerable significance and to be related to the subject of this symposium. For is it not the case that, although we are talking about African refugees, about refugees from one African country to another, or to countries outside of the continent, in one sense there is no such thing as an African refugee within his own continent? There is a tradition and practice of hospitality in the continent, so that an African is always an African. If he leaves one society he will be accepted by another. It seems to me that this is the secret of the opportunity raised by the creation of the OAU and the root of hopes for its continued existence. It is a continental forum where the challenge of African problems can be met, but met in an African way, by African means and through the efforts of African people. Despite the unhappy experiences of the past five hundred years, there is still a deep sense of mutual communication within the African continent. It means something to be conscious of being an African. This common consciousness creates a degree of coherence within the African continent which has made it possible to create the Organization of African Unity so soon after the end of the colonial experience. It is from this common experience, and from the universal desire in the continent to create a unified African community, that arises the best chance for dealing with this problem of African refugees. With this background, it is no exaggeration to suggest that Africans are probably better equipped than any other people in the world to meet the challenges provoked by the refugee problems of their continent.

COMMENT

GABRIEL D'ARBOUSSIER, Senegal's Ambassador to the Federal Republic of Germany

After the two world wars, the refugee problem has become so grave that there have been continual attempts to perfect the rules of international law which were to apply to individuals classified in this category. These rules were based on respect for the human condition and for individual liberties which should be guaranteed to every man whatever his situation. They were evidently imbued with the general conceptions of European law, and the very definition of displaced person, and the ideas regarding solutions to be found for his case, are in agreement with principles which have been acknowledged as having universal value. However, the problem of displaced persons, especially in Africa, had to show that the very idea of the displaced person and the solutions which must be found in order to safeguard his essential rights, must take into consideration the general and the special conditions existing not in any particular country, but at least in a particular continent.

In Africa there have always been large scale migrations, some due to desires for conquest, others to economic exigencies and these constant movements of people have brought about an extraordinary mixture of people and races, increased still further by the almost complete nonexistence of national states and of state borders. It has been possible to say that Africa has known Empires and not States, and this is true.

This mixture of peoples, races, and ethnical groups has created a basic general tendency in the African, and a particular mentality, which permits the assertion that if Africa knows tribal sentiments, it does not know what has been termed racism. Moreover, that which we could call "African way of life" is based on sentiments of tolerance and hospitality which could sometimes lead one to think that there existed there a kind of primitive socialism. Now, all these conditions are very important from the point of view of the problem of displaced persons in Africa, which has suddenly taken on a dramatic aspect during these last years.

It seems that until now, people have wanted to examine the problem of the displaced persons only from the humanitarian angle, certainly a very important aspect; and the praiseworthy work of the United Nations Commission for displaced persons is well known in this regard. But, in our opinion, one must go further and see the basis of the problem, trying to place the African case within the historical evolution.

It is to this aspect that the intervention of Mr. John Hatch, undertaken in accordance with the best verbal African tradition, so soundly documented and constructed, makes an essential contribution.

His reminder of the general conditions of existence of the African people, of their ideas and philosophy, of their social structure, is all the more necessary, as, since independence, there has been a tendency to forget them in the analysis of present situations.

We have sometimes seemed insistent when, in our battle for the assertion of the African personality, we continually came back to these historic events, and when we advanced arguments which appeared to pose problems to some of our questioners. But the historical facts are there, and the parallel drawn by John Hatch between the evolution of African society and that of European society up to the period of the colonial conquest, can today no longer be in doubt. Just as we must also take into consideration the evolution of these two societies after the colonial period. All this has left traces in both, and one can therefore not talk about the problem of displaced persons in Africa, without taking the historical evolution into account.

John Hatch has not omitted any of the important events which have stood out in the history of Africa in these last centuries, from the creation of African empires which were states, but not nations, to the great drama of the slave trade, to European political but also cultural penetration, which is going to upset all the foundations of African society in bringing to it new ideas concerning the relationship between man and his society. But this upheaval, however profound, has to this day been unable to efface what constitutes the very foundation of African civilization, whose conception of the organization of the world is based on the relationship between man and the universe. Thus, the historical categories which Europe has experienced in its evolution, the social and political structures, the yields of production due to technical evolution, must, in order to apply to Africa, take into consideration this basis of civilization, of this actual way of life of the Africans, the two essential qualities of which are patience and tolerance.

This patience is sometimes taken for passivity, and this is not absolutely inaccurate, as in the conception of African chieftaincy there is definitely a certain element of authoritarianism, and tolerance also can sometimes be taken for lack of zeal and conviction. But, there will also be objections that the present tragic events in Nigeria, as well as those in the Congo a short time ago, do not fit in with these assertions. Far be it from us to minimize the importance of these events.

But John Hatch very rightly draws the attention to the realization of the Organization of African Unity, which until now was the only continental organization in which the states of a continent coexist and cooperate almost unanimously.

Its establishment, its activities have run into, and are still running into, considerable difficulties, but despite this the organization continues its work, and this is absolutely remarkable.

Now, a problem like that of the African refugees can have no solution except one, thanks to the existence of such an organization. For this problem brings into question the right of individuals in confrontation with those of the different groupings of which they form a part—tribe, people, state, nation, regional groupings, and finally continental organization. One can see, therefore, that the problem of displaced persons in Africa is revealed in different terms from those which Europe, for example, has experienced and knows.

Certainly, the fundamental problem is respect for the human being, but this exercises its rights within limits which obey economic and social imperatives, historical and cultural traditions, philosophical and religious ideas of extreme importance.

The Symposium organized by St. John's University will have rendered a great service in allowing the attention of public opinion to be drawn to one of the most serious problems of our day, and, at the same time, making known in detail the fundamental conditions of existence of the African people, to American public opinion.

Nothing today seems more important to me than this mutual understanding, which is the basis of international cooperation.

BOUNDARY DISPUTES AND TENSIONS AS A CAUSE OF REFUGEES

THOMAS HOVET, JR., University of Oregon

It seems self-evident that there is a direct relationship between the movement of refugees from one African country to another, and their common political boundaries. The nature of the boundary, both its physical and political characteristics, is a key element in determining the direction and the extent of the flow of refugees from one state to another. Furthermore, the manner and the mode in which refugees are dealt with in the country to which they flee may have a direct bearing on the creation of tensions and possible conflict between this host country and the country from which the refugees have fled. It would probably be erroneous, however, to argue that disputes and tensions along a border cause refugees. It is more likely that refugees may become the cause of increased tension and disputes between bordering states. In all probability, the significant question for the African states is the question of whether they can continue to allow for an easy flow of refugees without, at the same time, increasing tensions and the possibilities of conflict between those states whose common boundary serves as an avenue for the flight of refugees.

In essence, a refugee, as defined in the 1951 Convention on the Status of Refugees and the 1967 Protocol Relating to the Status of Refugees, is a person who has left his country of nationality (or who will not return to it) because of a "well-founded fear of being persecuted for reasons of race, religion, nationality or political opinion." The possibility of a person becoming a refugee, however, is dependent upon his ability to flee the country of his nationality and his ability to obtain entry to another country. His ability in this regard may be determined by

21

the extent to which his country of nationality allows potential refugees access to cross the border, and the degree to which the country to which the refugee seeks to flee is willing to allow entry across their border.

A person in South Africa, for example, may have well-founded fears that he may be persecuted for reasons of political opinion, but his ability to become a refugee may be limited by controls on his possibility of exit from South Africa. Even if he evades, or overcomes, a controlled exit system, his ability to acquire access to another state may depend upon its system of entry control. If a person with well-founded fears of persecution for his political opinion seeks to flee South Africa and find refuge in Lesotho, his ability to seek refuge in Lesotho is dependent upon Lesotho. Surrounded as it is by South Africa, economically tied as it is with South Africa, Lesotho currently is fairly restrictive on allowing the entry of refugees. While most states will allow entry of political refugees, Lesotho will return to South Africa any person seeking refuge whom South Africa charges with a violation of a law, including violation of what in other societies might be called political crimes. Thus, although the internal situation in South Africa might seem conducive to creating refuge movements, the refugee flow may be very restricted.

For whatever reasons, if it is the policy of a country to prevent persons with fears of persecution for race, religion, nationality, or political opinion from leaving a country, there is unlikely to be a large flow of refugees from that country. Similarly, whatever the reasons, if it is the policy of a country to make it difficult for refugees to find refuge in their country, there is likely to be little flow of refugees into that country. This does not mean that there may not be persons able to evade the systems of controls in both exit and entry, but that the flow of such refugees will be diminished. This also means that large refugee flows from a country are indicative that there is a minimum of exit restrictions, and that if there are large flows of refugees into a country that there is a minimum of entry restrictions. One element then in determining the flow of refugees is the extent of exit and entry controls.

Assuming that the exit and entry systems are not limiting, the direction of the flow of refugees across borders is probably determined as a result of the formal and informal communication patterns of refugees, and the ease of physical access of refugees to a bordering state.

Refugees from Rwanda, for example, have in the past few years fled to Burundi, Tanzania, Uganda and the Democratic Republic of the Congo. With all four of these bordering states exerting little control on the entry of the refugees, the direction of flight is determined by such factors as those of communicated information and the ease of physical access. In the case of refugees from Mozambique who tend to go to Tanzania or Zambia, the direction of flight may be more a factor of the control systems of Southern Rhodesia or South Africa. Even in this case, the direction of flight may not be determined as much by the system of control as the fact that refugees perceive from their communications network anxieties that may preclude their flight in the direction of Southern Rhodesia or South Africa. (Note: a distinction is made here between refugees and persons from Mozambique who may migrate to these two countries.) In other words, the direction of flight of refugees, apart from the physical factor of access, and the factor of control, may be based on the perceived advantages inferred from the formal and informal channels of communications available to potential refugees. This information may come from all variety of sources—previous refugees, tribal contacts in another country, etc.

It may well be that the perceived advantages of flight to a given country may be based on the impression that conditions in that country are the opposite from the conditions in the country which they are leaving. One could argue that refugees fleeing Rwanda to Uganda may feel that the situation in Uganda is the opposite of the situation in which they found themselves in Rwanda. They may even have the impression that Uganda is opposed to the existing situation in Rwanda, and this impression, therefore, enters into their choice to seek refuge in Uganda. Whether based on valid information or not, the refugee may develop perceptions of tensions between countries, so that they seek refuge (assuming it is physically accessible) in a country which appears to them to be opposing events from which they are fleeing.

One might, therefore, make the erroneous assumption that

tension between states is likely to cause an increase in the flow of refugees. Such a fact is not apparent if one observes the major patterns of the flow of refugees across borders in Africa in the past few years. A substantial number of refugees have fled the Democratic Republic of the Congo, going to the Central African Republic, Uganda, Burundi and Tanzania. Few have gone to the Congo (Brazzaville), where there has been probably more tension with the Democratic Republic of the Congo than with these other states. Considerable tension and dispute over the boundary exists between Somalia and both Kenya and Ethiopia, but there is no appreciable flow of refugees between these states. (While there are reports of substantial numbers of Somali refugees in Ethopia, these appear to be migrants and not refugees at all.) Sudanese refugees have fled to the Central African Republic, Uganda and the Democratic Republic of the Congo, yet there have been greater tensions between the Sudan and Ethiopia, Chad and the U.A.R. (where there is a little flow of refugees). Refugees from Portuguese Guinea have tended to flee to Senegal, not to Guinea, although tensions between the Portuguese colony and Guinea are probably just as great as with Senegal. The explanation of these facts may be an indication that in the case of increased tensions between states there is more likely to be a higher degree of control exerted over exit and entry. States in dispute with other states may be more hesitant to permit free passage across common borders, fearing infiltration. There may be, however, an indirect flow of refugees between states with high degrees of tension. Refugees may flee one state, then a second, and even a third to arrive in a fourth state. This state may border their initial state, but the refugee flow to it may be indirect because the border tensions and control prevent direct movement.

In the case of the movement of Angolian refugees to Zambia or the Democratic Republic of the Congo—or refugees from Mozambique to Zambia or Tanzania—the direction of the flow is in part a factor of proximity, in part a perception that these alternatives are preferable to South Africa or Southern Rhodesia, and in part awareness that entry controls to South Africa and Southern Rhodesia are more restricted. In the case of refugees from Rwanda who flee to all the neighboring countries—Uganda, Tanzania, Burundi, and the Democratic Republic of the Congo—

proximity and communication patterns with previous refugees may be the primary determinents of the direction of flight. In this instance there have been few obstacles of control exerted on the borders.

Based on this overview of the evidence on factors influencing the direction of the flow of refugees, and the major patterns of that flow, it can be argued that border disputes and tensions are not a major factor in the cause of refugees. Rather, as the "international" definition of a refugee implies, the internal situation in which they find themselves creates the fears of persecution from which they flee. The artificiality of imposed colonial boundaries may, however, force the division of African tribal groups. Much of the refugee flow may be a result of this border division, which has a tendency in some states to make minorities of some tribal groups. Such a minority may flee to a neighboring state to join its own tribal group in order to gain a measure of security.

All the foregoing is not to say that there is no relationship between refugees and boundary disputes and tensions, but rather to suggest that if there is a relationship it is to be found in the fact that the flight of refugees from one African country to another may become a source of tension between the countries.

The presence of political refugees in a country may easily be perceived as a threat by the country from which they have fled. This is especially true in cases in which the flight of refugees takes place after a sudden or violent change of government. The Ghanian political refugees in Guinea are seen as a potential threat to the existing government in Ghana. The tension is even greater when there is the impression that Guinea is encouraging these refugees to engage in activities to bring about a change in Ghana. Similarly, the rather bitter exchange between representatives of Guinea and the Ivory Coast in the twenty-second session of the General Assembly revolved around charges that refugees in both countries were being encouraged by those governments to undermine each other's regime.

The perception by one country of the possibility that refugees may be an effective device to use in changing the internal situation in another country is in good part, a continuing reflection of the fight against colonialism in Africa. In the movement for independence in Africa, those African countries that had achieved independence sought to encourage the independence in the remain- ing colonial territories by not only accepting political refugees but by giving these refugees all variety of assistance so that they could evolve as liberation movements infiltrating back into the colonial territories. Certainly, the FLN in Algeria received such encouragement and assistance from Morocco and the United Arab Republic. Most African states that are militantly distressed with the continuing colonial regimes in Africa (the Spanish and Portuguese colonies) and the white-settler regimes in Southern Rhodesia and South Africa are still encouraging refugees to become elements hastening the liberation of these countries. This attitude on the role of refugees in promoting independence has been institutionalized in the Committee of National Liberation of the Organization of African Unity. The initial resolutions passed at the Addis Ababa meeting in May 1963, asked all independent African states to receive on their territories, nation- alists from the liberation movements in colonial territories in order that they could get training that would be of use in effecting a liberation of their colonial area. While the assistance to these liberation movements in the years since may not be as much as was hoped for in 1963, the principle of allowing and encouraging states to serve as a base of operations for national liberation movements among refugees has continued. In a sense, this prin- ciple was reaffirmed in the October 1965 meeting of the Heads of State and Government of the Organization of African Unity.

Such an attitude toward refugees from nonindependent territories in Africa has a number of implications, especially with regard to creating tensions between the independent African states, and Africa "south of the battle line". Tensions between the Demo- cratic Republic of the Congo and Portuguese Angola have increased as the numbers of Angolan refugees has steadily increased, and as some of these refugees have been involved in liberation activities. Similarly, the tensions between Tanzania and Portuguese Mozambique have increased. While the Portuguese have been distressed by these developments, the physical problems of the control of the border, and the fact that Tanzania and the Democratic Republic of the Congo are not subject to much eco- nomic pressure, has hindered the ability of Portugal to limit the activities of these refugees.

A somewhat different situation is apparent in the case of Zambia and Malawi with respect to both the Portuguese territories, as well as Southern Rhodesia and South Africa. With closer economic relationships with these territories, Zambia and Malawi have not served as significant sites for such refugee activities. They have not been as willing to allow their borders to serve as exit routes. They have been subjected to external pressures to prevent their territories from being used as bases for national liberation movements. In essence, Zambia and Malawi have had to face the fact that such refugee activity would increase border tensions with Southern Rhodesia, South Africa, and the Portuguese territories, to such an extent that it could possibly threaten their security. This is not to imply that Zambia and Malawi are not sympathetic, but they cannot economically afford to allow the refugee flow to become a deep source of conflict. Their apprehension in this regard was evidenced by their reluctance to go along with the economic boycott resolution of the Security Council against Southern Rhodesia. Both states have argued that they cannot jeopardize their economic relationships unless other independent African states are willing to come to their assistance. In pushing for independence "south of the battle line" many militant African states may see refugees as an easy road to establishing subversive national liberation activities, but Zambia and Malawi, in their vulnerable economic positions, cannot afford the increased tension that would result from such action.

The situation for Botswana and Lesotho is even more acute. Their isolation in the sea of South Africans means that they have to be very circumspect in the case of refugees. Although states normally may be willing to admit refugees, and permit forcible extradition only of those accused of criminal activities, most states would not consider political crimes as extradition offenses. But, in the case of Botswana and Lesotho, these states have agreed to requests from South Africa for the return of refugees who are charged with crimes that most states would consider as political crimes. It is, therefore, very apparent that even the movement of refugees into these two countries from South Africa creates a degree of tension and conflict. Their economic survival depends, in large part, on their ability to contain the refugee situation in such a way as to minimize tensions with South Africa.

There is another implication that follows from the fact that the independent African states, in their fight for decolonization in Africa, have placed pressure on the colonial areas by encouraging liberation activities by refugees. This implication is to be found in the fact that to some militant African leadership, questions can be raised as to whether the independence achieved by some other African states is really independence or simply a new version of colonial rule. In the eyes of some African leaders, the leadership in other African states appears to be just a front for the former colonial masters. There have been a number of cases in which some African governments were encouraging "liberation" movements in other independent African states. Refugees, called exiles, have been used as bases for subversion of what were considered to be neo-colonial regimes in the more "reactionary" African states. To the African states who were the subject of this sort of pressure, the refugees, in essence, became a source of tension. The tension now manifested between the Ivory Coast and Guinea is of this sort. As another example, Ethiopia's relations with the Sudan are certainly strained because of the presence of a "nationalist" movement among Eritrean refugees in the Sudan.

In fact, even if a host country makes every effort to contain refugees and to prevent them from constituting a source of tension, the refugees themselves have learned the lesson from the recent history of the African states in encouraging national liberation movements among refugees against the colonial areas of Africa. Tanzania, at the present time, is trying to contain Malawi refugees who are trying to mobilize themselves for internal changes in Malawi. This has been a factor in more restrictive controls on refugee entry into Tanzania, although the economic problems may have been a more important factor. This fact that the refugees, themselves, are a possible source of tension between states may explain the sudden action of Uganda in July 1966 in removing important numbers of Sudanese refugees from their immediate border with the Sudan. The tension caused by the presence and activities of Sudanese refugees near the Sudanese border has led to Sudanese negotiations with the

Central African Republic, Uganda and the Democratic Republic of the Congo, resulting in an agreement to resettle the Sudanese refugees a considerable distance from the common borders. In the case of Uganda these negotiations also resulted in an agreement whereby Uganda would refuse asylum to Sudanese refugees engaged in subversive activities.

Thus, the very existence of refugees in African states, in the light of the recent historical role of refugees in independence movements, can, of itself, constitute a factor in increasing tensions among African states. Refugees living close to African borders may constitute a Pandora's box for potential tensions.

The dilemma for the African states, therefore, is a dilemma between a humanitarian concern for refugees, and a realization that refugees can be a source of tension between the African states.

The attempts of the legal experts of the Refugee Commission of the OAU (September 1966) have stressed three paramount principles in proposing a draft African Refugee Convention:

1. that the granting of asylum to refugees is a peaceful and humanitarian act and shall not be regarded as an unfriendly act by any OAU member state;
2. that no person shall be subjected by an OAU member state to measures such as rejection at the frontier, return or expulsion, which could compel him to return or remain in a territory where his life, physical integrity or liberty would be threatened with persecution for reasons of race, religion, nationality or political opinion; and
3. that no refugee will be repatriated against his will.

On the other side of the dilemma, the question of subversion, the OAU Heads of State and Government in October 1965 adopted a Declaration on the Problem of Subversion, which stated that they:

1. pledged themselves not to tolerate subversion against OAU member states and to oppose it in every way;
2. resolved to strictly observe the principles of international law with regard to political refugees who were nationals of any OAU member state; and
3. to seek to promote the return home of refugees with their consent and that of their countries of origin.

One of the most hopeful aspects of the African refugee problem has been the extent to which refugees have voluntarily returned to their countries of origin.

Yet, the remaining dilemma for the African states is one of putting into practice a concern for the humanitarian needs of the refugees, while at the same time making an effort to see that the existence and activity of refugees is not a source of tension between bordering African states. If too many restrictions are placed on controlling the access of refugees to flight and re-settlement in order to prevent refugees becoming a source of tension, the humanitarian concerns for the refugees may be sacrificed. If too much emphasis is placed on the humanitarian needs of refugees, then there can be a problem of increasing tensions developing between bordering African states.

COMMENT

ALEXANDER MELAMID, New York University

I am a refugee and, therefore, the danger exists that I might be in favor of all refugees. Or, I might turn around completely, as quite a few refugee friends of mine have, and say that every refugee is a faker and not worth listening to.

I had the good luck to spend this summer in Africa and, as a former refugee, liked to talk to African refugees in the many bars and coffeehouses which now exist in Africa. My interest in listening to refugees gives away my obvious bias in favor of refugees. I talked to refugees in Ethiopia, Tanzania, and Malawi. Malawi illustrates best the point I wish to make, for that country contains an interesting group of so-called white Rhodesian refugees, most of them born in Africa, who fled from Smith's regime because they objected to his government. These refugees went to nearby Malawi because if and when Mr. Smith is kicked out they hope to jump into a car or bus and drive "home" in a few hours. Not only these Rhodesian refugees, but all refugees, try to minimize the return trip in order to be back in their country first and to grab jobs, including cabinet ministers' jobs, which have become vacant due to the change of government. Unfortunately, in Africa, this principle of choosing a nearby country as a place of refuge does not always work. It is no good to flee from South Africa to Lesotho, because Lesotho, being dependent on South Africa, will have to deport you back to South Africa. For various reasons, Africans can usually not take refuge in nearby countries. In many cases African refugees have to flee from one country to another. For example, this summer in Ethiopia I met quite a few refugees from South Africa who could not stay in any of the countries adjoining South Africa. They fled directly to Tanzania, did not like the politics there, and moved on to Ethiopia which is even further away from South Africa. In Ethiopia these persons were referred to as double refugees. Obviously, these refugees, be they "single" or "double" refugees, having had to travel great distances from their country of origin, suffer hardships. Yet, and this is important to our discussions, having travelled that far from their county of origin, these refugees cannot contribute to the inflammation of boundary disputes with their own countries.

However, there is another group of people, usually far less educated and without political ambitions, who found themselves on the wrong side of boundaries as a result of boundary demarcations by European powers. This was not too bad under European colonial rule, but with the advent of African self-government, these people fled across the border and became refugees in another country, although the inhabitants of that country include their own brethren. Usually these refugees do not own land in the country to which they have fled. They are, therefore, impoverished and desire to take action to reconquer the lands which they owned across the border. These refugees may inflame boundary disputes. The Kenya-Somalia boundary dispute is a good case study. Professor Hovet has also mentioned the southern Sudan which potentially is even more explosive. The Congo, Ethiopia, and several West African countries provide more case studies.

Does the African refugee problem therefore imply that most

of the boundaries created by European powers should be changed? Unfortunately, the geographical distribution of tribes or other groups in Africa is not as uniform and contiguous as the distribution of nations in Europe. Changing boundaries to accommodate refugees will therefore cause even greater upheavals and, therefore, more refugees than existed before. Misery will only increase. For this reason I recommend adjustment of refugees to the existing boundaries, and economic development within these boundaries to accommodate the refugees. Action of this nature will make African refugees of this type into "fake" refugees, which I referred to before; but, I hope that this action will make Africa into a better place for everybody.

SOME ASPECTS OF THE REFUGEE PROBLEM SOUTH OF THE SAHARA

3

GEORGE-IVAN SMITH, Director, U.N. Information Center, London, England

Please do not suppose for one moment that I toy lightly with the tragic human problems involved when I use the phrase—"what has been done for refugees so far in Africa may prove only to have been practice." The scale of the problems pulsing out of Rwanda and Sudan are terrible, but are even more so to the south of them, to the places of slowly bubbling anger where the African faces the European in South Africa, Mozambique, Angola and Rhodesia. Southern Africa is a cockpit for disaster, a compression chamber that could be ignited as easily, as irrelevantly as an American city is ignited by a hot night, an insensitive cop, a remark, a smashed skull under a baton.

Let us for a moment stop thinking about a study of refugees as though we mean people on the run. I know that the mandates of refugee and welfare agencies that help require criteria, proof that the man is on the run within the appropriate set of rules. I respect the work that such agencies do after the event, after the proof; it is not my aim to disparage them when I cry aloud for an agency that will warn us and act against impending human tragedy; direct us to avoid mistakes that may put a million starving peoples on the roads, fleeing from the little security they have known to an insecurity so deep, that most of us are too grounded, too committed, to comprehend it.

The Africa that I know best is south of the Sahara. So far it has produced a modest crop of refugees, if that agricultural term is permitted in such a context. Should we sit and wait for the bumper crop that comes from the tempest, the blowing down of the trees with the fruit?

Abraham Lincoln faced this nation with his first inaugural address, knowing that it was about to tear out its own heart in the tempest of passion roused up by race prejudice, and he uttered an anguished warning that might well be the text for what I must say about Southern Africa—"The dogmas of the quiet past are inadequate to the stormy present. Let us disenthrall ourselves . . . " As you well know, Lincoln was not one to use a word lightly nor loosely. To be enthralled is to be enslaved. In context he did not mean the physical act of bondage but the prejudice behind it, the thought that makes segregation possible. Another American with great perception, James Harvey Robinson, caught the same idea when he wrote in *The Mind in the Making,* "Creative thinking today is largely a process of searching about in our minds and experience for reasons to support what we already believe."

Let us disenthrall ourselves. A refugee problem in Africa that may engage us until we are too tired to stand, is being wound up like an old clock at this very moment; tension is being wound into the springs by a thousand fingers. Elements feed in upon each other. The Bantu education acts, as a policy, restrict education for Africans, the Labor laws restrict the training of Africans so that fixed low proportions are permitted to become highly skilled. There is segregation on public transport. Benches in the park are marked for whites and blacks. Sexual intercourse between the races is severely punished. All cases mentioned do not represent uncaged bias. It is policy, backed by law. And one must add an alarming fact with regard to this situation: the Afrikaaner sincerely believes that what he is doing to repress and restrict the African is right, necessary, and is supported by the Bible. The Africans are regarded as the hewers of wood, the drawers of water.

The meshing in of religion and politics, particularly religion with such a restrictive concept of man is yet another indicator of the deteriorating situation in the South. Business meetings, council meetings, and so on tend to start with a prayer. Again, that in itself is not culpable. Indeed, as a Christian I find the idea behind it admirable. Yet, once you have been through the reserves or African townships in South Africa or Rhodesia and have seen the contrast between living standards there and for Europeans in town, then you stop and wonder whether the public praying is backed by key principles governing human behavior, cardinal principles such as those expressed for Christians in the Sermon on the Mount and expressed in other great religions and philosophies in other forms.

For four years, and until recently, I worked as a U.N. representative in east central and southern Africa. I went back there on a private visit a month or two ago. Step by step, a dreadful confrontation between the races, simmering for a long time, has acquired a new and deep bitterness, a sharp crystallization of contrary determination that is immensely dangerous, not simply for Europeans and Africans, in southern Africa, or in the continent. Those dangers are obvious. Perhaps it is less obvious that if the fury and frustration bursts down there from one side or another, it may prove itself to be a manifestation of a world-wide condition of fury and frustration felt by underprivileged majorities or large groups in a society that feel, or are made to feel on grounds of race, color, religion, or simply because they are too numerous, that they are obliged to accept an inferior standard of rights, freedom of economic and political entitlements.

"The dogmas of the quiet past are inadequate to the stormy present." The seething convulsions in Asia are part of a popular movement, a slow response, after centuries of acceptance, against having to live their lives out "in quiet desperation", a response to the idea that it was an artificial curse put on them when man's knowledge was more limited and must come off in an age when modernization for them too is possible. It becomes an imperative. The same determination drives Africans whether they are the unfortunate subject peoples in the South or the pressed and harassed African leaders to the north.

Behind President Kaunda, President Nyerere, Kenyatta, Obote are millions of peoples for whom the standard of life is desperately low—and in this age and time—unnecessarily low. Why did colonial powers, when the responsibility was theirs, deal with development at such a slow pace, Africans may ask themselves. How could the Congo find itself at independence with no more than ten Africans with college training? How could Zambia at independence four years ago, find they had less than nine hundred Africans educated through secondary school level?

In the past, the answer to the Asians, the Africans (and dare I mention the Aswan dam) went along lines that there is no money on that scale for development, or on those conditions, that we must progress slowly, that you must help us by understanding the scale of the problem, keep your people quiet, cooperative and, in due course, things will be better for you.

If suffering people do not get a response, in due time they explode. It is true in Asia, Africa, the Middle East and among Black Power movements that are starting to coagulate in various parts of the world. It is not race, it is poverty and unfair distribution. Britain's Industrial Revolution produced social changes that profoundly changed the power structure in the world. It may be classical simplification for me to say in a sentence, that the failure of British authority at that time to ensure that standards of human life and dignity were maintained during the Industrial Revolution, was more truly the "shot heard around the world". It was lack of concern for man of his own color, race, and country that permitted conditions in which women and children worked in mines and factories, in filthy conditions, and were discriminated against politically and, particularly, economically. The protest led to a chain of events to redress the old balance—the formation of political groupings of workers, the socialist movement, the written protests of Marx and Engels whose words became weapons when yet another set of authorities, this time in Russia, lost contact with and concern for the people. Only fifty years later that nation of starving peasants has become one of the two super powers.

In a sense, one sees that the old struggle to redress the balance that went on inside the nation/state has moved out onto the world stage, encaged in a global grid; and, alas, the poor today are in the most highly populated parts of the earth. The popular power, and the political power, behind these continental and other groupings varies greatly, but in my view, they share the common feeling of angry frustration over the continued imbalance in their own societies or in the world society. If the economic, political or human rights gap is not reduced, and seen to be reduced, rapidly and drastically, it is obvious that circumstances will draw them together, not simply into the general front of mutual understanding that characterizes the world's present Afro-Asian grouping, but in process of time, into specific acts of support at many physical, political, and economic levels.

Unfortunately, today's massive societies of the poor are overwhelmingly what we indelicately call "colors." How much longer should they be expected to believe that the alleged shortage of funds and resources from the privileged donor countries of the West has nothing whatever to do with their color? Or leave that aspect of discrimination aside for a moment and consider this: How much longer should they be expected to believe that the failure of the West to make the massive and combined effort needed to bridge the development gap has nothing to do with the fear of a privileged minority about diluting, even putting their privilege or their high standards in jeopardy, by sharing the opportunities more equitably with the majority—a majority needing it badly.

Africans, and observers in other underdeveloped countries, not infrequently claim that the restrictive policy of some large western countries toward UNCTAD, the U.N. agency created to redress the balance in trading patterns and practices is based on that fear. A few years ago, attempts to establish SUNFED, the Special U.N. Fund for Économic Development, were frustrated by major powers. Critics in the underdeveloped countries claim that it was because the proposed agency would call for more and more funds from the rich nations to distribute to the poor, not only on favorable terms economically but also politically, since the distribution would be made on the basis of economic need without reference to ideological friendships or differences. That may be too harsh a judgement, but I stress the word may.

For the record, I should make clear that the SUNFED, The Special U.N. Fund to which I referred, is not the same program as one that emerged years later and was called Special Fund and has now merged with TAB to become the U.N. Development Program. It is an agency of immense importance in the context of reducing imbalance. It concentrates on the critical sector of preinvestment. It dispenses aid internationally, strictly in response, apolitically, to economic and social need. When it flies the U.N. flag on its product, it flies for all, rich and poor alike, because significantly, all make their contributions to it in cash and kind, rich and poor alike. It is technical cooperation on a worldwide scale.

I may have come a long way from refugees. I do so to stress the need to study and plan in the broader context of the whole convulsion that is seizing the world. The fury and frustration cannot be contained, should not be contained, if the poor fear that their situation gets worse while the privileged conditions improve for others. The accelerators for growth in the developed countries have become so fantastic that lack of resources is no longer the brake it was in the past. The U.S. alone is annually adding to itself a wealth of resources greater than that available to the African continent.

In Africa recently, I met and talked with a number of visitors from U.S. Black Power groups. I met them also with African refugees from the south, and despite basic differences in stated aims, (one group saying it is working for segregation, the other against it), one clearly heard the common language of frustration leading to their conclusion that talk is no longer any use, that solutions can no longer be expected by those means. Nor are Africans and Black Power delegates the only ones to hold dangerous conclusions. The white backlash, the extreme views of many Europeans in Southern Africa, say it too. How often have I heard the phrase "you cannot make the African understand" from Europeans who seldom try it. Rhodesia's UDI was triggered off by men determined to avoid being brought into consultation with Africans or into the "partnership" that Sir Roy Welensky claimed was the earlier aim. Huggins put it bluntly, but truly, when he defined the European African relationship as the partnership between rider and horse—and guess who is the horse. On my last trip I heard an Afrikaaner simply and sincerely say that the answer to what he called the native problem is to shoot them.

I accompanied the late Dag Hammarskjold on many missions to what are too simply described as crisis areas, a phrase neatly tieing together confluence of great streams of history, complex social relationships, the actions triggered by hunger, fear. I was on the very margins of his great work, but even from that modest role one learns to detect a few of the indicators of truly dangerous situations having a potential to explode in one region and to involve the world. Southern Africa is a clear example.

Hammarskjold's role as a peacemaker would not have survived a day had he begun by making statements based on value-judgements, or by trying to apportion blame. He judged that to change the world, one had first to face it as it was. Having done that, he knew that moves from the extreme positions had to be affected, step by small step if necessary. But when the parties get themselves in a quadrille of fear they take steps toward more extreme positions. Soon responses become automatic. Response becomes a substitute for policy, and Hammarskjold among others pointed out a stage at which people under the impulse of fear act against their own interests, and even against their own fundamental will. The course of events may take on aspects of futility to the point where, out of sheer weariness, no resistance to the gravitation into open conflict any longer seems possible.

His remarks, made in 1956, may have been brought to mind by tensions then current in the Middle East and to which they still apply. The same warning signs are clear to see in Africa, with the Zambezi River the dividing line. Twelve months passed between my last two visits to the region. In that time, the deterioration in the situation is far worse than I imagined from the fairly close study I have tried to make of current events there as a temporary academic, and as an individual deeply concerned for all of the peoples there, Europeans and Africans alike.

Some of the parties in the region probably do not agree that the situation is grave. They never all do. They wishfully believe that something is going to take care of it—strength of security, external aid, a rising of the peoples. Security is no substitute for policy towards conciliation if the wish is to avoid ultimate conflict—conflict in which hard won and often spectacular European economic developments have so much to lose, whereas many of the Africans, in those terms, have pitifully little to call their own. But this state of euphoria among many Europeans there simply has to be experienced to be believed. Their own fundamental will should certainly be expected to follow a desire for a society in which their own children hope for a future.

In the vast majority of cases, Europeans in South Africa and in the Portuguese territories have a long historical association with the land. The Rhodesians are different. Most of them came from postwar England and have no more claim to the country or to being a part of its traditions than I have. Very few of the ministers were born in Rhodesia, and in any case the first Europeans only came to Rhodesia about eighty years ago. However, generally speaking, the South Africans and the Portuguese Europeans have an African history, a role and a large stake in the region, and I would assume a fundamental will to secure that for their next generation. It can only be assured by the development of mutual understanding. Security strength lasts only for a time. Tougher security produces more desperate response after a time, so the cycle starts spiralling, people get to the point where not only are they acting against their own fundamental will, but they attempt to justify it too, thereby charging the pressure chamber with yet another combustible element in a chain of action and reaction.

Often the danger is greatest when people do not see, or pretend not to see, that it exists. On numerous occasions I have been with Europeans in Salisbury or South Africa, in beautiful cities where no African is allowed to live, and heard them almost pathetically draw attention to the fine European homes, to the beauty of the jacaranda trees, to the mellow sunlight on lovely colonial architecture and say, in effect, can't you, can't the world understand that everything is all right? Few had ever gone out into the reserves where Africans are obliged by law to live among themselves. They knew, of course, from the newspapers that there is a mounting crime wave among Africans on the reserves. Outside Johannesburg alone, Africans kill each other for money or in anger at an increasing rate, probably now measured in scores every week. And the word has probably got around that young, frustrated, deprived Africans on the reserves try to pierce each other with the sharpened spokes of bicycle wheels, and that there are hundreds now lying paralyzed in African hospitals. This, however, the European is apt to put down to character faults of the African and to an imagined "limited capacity to develop." Most of them do not appear to be able to see the link between standards of life and man, the effect upon the imagination of any poor and dispirited people, whatever their color, when they find themselves living at unnecessarily low levels of training, justice, opportunity, and dignity while another section of the community has access to higher standards. It bites more deeply when the higher standards are enjoyed by a minority, and an additional humiliating element is added when the unfair division is based on race.

Increasingly, some Europeans whom I know in Southern Africa are beginning to see that they are in a situation from which physical security alone cannot spare them. The conditions that a minority imposed against a majority carry with them the demand for redress. As Emerson wrote, "the dice of God are always loaded". Tough conditions produce a tough response, and then the horrible spiral begins in this area of action to security and counter-security. In recent months there was an outbreak of violence in the Wankie area of Rhodesia on a larger scale than ever before. *The Guardian* wrote "South Africa felt it to be serious enough to justify the dispatch of troops and police to Wankie to fight with the Smith forces. Indeed rumor says that Mr. Smith was forced to turn in desperation, for aid to Pretoria." When the Africans involved have all been killed and captured in this, or in other actions, the minority Governments may claim a victory without recognizing the immense danger to themselves and to their peoples through winning such Pyrrhic victories. No comfort may be taken from the fact that there is no immediate counterattack. The defeat drives deeply back into the heart of the village, the region, the continent, and coils the intention like a spring until it breaks out again here or there.

Basil Davidson, correctly described by the London *Sun* as "one of the world's leading authorities" when it published an article entitled "The Gathering Storm in Africa," wrote "a major race war in Southern Africa, always more than possible since the folly of Smith's rebellion in Rhodesia is now beginning to look more than probable."

He states his view that, whether they like it or not, South African leaders are being drawn ever more directly into conflicts to the north. Their policy had indeed been to avoid entanglements outside South Africa. The use of South African police in Rhodesia was a sharp departure. The use of napalm against African Nationalists in a Portuguese territory is a sharp departure. It was witnessed by Basil Davidson who also took a photograph of the canister and recorded the details in the *London Times* a few weeks ago. In the *Sun* article he refers to the mercenaries who came from Angola for illegal action in the Congo and sets it all in the context of a tougher and agreed line between South Africa, the Portuguese and Rhodesia and adds, "what we are witnessing are the ranging shots in a combined offensive to the northward, secretly agreed and secretly prepared . . . an offensive aimed at undermining the peace and independence of Zambia and her African neighbors". It is not my place, nor do I have data on which to do anything except to note with concern, that an observer as informed and as careful as Davidson should feel this to be the case.

From the southern side, in varying degrees, Europeans believe that the countries to the north harbor, train, or at the very least, permit to pass on their way south, armed African nationalists in revolt against South Africa, Rhodesia or the Portuguese authorities. Also, in varying degrees, they have been persuaded to believe that there is some external influence, some "ism" or other, behind all this. Again, it's not my place to weigh the elements. For the purpose intended, to sound a warning, it is enough, sadly, to note the cycle of action and reaction across the Zambezi has begun to spiral harshly, negatively, and that it is a familiar pattern to me from critical world crises at other times and places.

As though the situation were not complicated enough, one must refer to yet another damaging ingredient—the disenchantment, the desire for disengagement on the part of the British—and possibly here in the U.S.A. The battle for the pound, the controversy about unemployment, the complexity of African affairs as seen by newspaper readers ignorant of the continent, Congo, Ghana, and Nigeria all help to have the subject quietly shelved if at all possible. In addition there are those who wrongly feel that in some curious way the tragedies in Ghana, Nigeria and in other former colonies "let the side down . . ." The truth is that we have in the West, for too long, been attempting to judge the success or failure of African states by false indicators. If they create themselves in our image, make a success of federations and institutions created by us for them on European lines, they are good chaps. If they fail, we seldom stop to ask if the idea we planted was appropriate.

If I have learned anything from Africa, above all else it is the fact that political stability depends upon African leadership that is close to, attuned to, sets an example for, the people. Nyerere's Arusha declaration and Kaunda's doctrine on Humanism are the programs most likely to engage peoples on positive constructive lines of development. Yet, how often do we hear criticism in the West, especially of the Arusha declaration, because a small element in the program appears to affect our interests by nationalizing some banks and a few industries. That was a bit in the tip of an iceberg. Below, in the body of it, is a really tough regime, a set of disciplines to root out corruption in government—many factors that critics from European countries often gratuitously tell Africans they should do. Kaunda also has a tough program for his government and people. How much have you seen in your papers about that side of the program? How much on the other hand appeared when the extent of Nkrumah's lapses were revealed? These programs in Zambia and Tanzania provide the African peoples with an example of leadership without which the critical link for political stability would not be possible, i.e., the link between central government and the needs of even the most remote and poorest people in the land. Our external interest, incidentally, is more likely to find protection in that setting because protection of investment is only achieved by protecting people as a whole.

Disengagement, a break in the dialog between African states now, would be disastrous for Africa and the West alike. I urge you, through your organizations, to use what influence you have to keep Africa's problems before us, and the pressure on for positive peaceful solutions. Should violence begin in southern Africa, and one prays that all be spared it, it could spread like a sheet of flame through the tindery bush of that region, in the world of fear and of anxiety it represents.

Europeans are naturally concerned when Africans come from the north to commit sabotage south of the Zambezi, and although one knows that the perennial "man in the street" does not necessarily reflect government opinion, it still is a shock to hear so many of them saying that it may be necessary to teach the African States "a lesson", and in that context, quoting recent events in the Middle East as an example, of the "salutory pre-emptive strike." And, on the other side of the Zambezi it is also a shock to hear African friends, who even twelve months ago talked seriously and hopefully about support to bring about a positive and peaceful solution to the problems in Southwest Africa, Rhodesia and the Portuguese territories, now more often conclude that the West is too engaged in other problems in other regions, too inhibited by virtue of their commercial investment in southern Africa to do anything substantial. Therefore, they must find ways and means, perhaps with others, and you can imagine some of the possibilities that come to mind. Again, without attempting to weigh charge and counter-charge, these are some of the signs of growing tension that intensifies Britain's argument that force couldn't be used against "kith and kin" in Rhodesia strikes them as racism, and they say that they have been let down.

Should violence occur, one must face the prospect of large movements of refugees, European as well as African. Refugee movements might well start from Rhodesia when more Africans there begin to learn that recent legislation is shaping a pattern of apartheid for that country. The Tribal Trust Land Act passed in the last twelve months, The Emergency Power African Affairs, Regulations, The Citizenship Amendment Act, and now the Property Owners Residential Protection Bill, foreshadow and provide the powers for the South African pattern of apartheid.

It is a grim and tragic thing to have to observe the vast area of Africa below the equator, so rich in human and natural resources as to be able to put a thumping pulse of vitality into the continent, providing examples of European enterprise like the Portuguese Zambezi Valley scheme, and many in South Africa which are great projects, examples of the way in which countries like Zambia and Tanzania have, since independence, put fantastic effort and priorities into educating and training their peoples. It is grim and tragic to observe that, instead of being able to function as Africa's powerhouse, the regime is instead being dragged by events towards a vortex of human tragedy because, yet again, the dignity of man has been disregarded.

In Britain's last century, it was the horror of their conditions that forced working people to bring about changes, peacefully, thank God. In southern Africa it will be the conditions of degradation, conditions that cause so many Africans to murder each other, conditions that limit the education, freedom, and the sense of dignity of the African, that will spark action—unless, urgently, men see that impoverished conditions, impoverished thought, impoverish the whole society in which it exists, and finally, driven by despair, as I said earlier, a compression chamber may be ignited as easily and irrelevantly as an American city by a hot night, an insensitive cop, a remark, a smashed skull from a baton.

The dogmas of the quiet past are irrelevant to the stormy present. Let us disenthrall ourselves.

LEGAL ASPECTS OF THE
REFUGEE PROBLEM

4

OSCAR SCHACHTER, United Nations Institute for Training and Research

That refugees have manifold legal problems is obvious, and that they present legal problems for others, and especially for governments, is also plain enough. One would, in fact, need a treatise to cover these problems, and that would require more knowledge than I have. But fortunately for you, as for me, our time is limited, and, consequently I shall only point up the main issues.

One naturally thinks first of the refugee as an individual—homeless, without papers, often uncertain as to nationality, and domicile. His right to remain in the country is frequently in jeopardy, he may be denied the opportunity to work, his children excluded from schools, he and his family cut off from social welfare, his mobility restricted. All of this has become familiar in the successive waves of refugees we have witnessed in this century.

Somewhat less obvious are the legal problems facing governments in regard to refugees. What are their obligations to those who come for a safe haven, who may be fleeing from neighboring states, who present an economic and social burden and often a political liability? May a state grant asylum to nationals hostile to a neighbor—should they tolerate political activities or propaganda directed against that neighbor? Shall international law, traditionally concerned with states, not individuals, as subjects, be expanded so that individuals may claim rights on the international level simply because they are refugees? These are the questions that have concerned the international bodies which since the end of World War I have endeavored to meet the problems of refugees.

WHO IS A REFUGEE?

You would expect a lawyer to give a complicated answer to a question as simple as that, and you would be quite right. Defining

45

the term "refugee" for the purpose of international protection is not simply a technical or semantic task; it is, in fact, a crucial step in determining which individuals shall receive international protection and which shall be denied such protection. In the early instruments, the problem did not seem so great; they merely referred to a specific group—Armenians, or Assyrians, or Russians—who had been displaced as a result of a particular event or series of events. Later as the groups multiplied, and international bodies were given comprehensive tasks for many groups, efforts were directed to reaching general definitions. A whole series of such general definitions of refugees eligible for aid or protction—beginning with UNRRA resolutions in 1944— culminated in the definition contained in the 1951 Convention relating to the Status of Refugees.[1]

The key elements in that definition may be summarized as follows: The refugee must be outside of the country of his nationality owing to well-founded fear of being persecuted for reasons of race, religion, nationality, membership of a particular social group, or political opinion. He must also be unable or, owing to such fear, be unwilling to avail himself of the protection of that country. If a person has no nationality, and he is outside the country of his former habitual residence, he must be unable or, owing to such fear (as described above) be unwilling to return to it.

In the 1951 convention, there was a time limit—namely, it was limited to refugees created as a result of events before 1951. However, a Protocol which recently entered into force for several states has the effect of removing that limit.[2] I should note here that 21 African States are parties to the 1951 Convention, and that the recent OAU meeting in Kinshasa recommended that all African States adhere to the 1951 Convention and the Protocol which removes its time limit. At the October meeting in Addis Ababa on refugees, it was recommended that "African States should take into account the specific aspects of the African Situation with regard, in particular, to the definition of an African refugee."[3]

PERSONS EXCLUDED FROM BENEFITS

Not all refugees who fall within the definition of a refugee are entitled to the protection and benefits of the convention.

One excluded category are persons receiving protection or assistance from agencies of the United Nations other than the UNHCR (for example, the refugees receiving assistance from the UNRWA).[4]

Another group excluded are the so-called national refugees, that is, those whose country of residence accords them rights and obligations attached to the possession of nationality. Of more importance are the several classes of refugees who are not considered as deserving protection or assistance by the United Nations. These include the following:

1. persons who have committed crimes against peace, a war crime, or a crime against humanity as defined in the international instruments relating to such crimes;
2. persons who have committed a serious non-political crime outside the country of refuge prior to their admission to that country;
3. persons who have been guilty of acts contrary to the purposes and principles of the United Nations.[5]

It does not take much reflection to discern in these three exclusionary clauses the issues that have complicated the problem of protecting individuals under charges in their countries of origin. The clauses reflect the attitude of states which oppose international protection of persons who have engaged in activities that are considered seditious or subversive or "against peace". They bring to mind the sharp and bitter debates through which I sat in UNRRA in 1944 to 1946[6], and then for many years in the United Nations, when it considered the treaty establishing the International Refugee Organization, the statute of the Office of the High Commissioner, and the 1951 Convention. Few discussions in international bodies have exhibited so much emotion and vehemence as these debates, particularly when they related to persons who had left the countries of eastern Europe.

WHO DETERMINES ELIGIBILITY

The 1951 Convention does not prescribe any particular procedure and thus leaves it to the parties. In European countries individual determinations have been used; in some cases the High Commissioner for Refugees participates in these procedures.[7] In Africa it has been difficult to resort to individual eligibility decisions in most cases, and as a result it has become necessary to deal with refugees *en bloc*. Those members of these groups have been declared as *prima facie* eligible and the High Commissioner for Refugees has taken action to protect them.[8]

RESTRICTIONS AGAINST EXPULSION
AND THE RIGHT OF ASYLUM

The first legal need of the refugee when he crosses the frontier of his country of origin is that he should be protected against forcible return. In the 1951 Convention, the Contracting States undertake not to expel a refugee who is lawfully in their territory except on grounds of national security or public order; the exceptions, moreover, may be taken under a decision reached in accordance with due process of law.[9] If a refugee is in the country illegally, the contracting states agree not to impose penalties on account of such illegality on refugees who come directly from a territory where their life or freedom was threatened, provided they have presented themselves without delay to the authorities and show good cause for their illegal entry or presence.[10] Moreover, the Convention has a general provision under which no contracting state shall expel or return a refugee in any manner whatsoever to the frontiers of territories where his life or freedom would be threatened on account of his race, religion, nationality, membership of a particular social group or political opinion.[11] This benefit may not, however, be claimed by a refugee if there are reasonable grounds for regarding him as a danger to the security of the country in which he is.

Although the Convention does not use the expression "right of asylum", the provisions just referred to against expulsion obviously involve an implicit recognition of that right. A few words may be appropriate on that subject, which only the other day was dealt with in the Legal Committee of the U.N. The Committee approved a Declaration on Territorial Asylum which has been many years in preparation.[12] A declaration—it should be noted—is not a treaty, but a statement of principles which may through application by states develop into customary law.

The main principle in the declaration recognizes the right of the state to grant asylum, and to have that right respected by others. It does not involve recognition of the right of the individual to receive asylum. Moreover, it is made explicit that the state granting asylum has the right to evaluate the grounds for such asylum. At the request of several African States, the declaration refers specifically to the grant of asylum to persons struggling against colonialism—a reference which some delegations favored as an encouragement to persons fighting against colonial domination. A series of recommendations on territorial asylum, similar in part to those in the United Nations Declaration, was adopted at the Addis Ababa Conference of October.[13]

These recommendations include an explicit provision requiring the refugee to abstain from subversive activities against any African country, except for countries under colonial and racist minority domination.

For most individual refugees the most important legal right, next to that of admission and nonexpulsion, is the right to earn a living. That right is set forth in the Universal Declaration of Human Rights, which is a statement of aspirations rather than law—and in the new International Covenant on Economic, Social and Cultural Rights which has recently been concluded, but is not yet in force. With regard to refugees, the 1951 Convention has several provisions on the right to work and to earn one's living. One of these provides that a refugee who has completed three years residence or who has children having nationality of the country shall have the same rights as citizens of the state of residence—in other words, shall be free of restrictive measures. Refugees who do not fall within these categories are given the most favorable treatment given to foreigners in the same circumstances.

Apart from wage-earning, rights to engage in self-employment and to practice the professions are to be at least as favorable as that accorded aliens generally. This provision is not always helpful; alien lawyers and schoolteachers are often denied the right to engage in their profession.

The Convention of 1951 also accords refugees with three years or more residence the same treatment as nationals in regard to public assistance, labor legislation and social security.

The refugee's need to travel is especially important. He often will have to settle in a country other than his country of first asylum, and frequently he will need to visit another country for employment or for study. Since he often cannot receive a national passport from his country of origin, it is necessary for him to get some documentation which can be recognized by the authorities of countries other than those in which he is resident.

The importance of this need for an internationally recognized document is evident from the history of international protection. The first example is the well-known Nansen passport issued to Russian refugees under an arrangement in 1922. Many of the other arrangements for specified groups adopted in the 1920s and 1930s were premised on the need for certificates of identity that served as travel documents. In the period after World War II, the London travel document was widely used. The 1951 Convention which consolidates the previous agreements also provides for a travel document to refugees who fall within the scope of that Convention.

The Convention travel document gives the holder the right of return to the country of issue. In form, it is a booklet resembling a national passport, and most States issuing the document have used the recommended model document prepared by the High Commissioner. Although the Convention itself has the 1951 dateline, a number of African countries have issued the travel document based on the recommendation that it be issued to post-dateline refugees. Of course, as states become parties to the new protocol eliminating the time limit, the problem of a dateline will disappear.

While it is normal for the country in which the refugee first obtains asylum to issue him a travel document, the Convention permits other Contracting States to issue the travel document and, in particular, recommends that such travel document be issued to such refugees who are unable to obtain one from the country of their residence. All Contracting States must recognize the validity of the documents issued by any State under the Convention. The right of the holder to return to the country which issued the document is of great importance in enabling him to take full advantage of the document, since visas generally are only issued to refugees who have the right of return to a particular country.

My remarks have centered largely on the 1951 Convention, a document of transcendent significance for the legal problems of refugees. It is fortunate, and even remarkable, that more than fifty countries have become parties to the Convention and, as I have indicated, that includes twenty-one African countries. On the other hand, these figures mean that a fairly large part of the world has not yet accepted the Convention including, for example, the United States. Nor has it been accepted by a number of African countries. For these governments, the treatment of refugees is still a matter entirely for national determination—and, often enough, governed by current political, racial, or social attitudes. One cannot assume that the refugees in these countries are being accorded the treatment provided under the 1951 Convention, though in some cases they probably are. In other cases, they are still subject to the discrimination and prejudice resulting from their peculiar situation. Many governments still reject the idea of international protection for individuals in their countries, and even more strongly reject such protection for persons who have left their country because of fear of persecution.

A more hopeful aspect can be seen in the efforts of international agencies, which are in many respects more effective than they have been at any time in the past. One must note with particular approval the Office of the High Commissioner for Refugees of the United Nations, which has carried on for so many years a valiant and courageous operation to bring legal protection to millions of displaced persons.

COMMENT

FRANCISCO URRUTIA, UNHCR Regional Representative at UN Headquarters, New York

There is very little to discuss when as, in my case, I agree completely with my old and good friend, Mr. Schachter. He has submitted a really outstanding paper. I would only make a few comments, not to discuss, but to support his views and maybe to explain some of the more important issues that he raises. Along these lines, and to permit you to evaluate the kind of legal problems faced by the refugee, I would like to draw your attention to the fact that, in this twentieth century, the governments on the one hand are facilitating traveling by even abolishing visas and sometimes passports, but on the other hand they often restrict the permits needed to work so that the foreigner can make a living in a foreign country. Now, for an ordinary migrant or foreigner this creates a problem, but for the refugee it is not just a problem, it is a tragedy, because the refugee cannot choose where to go and work. A refugee technically may be able to obtain with ease an entry permit to be admitted to a country, but it becomes more difficult every day for this refugee to be permitted to work, and this is a tragedy we are facing. Mr. Schachter pointed out very well that, for the refugee, the right to work is essential. To admit the refugee as a simple visitor without the right to work really is not granting him the right of asylum. He must be able to work, and this is why the Convention is important.

This leads me to another observation—the Convention, of course, is the basic instrument to implement the status of refugees. But we cannot expect the convention to solve all the problems. Many problems are not solved by it, and I can enumerate a number of them. For the moment I can think of at least two very important ones. One of them is the problem of students, teachers and intellectuals, who in many cases cannot be easily resettled in the country of first asylum. Take especially Africa, where it is not very easy for an intellectual, a professional, or a teacher to get a job in the first neighboring country where he arrives. In this case, in a humanitarian spirit, all the countries ought to be ready to give second or third asylum, but more than that, ought to be ready to make an effort to find jobs for these refugees because the most tragic case is the refugee, member of the intelligentsia of his country, going abroad and being unable to work. Also tragic is the problem of proof of civilian status. I know of many people who could not marry because they lacked proof of their civilian status. In some countries no one can be buried if someone does not submit a certificate, either a birth certificate or identification certificate, and most refugees have arrived without any kind of papers. A refugee without a paper in a new country sometimes is nobody —he doesn't exist. Not all these problems are solved by the Convention.

Now, going back to the paper by Mr. Schachter, he listed among the persons excluded from the benefits of refugees, those who are receiving protection or assistance from other agencies of the United Nations. It is not that they are not refugees. They are not refugees under the mandate of the High Commissioner, but, of course, they *are* refugees also. The Palestine refugees are not under the mandate of the High Commissioner, but they are refugees under the mandate of another agency of the United Nations. Another explanation I want to give to you is on what is called the "national" refugee. A refugee from East Germany in West Germany, for us, is not a refugee because there is only one Germany. If a German from East Germany comes to West Germany, he is in his country. He is not outside his country so he is not a refugee. This is also the case in Vietnam. People are called "refugees" in South Vietnam, but are not refugees under our terms of reference. A North Vietnamese in South Vietnam is not a refugee. He is in his country. He is in Vietnam. He may be a displaced person. Sometimes you call refugees people from one part of South Vietnam who had to go to another city in South Vietnam. When both cities are in South Vietnam and he is in Vietnam, he is in his country. In that case he is technically a displaced person, much more than a refugee. A person must be outside of his country to be a refugee.

Another observation he did not mention but I want to raise, because in other symposiums the question has been asked—is a deserter a refugee? A deserter, as such, is not a refugee, cannot be a refugee, but if a deserter fears persecution for political reasons, then he can be considered a refugee.

Regarding eligibility, Mr. Schachter asked me to tell you if your office has made decisions *en bloc, prima facie*. Yes. Obviously, if you have, in a few hours, several thousand refugees crossing a border, it would be ridiculous to think that we could interview the refugees one by one. If you see a whole group is crossing the border because they are afraid for political reasons, then a decision is made *en bloc, prima facie* for the whole group, and this has been done in Africa.

Two last remarks on the Convention. Mr. Schachter pointed out very well that, unfortunately, of the fifty-three countries which have now ratified the Convention, neither the United States or other important western countries have ratfiied this Convention.

As a matter of fact, neither Canada or the United States, or Mexico have ratified it, and in Latin America only five countries: Brazil, Argentina, Peru, Ecuador and Colombia have ratified it. But, I think one of the reasons why those countries have not acceded to this Convention is because of the time limit.

Now that the Protocol has been signed, extending the date line, I am confident that many other countries will accede both to the Convention and the Protocol. As a matter of fact, only a few weeks ago the Human Rights Commission of the Organization of American States approved a recommendation for all governments to accede both to the Convention and the Protocol and even dropped the idea of having a special convention for America. As far as the United States is concerned, I would like to point out that today, the United States, in fact, is giving to the refugees practically all the benefits of the Convention. As for travel documents, if a refugee wants to leave the United States, he is given what is called a reentry permit which is almost a passport of the same format as the United States passport. The only difference is that, instead of the word "passport" it says "Reentry Permit", but it has exactly the same form and pages for visas. We are confident that with the intervention of many of the voluntary agencies who have been urging the State Department to accede to the Convention, sooner or later the United States will also accede to the Convention.

NOTES

1. Convention Relating to the Status of Refugees signed at Geneva on 28 July 1951. The Convention entered into force on 22 April 1954. United Nations, *Treaty Series*, 189 (1954): 150.

2. The complete text of Article 1 reads as follows:

Article 1
DEFINITION OF THE TERM "REFUGEE"

A. For the purposes of the present Convention, the term "refugee" shall apply to any person who:

(1) Has been considered a refugee under the Arrangements of 12 May 1926[1] and 30 June 1928[2], or under the Conventions of 28 October 1933[3] and 30 June 1938[4], the Protocol of 14 September 1939[5] or the Constitution of the International Refugee Organization[6];

Decisions of non-eligibility taken by the International Refugee Organization during the period of its activities shall not prevent the status of refugee being accorded to persons who fulfill the conditions of paragraph 2 of this section;

(2) As a result of events occurring before 1 January 1951 and owing to well-founded fear of being persecuted for reasons of race, religion, nationality, membership of a particular social group or political opinion, is outside the country of his nationality and is unable or, owing to such fear, is unwilling to avail himself of the protection of that country; or who, not having a nationality and being outside the country of his former habitual residence as a result of such events, is unable or, owing to such fear, is unwilling to return to it.

In the case of a person who has more than one nationality, the term "the country of his nationality" shall mean each of the countries of which he is a national, and a person shall not be deemed to be lacking the protection of the country of his nationality if, without any valid reason based on well-founded fear, he has not availed himself of the protection of one of the countries of which he is a national.

B. (1) For the purposes of this Convention, the words "events occurring before 1 January 1951" in article 1, section A, shall be understood to mean either

(*a*) "events occurring in Europe before 1 Jaunary 1951"; or

(*b*) "events occurring in Europe or elsewhere before 1 January 1951"; and each Contracting State shall make a declaration at the time of signature, ratification or accession, specifying which of these meanings it applies for the purpose of its obligations under this Convention.

(2) Any Contracting State which has adopted alternative (*a*) may at any time extend its obligations by adopting alternative (*b*) by means of a notification addressed to the Secretary-General of the United Nations.

C. This Convention shall cease to apply to any person falling under the terms of section A if:

(1) He has voluntarily re-availed himself of the protection of the country of his nationality; or

(2) Having lost his nationality, he has voluntarily reacquired it; or

(3) He has acquired a new nationality, and enjoys the protection of the country of his new nationality; or

(4) He has voluntarily reestablished himself in the country which he left or outside which he remained owing to fear of persecution; or

(5) He can no longer, because the circumstances in connection with which he has been recognized as a refugee have ceased to exist, continue to refuse to avail himself of the protection of the country of his nationality;

Provided that this paragraph shall not apply to a refugee falling under section A (1) of this article who is able to involve compelling reasons arising out of previous persecution for refusing to avail himself of the protection of the country of nationality;

(6) Being a person who has no nationality he is, because the circumstances in connection with which he has been recognized as a refugee have ceased to exist, able to return to the country of his former habitual residence;

Provided that this paragraph shall not apply to a refugee falling under section A (1) of this article who is able to invoke compelling reasons arising out of previous persecution for refusing to return to the country of his former habitual residence.

D. This Convention shall not apply to persons who are at present receiving from organs or agencies of the United Nations other than the United Nations High Commissioner for Refugees protection or assistance.

When such protection or assistance has ceased for any reason, without the position of such persons being definitively settled in accordance with the relevant resolutions adopted by the General Assembly of the United Nations, these persons shall *ipso facto* be entitled to the benefits of this Convention.

E. This Convention shall not apply to a person who is recognized by the competent authorities of the country in which he has taken residence as having the rights and obligations which are attached to the possession of the nationality of that country.

F. The provisions of this Convention shall not apply to any person with respect to whom there are serious reasons for considering that:

(*a*) he has committed a crime against peace, a war crime, or a crime against humanity, as defined in the international instruments drawn up to make provision in respect of such crimes;

(*b*) he has committed a serious nonpolitical crime outside the country of refuge prior to his admission to that country as a refugee;

(*c*) he has been guilty of acts contrary to the purposes and principles of the United Nations.

---

1 League of Nations, *Treaty Series,* vol. 89, p. 41.
2 League of Nations, *Treaty Series,* vol. 89, pp. 53, 63; vol. 93, p. 377; vol. 204, p. 445, and vol. 205, p. 193.
3 League of Nations, *Treaty Series,* vol. 159, p. 199; vol. 172, p. 432; vol. 181, p. 429; vol. 200, p. 530; vol. 204, p. 464, and vol. 205, p. 214.
4 League of Nations, *Treaty Series,* vol. 192, p. 59; vol. 200, p. 572, and vol. 205, p. 218.
5 League of Nations, *Treaty Series,* vol. 198, p. 141, and vol. 205, p. 219.
6 United Nations, *Treaty Series,* vol. 18, p. 3, and vol. 26, p. 416.

3. UNHCR Document No. AFR/Conf. 1967/No. 2. See Appendix III.

4. See par. D. of Art. 1. in note 2.

5. See par. F. of Art. 1. in note 2.

6. Woodbridge, *UNRRA History of the United Nations Relief and Rehabilitation Administration* (1950), 2:469-543.

7. Weis, "International Protection of Refugees," *American Journal of International Law,* 48, no. 2 (April 1954) 193-221.

8. Schnyder, *Hague Academy Recueil des Cours,* I, 114 (1965): 339-446.

9. Article 32 reads as follows:

Article 32

EXPULSION

1. The Contracting States shall not expel a refugee lawfully in their territory save on grounds of national security or public order.
2. The expulsion of such a refugee shall be only in pursuance of a decision reached in accordance with due process of law. Except where compelling reasons of national security otherwise require, the refugee shall be allowed to submit evidence to clear himself and to appeal to and be represented for the purpose before competent authority or a person or persons specially designated by the competent authority.
3. The Contracting States shall allow such a refugee a reasonable period within which to seek legal admission into another country. The Contracting States reserve the right to apply during that period internal measures as they may deem necessary.

10. Article 31 reads as follows:

Article 31

REFUGEES UNLAWFULLY IN THE COUNTRY OF REFUGE

1. The Contracting States shall not impose penalties, on account of their illegal entry or presence, on refugees who, coming directly from a territory where their life or freedom was threatened in the sense of article 1, enter or are present in their territory without authorization, provided they present themselves without delay to the authorities and show good cause for their illegal entry or presence.
2. The Contracting States shall not apply to the movements of such refugees restrictions other than those which are necessary and such restrictions shall only be applied until their status in the country is regularized or they obtain admission into another country. The Contracting States shall allow such refugees a reasonable period and all the necessary facilities to obtain admission into another country.

11. Article 33 states:

Article 33

PROHIBITION OF EXPULSION OF RETURN ("REFOULEMENT")

1. No Contracting State shall expel or return ("refouler") a refugee in any manner whatsoever to the frontiers of territories where his life or freedom would be threatened on account of his race, religion, nationality, membership of a particular social group or political opinion.
2. The benefit of the present provision may not, however, be claimed by a refugee whom there are reasonable grounds for regarding as a danger to the security of the country in which he is, or who, having been convicted by a final judgment of a particularly serious crime, constitutes a danger to the community of that country.

12. The Declaration was adopted by the General Assembly on 14 December 1967 by unanimous vote. Res. 2312 (XXII).

13. UNHCR Document No. AFR/Conf. 1967/No. 3.

NON-CONSTITUTIONAL CHANGE OF GOVERNMENT AS A CAUSE FOR REFUGEES THROUGHOUT SUB-SAHARAN AFRICA

THOMAS R. ADAM, New York University

The growth of a refugee problem in tropical Africa presents a harrowing addition to current world tragedies. Exploration of timely remedies requires allocation of responsibility as an initial step. For practical purposes a distinction should be drawn between underlying causes, historic and otherwise, and the means to meet the situation as it exists at the moment. It is the latter that alone presents reasonable hope of alleviating the tragedy through institutional action. As the use of power is clearly indicated, responsibility lies with the institutional monopoly of social force centered in the political organization of the nation state.

It is the thesis of this contribution that the structural form of many of the emergent African governments is a major factor in permitting a breakdown of social tolerance. More specifically, it is suggested that the constitutional framework prevalent in African countries is inadequate to meet the stresses that have arisen since independence. There are two separate aspects of a political constitution that may be distinguished from each other. In the first place, the allocation of governmental powers and the arrangement of the apparatus of rule is an essential feature of any constitution. However, in the context of the problem under discussion, patterns of formal organization may be considered of lesser importance. The significance of constitutionalism as a political issue lies in the setting of standards acceptable to the community as the basis for their political union. It is this aspect I propose to stress. I am enough of a traditionalist to hold that an Agreement of the People is basic to constitutional rule anywhere, at any time. There are two features to such an agreement. First, the honest determination by a substantial majority of the community of standards that they approve, or at least tolerate, as foundations and limitations defining political authority. Let me interpose at this point that I have little criticism to offer of the integrity of the original constitutions of independent African states as expressions of popular acceptance. It is the second essential for constitutional government that may be questioned in the context of present African circumstances.

Each generation of citizens serves not only as guardians of the original constitutional agreement, but as the originators of change. This is the gravest responsibility facing the individual citizen in his relation to the political community. If, however, adequate machinery does not exist to provide unhampered discussion, based on honestly presented information and time for mature consideration, the safeguards of constitutionalism collapse. Another factor is the need for pragmatic interpretation of the existing constitution by an uncommitted authority possessing the means to make effective rulings.

These conditions for constitutional government may appear too biased in favor of Western legalism, to meet African conditions. On the other hand, the political process in any form of society is either based on acceptance of agreed standards, actively or passively, by the overwhelming bulk of the citizenry or it constitutes tyranny, at least in the Aristotelian use of the term. The preamble to the Constitution of the United States gives, in my opinion, a meaningful statement of the purpose and necessity of constitutional government. "We, the People of the United States, in order to form a more perfect Union, establish Justice, ensure domestic tranquility, provide for the common defense, promote the general welfare, and secure the blessings of liberty to ourselves and our posterity, do ordain and establish this Constitution for the United States of America." I would add my personal conviction that the political obligation of every individual to the state, his obedience and loyalty in short, depends upon the observance of this Constitution in its present form. It is difficult to envisage some different kind of bond that would unite citizens of an African state in a common political union.

As it is the element of social union that is being stressed in reference to a refugee problem, it is worth examining some exemplars of constitutional change or abrogation that affect political solidarity under African circumstances. Perhaps the constitutional provisions that condition the willingness of the individual to accept the obligations of citizenship should be isolated. These would appear to be, first, a Bill of Rights determining effectively the limits of government authority as exercised against the individual. Second, the degree of self-government agreed upon for regions and localities, as opposed to centralized authority, is a major factor in determining the willingness of the individual to enter into and preserve the union of a nation state. Interference with either or both these postulates constitutes a major breach in the original Agreement of the People and may be undertaken only under safeguards essential to honest popular consideration.

Ghana may serve as an exemplar of constitutionalism, as a factor in contributing to the political stability of an African state. The original Constitution came into formal existence as an Order of Council of the British sovereign. Though independent, Ghana remained within the British Commonwealth under the titular sovereignty of the Queen. As in the case of many constitutions, our own included, major issues dividing the nation at the time of writing the fundamental charter were compromised. A powerful opposition to Nkrumah's Convention Peoples Party sought to delay independence until the new state was guaranteed a federal structure. Nkrumah and his followers were equally insistent on a unitary form that would allow for a strong central administration on a democratic base.

The conflict verged on the brink of civil strife. Final constitutional provisions gave neither side a clear-cut victory. The British practice of granting a sovereign law-making power to the Cabinet acting with and through the national assembly was adopted. However, Article 63 gave constitutional standing to five regions—the eastern, western, Ashanti, northern and trans-Volta Togoland regions. Another article (Article 33) prohibited alteration of the boundaries of the regions without prior approval of the assemblies of the regions affected. While the powers of the regional assemblies were to be prescribed by the national assembly, Article 64 listed local government, agriculture, education, communication, health, public works, housing, police, and town and country planning as subjects for regional control. Furthermore, Article 87 provided for a political regional constitutional commission to report to regional assemblies on the devolution of powers and functions.

Tribal organization presented another point of bitter controversy. At the time of independence, opponents of Nkrumah's regime, led by the powerful Ashanti hierarchy maintained that independence would be used to destroy traditional ties in favor of the mass organizations through which Nkrumah had risen to power. Accordingly, the 1957 constitution stated in Article 66 that "The Office of Chief in Ghana as existing by customary law and usage is hereby guaranteed". Article 67 provided for the establishment of a House of Chiefs in each region. These houses were to possess advisory powers in relation to the executive and assembly, and in their own right, determined by declaration the nature of customary law in their own areas. Attempts to legislate away existing chiefly powers was countered by a provision that a bill affecting the functions of any chief had to be referred to the regional House of Chiefs three months before its second reading. The Constitution also ordained that each region should have a Head of the region, chosen by the regional House of Chiefs except in the case of the Ashanti region, where the Asantehene became Head of the region by hereditary right.

The original Constitution condensed civil rights into three propositions. The first declared that "no law shall make persons of any racial community liable to disabilities to which persons of other such communities are not made liable". The other two clauses guarded the right to freely profess, practice, or propagate any religion, and prohibited compulsory acquisition of property without just compensation. Any law contravening these three basic propositions was to be held null and void. The Supreme Court was given original jurisdiction in cases involving these rights.

The process for the amendment of the 1957 Constitution proved, in retrospect, its Achilles heel. Minor alterations in the constitutional structure were to be effected by a two-thirds vote of the total membership of the National Assembly. Vital changes affecting the existence, functions, or powers of a regional assembly required more deliberate methods. At an early stage of consideration such a measure had to be referred for deliberation to all the regional assemblies, and in some cases to the House of Chiefs. The final form of the amending Bill had to be passed by two-thirds of all the regional assemblies, including the Assembly of the region most affected. Then, if passed by two-thirds of the total membership of the National Assembly, the Constitution stood amended.

It is my suggestion that if this constitutional base of government for Ghana had been observed over a reasonable "shake down" period, it may have ensured limited government, a consensual evolution of traditional ties, and a good measure of political stability. Nkrumah, however, by 1960 had maneuvered his CPP into a sufficient monopoly of political power to undertake radical constitutional revision. Unquestionably he was aided in this by violent and unlawful activities of opposition elements. The ostensible purpose of formulating a Constitution drawing its authority directly from the popular will, and embodying African characteristics in place of colonial traditions, was acceptable as a principal of constitutional evolution.[1]

The major change, however, apart from the declaration of a Republic, consisted in the abolition of federalist provisions. Ghana was declared a "sovereign unitary Republic" (Article 5[1]). The provisions of the 1957 Constitution establishing regional assemblies were struck out, though Article 8 recognized division into regions now increased from five to eight. Formal existence of the Houses of Chiefs for each region was preserved with their functions placed wholly at the mercy of the central government. "A House of Chiefs shall consist of such Chiefs and shall have such functions relating to customary law and other matters as may be provided by law." It must be noted that Article 14 stated that "chieftancy in Ghana should be guaranteed and preserved" and that this article could be changed only through a popular referendum.

Certain fundamental principles limiting the power of government were inserted as part of a Presidential Declaration to be made on his assumption of office. These appeared to have the force of a Bill of Rights, subject to alteration only through a popular referendum. Among them was the provision "that subject to such restrictions as may be necessary for preserving public order, morality or health, no person should be deprived of freedom of religion or speech, of the right to move and assemble without hindrance or of right of access to Courts of law." The significant departure from the 1957 Constitution was that the President became the guarantor of civil liberties in place of the courts of law.

If, however, means had been provided for the implementation of the 1960 Constitution above the level of executive or legislative caprice and if its permanence had rested on a more substantial base than referendums conducted under a one party regime, constitutionalism could have probably survived in Ghana. The repudiation of constitutionalism was completed by the 1964 referendum which clothed the one-party system with the cloak of fundamental law. For all practical purposes, representation through the electoral process was rendered obsolete. In fact, no ballots were cast in the June 1965 election for the national assembly on the grounds that CPP candidates were running unopposed in all constituencies. It is a singular fact that no general election involving a vote count was held in Ghana after 1956, the year before independence. The popular referendums were marked by large scale fraud and the affirmative response to their loaded questions may be viewed as meaningful as the acclaim accorded Hitler or Stalin. Nkrumah's dismissal of the Chief Justice of the Supreme Court for refusal to follow the party line in treason cases shattered the last remnants of constitutional safeguards for civil liberties.

Nkrumah's theoretical concept of democracy, as embodied in the one party state and the popular referendum, does not appear rooted in the practices of traditional African society. I quote Rupert Emerson's reflections on this point: "It is relevant to ask whether democracy is an alien importation or an authentically African concept and practice. Although I am sure that a case can be made for the latter view, and a number of both Africans and non-Africans have made it, I would be strongly inclined to see political democracy in its modern guise as more alien than traditional in origin. Undoubtedly, the principles of consensus, of general discussion until agreement is reached, and of the selection of chiefs with an element of popular consent, are well established institutions in many African societies; but I have always been skeptical of the proposition that the democratic procedures and other attributes of the small face-to-face society can with any ease be translated into the political systems of large post-colonial states. And it is surely legitimate to ask how much of a working democracy, in the kind of terms I have been suggesting, was to be found in the Kanu emirate, the kingdom of Buganda, the Zulus under Chaka, or for that matter in any of the greater African states and empires."[2]

Perhaps the major consideration leading Nkrumah to his destruction of constitutionalism was his belief that social and economic development was the paramount consideration and could only be achieved by riding roughshod over all opposition. "Development" conceived of as the primary function of government overruled all but tactical questions of social consensus and political cohesion. Under African circumstances, planning for development will remain unavoidably a prerogative of elite groups for at least a generation to come. With limitations on government authority over the community and individual freed from the machinery of constitutional safeguards, the political process is diverted into the arena of violence and countersuppression. A bare century and a half has elapsed since the "wars of wandering" disrupted African society. Fear of persecution, and loss of economic security derived from customary possession of their land, reactivates the tradition of movement among tribal groupings to a breaking point of recently acquired national bonds.

The part played by constitutional forms in Ghana in determining the degree of political stability has been explored as an exemplar for other anglophobe African states. Ghana, through its comparative homogeneity, its educational and economic advancement, may be considered as possessing a high level of opportunity for combining social and economic development with political progress along the path of limited government on a popular basis. Absence of suitable machinery, in structural terms, to curb and balance the various power-seeking elements in the community appears to have had a significant role in reducing government to its present transient level of administration. Many other African states are troubled by deeper obstacles in their path to nationhood. Their political stability, lacking the continuity of effective constitutional safeguards, tends towards dangerous dependency on the quality of personal leadership.

The tragic situation of Nigeria falls within a category of its own. Perhaps the regional rivalries, inherited from the colonial regime were insoluble through orderly processes of popular government. Certainly our own Civil War indicates limits to resolving divisions through the binding strength of constitutional structure. However, the Constitution of independent Nigeria provided means for the resolution of conflicts between central and regional governments through the rule of law. The American bulwark of judicial review was written into the Constitution (#104[3], #107[1], #108, #109) granting authority to the Federal Supreme Court to interpret both Federal and Regional constitutions. Test cases arose in 1962 from the dispute between the central government and the Western region. On the major question of the powers of the central Parliament to declare a state of emergency in the Western region, the Supreme Court declined to pass judgement on the grounds, familiar to American constitutional law, that the matter involved a "political" question intended by the Constitution to be determined by the subjective will of the legislature. This failure of the Court to establish its authority, to arbitrate a constitutional crisis, may indicate the inapplicability of judicial review as a factor in preserving political stability under African conditions. On the other hand, alternative means for providing an institutional framework for a federal union are difficult to envisage.

The heritage from the British system to anglophobe Africa was reliance on the absolute sovereignty of the representative legislature as the guarantor of popular rule. With the exception of Southern Rhodesia, the United Kingdom government took scrupulous care to prevent its authority over African communities being transferred to a minority group within the new state. Less successfully, through the instrumentality of a constitution negotiated before independence, the abdicating colonial regime sought to provide adequate protection for internal minorities against transient majorities. The operative structure needed, however, now appears to have been beyond the contribution possible from Britain's own constitutional experience. The unwritten, historic conventions that balanced the legal assumption of Parliamentary sovereignty in England could not be transmitted to peoples not sharing the full experience of English history. In consequence, the anglophobe African states were launched into independence with a constitutional keel insufficiently welded to the hull of partisan politics. Constitutional changes, disruptive of the original conditions for political solidarity, could be effected without meaningful consideration by the bulk of the citizenry. It is to the credit of African statesmanship that the temptation presented to leaders and their temporary majorities to impose their will, in absence of a known consensus, has been so generally avoided.

The prospect of future strains on national unity, however, requires greater reliance on the continuity of an established institutional structure. The rule of law means, in essence, that every individual within the political state can have confidence that basic rights and equal treatment are ensured above the level of partisan politics. The constitutional structure should provide an effective limit to political experimentation not based on a true consensus. This may be considered too cautious a viewpoint to apply to the urgencies of African social and political organization. Perhaps it is, but the alternative to be faced is that violence, persecution, and a tragic movement of peoples may prove the price of change by a wilful minority that has moved too fast for the acceptance of their views by the bulk of the community. When constitutional limitations are disregarded in favor of emotional appeals to economic or social objectives, the devotion of the individual to traditional ties may be brought into sharp opposition to his loyalty to a recently formed, and artifically conceived, political state.

Institutional barriers serving to curb the impatience of even an idealistic and competent elite may prove essential to anchor the ship of state against blasts of civil disunity. To quote an African scholar: "If we interpret relationships between individual citizens as being partly based on a 'covenant' promising mutual respect of each other's person and property, it could be maintained that such promises of mutual respect are useless without a sword to enforce them. The 'sword' may be taken to be the armed forces. And the person who is supposed to use the sword is the sovereign."[3] The turning of the sword on its official wielder in a succession of military coups d'etats indicates that the armed forces in many African countries do not consider that their monopoly of force has been properly employed for the guardianship of the basic social compact.

As a final example, Kenya may be cited as an evolving nation state that has met successfully transition to independence. The continuity of political stability within Kenya, however, appears to lack institutional safeguards. So long as the present leadership endures, confidence seems warranted. But after Jomo Kenyatta, what? The original Constitution granting self-government recognized the need to make binding provisions for the fundamental rights and freedoms of the individual. "Whereas every person in Kenya is entitled to the fundamental rights and freedoms of the individual, that is to say the right whatever his race, tribe, place of origin or residence, or other local connection, political opinions, colour, creed or sex, but subject to respect for the rights and freedoms of others and for the public interest to each and all of the following, namely life, liberty, security of the person and the protection of the law; freedom of conscience, of expression of assembly and association, and protection of his home and other property and from deprivation of property without compensation: the following provisions shall have effect provided that the rights and freedoms of any individual do not prejudice the rights and freedoms of others or the public interest".[4]

The provisions that followed were sufficiently explicit to support actions against their breach in impartial courts of law. It is proper to inquire whether the existing constitutional structure of Kenya has maintained the means to implement these conditions of political union beyond the level of administrative convenience, or temporary majority opinion. If so, why have the 175,000 residents of Asian extraction become a probable refugee problem? I have been informed, through I have not been able to check the figures, that not more than ten percent of the Asians have surrendered their British passports and opted for full Kenyan citizenship. This reluctance indicates distrust of equality of treatment and basic protection of personal liberty and property rights. A question of confidence is posed which would appear unanswerable except in terms of effective constitutional guarantees for minority cultural groups.

In conclusion, I will quote the reflections of Sir Ivor Jennings on the problems of constitutional government derived from British practices. "I merely say that it is not beyond the wit of man to produce formulae which will provide protection. One could even extend the examples to social customs and tribal organization, though that might be more difficult. People usually think not in terms of protective clauses but of Bills of Rights. But Bills of Rights have a different purpose, to protect the individual rather than communities. They protect the individual against harsh or

unjust legislation . . . Also all Bills of Rights depend on the existence of a strong judiciary whose decisions are generally acceptable. Nevertheless, we have had considerable experience of different forms of Bills of Rights in the United States, Canada, Nigeria,
India, Pakistan and Malaya: and so it is possible to devise a Bill
of Rights which suits the conditions of a particular country. Constitutional devices give protection to groups and individuals, but
they cannot replace good will and this means good will on
both sides."[5]

It is the thesis of this paper that the undoubted good will
present in the independent states of Black Africa requires to be
cast into more effective constitutional forms, in order to provide
a structure of government that will prove strong enough to with-
stand the violent communal divisions that underly refugee
problems.

DISCUSSION

EDWARD SCHILLER, Nassau Community College, New York

I thought perhaps some queries to Professor Adam would help
explain and illuminate some of the questions I have as to constitutionalism or lack of it. The first comment I might make is
that the constitutions of the new African states, indeed the nations
themselves, were of colonial manufacture. Bills of rights, checks
and balances, and judiciary controls all grew out of the western
intellectual tradition supported by the middle classes of Europe,
and I don't quite understand how you can expect a consensus or
approval of such constitutions from an indigenous people who
have hardly even developed any sense of nationalism.

DR. ADAM: My impression is that all the constitutions of the
African states were probably actually made in London, but they
were made by African groups. Admittedly, these African groups
were elite groups and groups in the Western tradition, but from

my knowledge of the making of these constitutions, there was very, very little imposition of the views of the Colonial Office of her Majesty's government, or what the African groups drew up as their constitution. There were no constitutional conditions laid down and I would say the consensus by the least articulate groups to the original constitution was pretty great, as good as the United States regards its constitution.

DR. SCHILLER: You mentioned two major factors that must exist in constitutions of Sub-Saharan Africa; a bill of rights, and a proper balance between regional self-government and centralized authority. I think you made this point particularly in reference to Ghana where the balance was altered after a short while. I wonder if the federal principle can be built into any African constitution when each country's nationalism was, for the most part, anti-colonialism to begin with, and then when independence came, tribal loyalties emerged to challenge the conception of a national state.

DR. ADAM: I would say that any hope of the African communities continuing with nation status if they want to, is for them to find a belief in themselves, as a nation, in something more than the freedom from colonial rule, and they cannot do that by abolishing bylaws of their regional and ethnic divisions. They have got to do it by agreement and by fairly slow processes. Again, I would refer to American history and the slow process by which we managed to overcome our states rights concept. If George Washington had gone dictator and slammed us all into one group, we would probably have had a refugee problem in Canada.

DR. SCHILLER: I feel the African problem is that they have much less time to mature their nationalism then we had.

DR. ADAM: I think it was patience more than time.

DR. SCHILLER: You mentioned Ghana's constitution, I wonder really was it the seizure of political power by Nkrumah and the altering of the federal constitution into a unitary one which led to his downfall and the military regime or was it really the violation of individual rights, the failure of economic progress and actually the bankruptcy which caused the breakdown in government? Was it a constitutional problem, or was it something that could have happened regardless of the kind of constitution?

DR. ADAM: I would say it is a constitutional problem because had there been an operative constitution, Nkrumah would not have been able to violate individual rights, and regional rights opted. He wasn't up against a structure which offered him opposition. We have many politicians both in the United States and Britain and elsewhere, sometimes even in France, who would violate all sorts of rights if they could, but the structure of government hinders them doing it and only in very extreme cases can they overcome that structure. I think Nkrumah suffered from the lack of any structural resistance to his ambitions.

DR. SCHILLER: Referring to Nigeria again, you mentioned that the Supreme Court power to interpret was built in, but when the time came for the Court to use it, it delegated it out and gave it back to the Parliament. Wasn't it really the impotence of the central government which, in fact, was controlled by northerners, that was at the root of the genocide that took place and the present refugee problem? What difference would there have been if the Supreme Court at that time had acted in the western Nigerian situation? Would it have resolved the crisis which was political in nature?

DR. ADAM: It might not have made any difference at all. It would have been a gesture, if tested. I don't know how close the balance was at the time. After all, our own constitution collapsed with the Civil War, and I don't pretend a judicial review is at all an infallible method. It is sad it wasn't even tried in Nigeria, even after it was built in, or it might have made history.

DR. SCHILLER: You say the United Kingdom took scrupulous care to prevent its authority from being transferred to a minority group within any new state. I wonder about Zanzibar. Would it not be an exception to that?

DR. ADAM: Who would you say was the majority in Zanzibar —the Arabs?

DR. SCHILLER: No. The Arabs were the minority. You said the United Kingdom took steps to prevent this authority from being transferred to a minority group. Did they not give it to a minority group; i.e., the Arabs?

DR. ADAM: No. I would argue that point about Zanzibar. The political party that took over had been elected by a majority.

NOTES

1. The machinery adopted for constitutional change, however, amounted to an evasion of popular consideration. A plebiscite was held on a draft of a Constitution which the government bound itself to implement. In subsequent fact, fundamental discrepancies appear between the draft and the final instrument. Among the most significant of these was the destruction of the principle of Parliamentary sovereignty by an article authorizing the President "to give directions by legislative instruments" if he considered the national interest was involved. Only 54 percent of the registered voters cast their ballots on the new Constitution whose validity as an expression of popular will was questionable. See Leslie Rubin and Paula Murry, *A Review of the Constitution and Government of Ghana* (London 1961).

2. Rupert Emerson, "African States and the Burden they Bear", *African Studies Bulletin* (April 1967); pp. 9-10.

3. Ali A. Mazrui and Donald Rothschild, "The Soldier and the State in East Africa; some theoretical conclusions on the army mutinies of 1964" *Western Political Quarterly* vol. 20, no. 1 (March 1967), p. 93.

4. Abridged extract from the Kenya Order in Council, 1961, no. 791, (Her Majesty's Stationery Office).

5. Sir Ivor Jennings, "Is a Party System Possible in Africa", *The Listener* (16 February 1961).

EFFECTS OF REFUGEES ON THE NATIONAL STATE

6

GEORGE L. METCALFE, Michigan State University

A Russian proverb has it that man consists of a body, a soul, and a passport. For millions of displaced persons in this world, that proverb is more than a clever remark. In a very real sense, in a world of increasing conflict, in a period of history described as the era of the Cold War, we can agree with Edgar Chandler's contention that this is, among other possibilities, the Age of the Refugee.

Whole areas of the globe have been drastically redefined in this century. Political systems and boundaries have been reconstituted at a pace and under conditions intolerable to millions of individuals. The complete political division of the world into sovereign nation-states—often in a violent manner—has made possible the virtual exclusion of persons from the world community, with the loss of basic civil liberties and security offered most individuals by common law.

The burden of complex political and economic conditions has made the refugee something of an institutional problem to be solved with objectivity and haste. The basic purpose of most assistance provided the refugee is how to deal with his physical displacement rather than his personal concern for having been denied what he feels are fundamental human rights. There is a sustained tendency to regard the refugee solely in terms of his potential threat to political and economic stability. Thus, for the pragmatic, honorable goal of maintaining world peace, it is the symptom and not the cause of refugees that occupies most of our attention. In a deeply dangerous sense, the refugee has come to symbolize the agent of separation, the hardening of attitudes in conflict. He is often able to drive real or potential combatants further apart. He can become the symbol of the enemy across the border.

It is not unreasonable to suggest that the exile, in a unique way, is the price the world community pays in the interest of maintaining international order and peace. So long as the ideological balance of power on an international scale can be conceptually defended, the price of pacifying the refugee is viewed as the more reasonable course when the only other alternative is aiding him in his cause. Thus, the refugee strives for physical and psychic survival, largely in the absence of improving the essential meaning and value of country and human dignity on a personal basis.

It is not surprising, therefore, that the general attitude of the refugee to assistance, and opinions about his place in the world, is one of distrust. And why not? He is convinced of the need for change. But the world, in its infinitely abstract wisdom of what is best for all, posits a continuing maintenance of the status quo. Thus, decisions about the refugee tend to be coldly objective since, in most cases, a very obvious policy of pacification is built into the resettlement programs on his behalf. In my own experience with African refugees, in Africa and here in America, I am quite convinced that the ultimate significance of their being in exile is systematically discounted in the total perspective of the formalized programs initiated for them. Though southern African refugees get some support from the Liberation Committee of the Organization of African Unity, the West—particularly Britain and the United States—and the United Nations, offers them obscure moral support for liberation, while at the same time pursuing programs which encourage a posture of rehabilitation with the promise of a new life serving free Africa, and not the cause of liberation for which they seek support. Consistent respect for the southern African refugee's right to violently protest against white minority rule in southern Africa is lacking in any substantive degree. This is a critical example: here we have refugees who believe that racism is the common enemy of all man, that support for such a belief will be found in significant ways in the West and in the United Nations. But once in exile, the refugee finds the obvious merits of his position considerably dulled when confronted by foreign policy decisions based on the complexities of self-interest and ideological stalemate. This situation rather painfully informs the refugee that most host countries have two faces: one for the casual visitor to Africa and another face for the displaced person.

For the politically active refugee, rehabilitation often causes the fundamental loss of purpose and identity. Facing this loss in a strange culture, with a foreign language and different traditions, can generate a deep sense of grief and insignificance. It is in this context that the refugee discovers the real meaning of becoming a political exile. Rather than seeing himself as a liberated human being and potential freedom fighter, the refugee is estranged from himself and his cause. Indifference, despondency and determination occupy his life on an erratic basis, with determination—the belief in his cause and his rights—the most difficult to sustain with clarity and purpose, through time. Again, in my experience, this is particularly true for many southern African exiles.

But it is equally important to recognize that the vast majority of refugees in Africa are not freedom fighters. Many have fled their homes in fear of escalating violence between leaders of political pressure groups engaged in power struggles which prey upon ethnic loyalties and larger racial and religious divisions between White and Black, Arab and African, Muslim and Christian. According to the United Nations High Commissioner for Refugees, the African refugee situation—divided as it is between what John Marcum has called the "race curtain" of southern Africa, and those caught in the violence and uncertainty of political evolution in free Africa—constitutes the most difficult problem facing U.N. agencies, individual states, and private groups concerned with the refugee in the contemporary world. From Senegal in West Africa to the heart of the continent, stretching from the Sudan through South Africa, the African refugee problem continues to grow more critical each year, even though the United Nations High Commission for Refugees has been involved since 1961.

Today there are over nine hundred thousand refugees in Africa accounted for by the High Commissioner. Although refugee movements in West Africa are generally reported only from Portuguese Guinea to Senegal, it is known that a problem exists with refugees from independent Guinea to the Ivory Coast, and the possibility of more refugees from Nigeria on an increasing basis is not an unrealistic expectation. Also, since the beginning of the year, an estimated 25,000 refugees have fled Ethiopia for the Sudan, and some 33,000 southern Sudanese have fled to the Congo.

But of the nine hundred thousand counted by the Commissioner, some 450,000 are viewed as settled through refugee programs, mainly on behalf of Angolans in the Congo and refugees from Portuguese Guinea settled in Senegal. Another one hundred thousand refugees have been settled on what is a rather tenuous basis, most of whom are from the Sudan and Rwanda, living in neighboring states.

There is a particularly unique factor about refugees in Africa: the problem is not generally one of displaced individuals, but rather whole ethnic groups, particularly in free Africa. Also important is the fact that the ethnic origin of refugees in some host African states is often the same as in the country being fled. Thus, the arbitrary boundaries of ex-colonial Africa have not entirely separated the unity of language, tradition, and psychological bonds which help alleviate the problem of resettling some of these displaced persons.

But, even with the remarkable efforts of U.N. agencies, private groups as well as individual African states, and the OAU., there are some 250,000 known refugees in a state of political suspension, unsettled, and dependent on assistance of a continuing emergency nature. Settling large groups of refugees takes an average of two years, though a continuing influx and security dilemmas in host states greatly complicate the resettlement process.

The rehabilitation of non-violent African refugees, most of whom must be resettled in African states other than their own, has cost the U.N. High Commission for Refugees some $10 million in the past six years, and the budget for 1967, including emergency grants for new refugee movements, is over $3 million. Since the states of asylum in Africa are not generally equipped to handle the economic and political problems of refugees alone, this work of the United Nations is most important. By channeling the problem of refugee settlement through the U.N., a multilateral solution can be financed and executed in the overall interests of maintaining international order in the face of potential crisis situations caused by refugee displacement.

Though humanitarianism and the preservation of order are important principles in this work of the U.N. High Commission for Refugees, the aid and planning initiated is not provided as a substitute for a negotiated settlement of conflict between refugees and their own governments. Nor is material assistance provided at a level which might act as a positive incentive for other persons to become refugees. (The innovative ability and economic rationality of the rural African is not to be underestimated!)

Legal concerns for refugees are very complicated sometimes, but concerted efforts are made to guarantee at least basic civil liberties and safety for the exile. In this regard, in Africa the Commission works closely with the Organization of African Unity, as well as with other international agencies such as UNESCO, the FAO, WHO and the ILO. Africa, too, works with other agencies to solve these legal problems. Of the 50 countries represented in the Convention concerning the Status of Refugees, 19 are in Africa. Church bodies, the International Red Cross, and other private groups also are significantly involved, contributing greatly to the desired quality of neutrality in dealing with African refugees.

Crucial in all this work, of course, are the attitudes of the refugees themselves. Thus, efforts are made to encourage the refugee to recognize his responsibility to his host government by demonstrating interest and effort in solving his own problems, by becoming a useful member in society in the country of asylum. This point is stressed particularly when dealing with refugees from free African states, but is not entirely relevant for refugees from southern African states, many of whom may be supported as freedom fighters in independent Africa.

Though these are remarkable efforts on behalf of refugees, it must be made clear that the causes of national displacement are not being effectively met. Except in the case of southern African refugees—and this varies the closer one gets to the Republic—the sovereign rights of individual states, constitutional or not, have paramouncy over the individual rights of exiles, who by political conviction or fear of violence have been forced from their homes and face permanent resettlement in a foreign land. The maintenance of stability and order for their own sake has been equated with the right of the individual state and its leaders to define the process of change in Africa. The growing crisis of expectations, the continuing threat of civil war and violent change through military coups, has been met with a policy of crisis commitment to stability and peace at any cost in human terms, in both independent and white southern Africa.

Though hopes for long-run solutions to refugee problems are often voiced, the reality of African conditions today does not suggest a cause for high optimism about such hopes in the foreseeable future. (The United States has still not signed the 1951 Convention on Refugees.) Certainly the real and potential threat of violent conflict in southern Africa is nowhere near negotiable phase. Equally significant, however, is the rapidly escalating refugee problem in independent Africa, a fact often overlooked in public forums outside the African continent. Sudanese refugees in the Congo, Uganda, and the Central African Republic total some one hundred-fifteen thousand persons, and the number is growing. Over 74,000 Congolese refugees are in Burundi, Uganda, the Central African Republic and Tanzania. Ethopian refugees in the Sudan are estimated to number nearly 25,000, and over 50,000 Rwandese have fled to Burundi, the Congo, Tanzania and Uganda.

Such figures, though far from complete, give graphic evidence that the overall climate of change and political evolution in white and free Africa is non-negotiable conflict in varying degrees. The effect of the refugee on the national state in Africa, therefore, must be studied in terms of varying degrees of potential or actual violence. The refugee, it seems to me, is testament to the fact that violence is part of the normal condition in the political life of much of the African continent.

Evaluations of degrees of political expertise, superior levels of civilization, and varying degrees of economic progress seem to have little to do with either the presence or absence of a refugee problem. Tanzania, however, that remarkable, poverty-ridden expanse of non-aligned self-reliance; surrounded by states who continually flood her with refugees, and deeply involved as she is in the violent struggle against white southern Africa, is an incredibly important exception worthy of serious attention, particularly by those who believe that coercion is a reasonable force in effecting political unity in the development process.

In other African states, where coercion has created the refugee, the respect for violence is a growing phenomenon. Refugees tend to accept the role of violence, and in the opinions of those I have known—most of whom considered themselves freedom fighters, not just exiles—violent conflict is seen as the only meaningful way in which artificially constituted nations might come to grips

with the need to create truly representative nationalistic consciousness. In this regard, the refugees agree with Frantz Fanon, that in
some inextricable way, particularly peculiar to Africa today, violence integrates and creates the nation. Violence is becoming
significant where leaders—white or black—pursue a narrow, abstract nationalism which speaks to issues instead of people, and
supports vested interest groups at the expense of wider participation at the grass roots level. Where leadership and minority groups
use power to coercively limit and control participation by the
masses in a narrow nationalism, violent conflict is not only possible
in the eyes of the refugees, but must be conceivably expected by
those in power. Because a narrow nationalism is founded on the
principle of arbitrary rule, conflict on a violent basis is viewed by
the refugee as reasonable. In a most significant sense, therefore,
the liberation-prone refugee sees his primary function as that of
testing the paramountcy of "legalistic" rule, constitutional or otherwise, through violent conflict. The degree of violence involved
depends partly on the strength of the central authority as well as
on the overall range of participation of the people caught in the
arbitrary rule process, toward goals set forth by the ruling
authority.

In such a situation, therefore, as Paul Goodman suggests, freedom becomes purely a juridical process through time. The individual is not born free, but he has the right to wrest it from his social
and political environment. The individual caught in a rigidly
controlled change process must decide the right relationship with
reality, to achieve what is viewed as just by the individual or group
for human and social survival. Likewise, in judging the merits of
their participation, some decision must be made on when the price
of involvement or noninvolvement is too high to be accepted. In
my opinion, it is reasonable to assume, particularly for those refugees bent on liberation of their homelands, that most have decided
that the price of participating in the status quo—in both white and
free Africa—has risen to the level where violent conflict is the
most logical, just course of action they can accept.

St. Clair Drake has noted that the attitude of many Africans,
leaders and nonleaders alike, is that independence means nothing
if not the right to make one's own mistakes, or to decide in the
incredibly heterogenous environment that is Africa which values,

and therefore goals, are to receive national priority. It is obvious, I believe, that the non-humanistic pragmatism of contemporary African development forges an attitude about value-goal decisions which often leads to the creation of some highly inflexible political institutions—and, I must add, political leaders. Once again, however, I mention that in my opinion, Tanzania and President Nyerere represent at least one important exception to the general rule.

In nearly all of Africa, the fundamental imperative to change is economic development. The role of the individual or groups of individuals in this change process is determined largely from central authority, based essentially on a wide variety of methods and procedures about producing and dividing the national pie. With differing degrees of moral integrity, special problems related to forced economic growth demand the sacrificing of some democratic values for the often accepted principles of achieving abstract national unity—sometimes referred to as securing the political kingdom—and the vaguely reasonable goal of rapid modernization. The cost of this economic determination, and the philosophy that high consumption means development, linked with modern mass communication so vividly separating rich and poor in white and free Africa alike, has caused what Raul Prebisch has called the rising sense of humiliation, a tremendous sense of humiliation among the masses whose participation in the nation-building process seems at once very limited and unfulfilling. It is in this psychological environment that the crisis of expectations in Africa must be appreciated. Rooted in goals of economic development, the promises of independence, the escape from subjugation, are the fundamental causes of anxiety on the individual level which produces one of the most dangerous potential revolutionaries in the world today: the African refugee. By legitimizing human dignity and civil liberties only within the matrix of economic growth, the panacea of development has relegated the choices of men on an individual level to a very subordinate role. Control of the development process, and the degree of individual participation therein, by political elites or minority groups, forms the basis of what I have called a narrow nationalism, and what my refugee friends refer to as the artificial nation-state. With the systematic use of coercion through law and enforcement, white southern Africa has dedicated itself to a narrow nationalism where participation is determined on the basis of education, income, religion, race, culture and anti-communism, so long as they do not conflict with the vested interests of the white minority, which rigidly determines the degree and direction of nonwhite participation through time. In this environment, the southern African unit of labor becomes the active refugee with unique problems to solve in his achieving his goal of liberation at any cost, including total race war. This violent challenge of the refugee to the national state in southern Africa has been indefinitely accepted.

In free Africa, generally, without the coercive means to control political and economic participation, African governments are forced to try to satisfy insistent demands for higher standards of living while also being forced to cope with a rapidly evolving social system. By accepting the imperative of economic development in their difficult situation, African leaders in free Africa, as Skarrs suggests, have laid claim to, and denied the human condition at the same time. This contradiction is so explosive that there has emerged in Africa a politics of violence, born in a growing crisis of expectations, both symbolized by the African refugee.

In a paradoxical manner, however, free Africa has the potential to reevaluate its goals and priorities precisely because of its refugee problem. The rapid growth in size and mobility of refugee groups in free African states, has demanded a new sense of urgency about the need for some structural unity, not only in dealing with refugees in a manner consistent with maintaining political stability in and between the states involved, but also in coming to grips with the root causes of refugees. Thus, it is quite possible that the continuing difficulties of African economic development and the persistence of white domination in southern Africa, may very well forge new meaning and purpose in the cause of unity among African states.

Should this reevaluation not take place, and should this urgency for order in unity fail, then the critical significance of the refugee problem is likely to increase. In such a situation, it is only reasonable to expect that narrow-minded national goals and ambivalent leadership will generate a politics of revolutionary violence for its own sake, and on its own terms. The frustrations of the national state combined with those of the refugee turned revolutionary could lead to greater factionalism and fanatic nationalism in free Africa, while drawing more closely together the great power of the white minority states of southern Africa. It is particularly significant to realize at this point, that the continuing frequency of rule by authoritarian civilian and military regimes in free Africa has had an inward turning effect on the states involved. The most dramatic effect of this trend has been the substantial loss of commitment to the liberation of southern Africa.

In its attempts to deal more realistically with these realities in Africa today, the Organization of African Unity meeting of the Commission on Refugees in September 1966 proposed six policy guidelines for dealing with refugees in free African states:

1. Refugees who wish to return to their countries should be helped to do so.
2. Refugees electing to remain outside their homelands should be settled as far as possible from the frontiers adjoining their country of origin.
3. The term "refugee" when applied to persons departing independent African states should be reserved to nationals of countries whose political, racial or religious regimes have made it necessary for them to expatriate themselves for fear of their opinions, or of their race or their religious beliefs.
4. Countries of asylum should prohibit refugees from attacking their countries of origin either through press or radio or with arms, while the countries of origin should refrain from like attacks against countries of asylum.
5. Countries with refugee problems whose boundaries are not clearly demarcated should take immediate steps to demarcate them.
6. Countries with refugee problems should initiate or continue bilateral talks aimed at solving such problems.

Though these guidelines are very much in keeping with the spirit of United Nations policy regarding refugees, it is obvious that they conflict with the policies of the Liberation Committee of the O.A.U., as well as with problems between individual states with widely conflicting ideologies and policies of national development. Southern African refugees are not encourged to settle as far as possible from the frontiers of their homelands, but the special problems facing free states such as Botswana, Lesotho and Malawi do not always aid the cause of unity between free African states against white-dominated southern Africa. Then, too, states like Zambia, the Congo and Tanzania, whose official policies toward southern white states is the support of liberation movements against them, places them in a very dangerous crisis environment, since it is painfully obvious that other independent African states are not in a strong enough military position to assist them in the event of attack from Portugal, South Africa or Rhodesia.

But, even between independent African states, policies in support of refugees bent on liberating African ruled nations are directly and indirectly evident. Such is the case between Kenya and Somalia, Somalia and Ethiopia, Guinea and Ghana, Malawi and Tanzania. More than many people care to admit, therefore, the African refugee increasingly symbolizes the character of the enemy across the border. Crucial also is the growing ability of the refugee to obscure the significance of whether the Enemy is White or Black, Arab or African, Christian or Muslim. I wonder if it was through the eyes of the African Refugee that Chou En-lai could predict that Africa is "ripe for revolution?"

How is the effect of the African refugee on the national state viewed in the United States? Is there evidence that the refugee problem is seriously considered in our foreign policy toward Africa? Let me answer these questions briefly by saying, first, that Africa as an entity is a continuing peripheral matter both in and out of Government, and, second, that both in the interests of maintaining international peace and indirectly to protect American vested interest in southern Africa particularly, official and unofficial policy towards Africa is to preserve stability. Who runs the show, or how they run it, is not particularly important to Americans generally, so long as ideological warfare between ourselves and the Communist world is not involved. Furthermore, because we are largely incapable of functioning in political relationships in developing nations where we do not play a rather major role in the self-determination process, both the free African policy of non-alignment and the white African policy of racism in varying forms have left us somewhat willingly, I am afraid, in the doldrums. When I first came back from Africa in 1966, I was told by several American officials that it is easier from our point of view to push for stability rather than high-minded positions of justice.

Our foreign policy toward Africa continues to be formed on a very short-run basis, the idea being that we are more effective in the use of power during a crisis, than in diplomacy and influence prior to a crisis situation. The irony of this policy of stability is the knowledge that the refugee, particularly in his efforts to liberate white-dominated southern Africa, has more chance of gaining our support—or the support of major powers against us and his enemies—only when he is able to cause a major conflict situation to occur. American foreign policy in Africa, based as it is on continued stability and non-ideological confrontation by world major powers in Africa, gives the greatest possible incentive to the African liberation fighter to pursue a continuing policy of violence for its own sake until adequate power can be mustered from outside Africa to help him achieve his goals.

The cost of our indecision about the justice of some liberation movements, and the insignificance of the quantity and quality of our moral and material aid in Africa, has lead us in our efforts to find an easy way out of involvement in African evolution, to accepting blindly the virtue of stability for its own sake, thereby encouraging those who believe in the worth of violent revolution to side with the African refugee and his cause. In this regard, therefore, America as a nation supports tacitly the intensifying trend in Africa to evolve many forms of authoritarian rule, with an increasing cost in human terms, through a politics of violence.

The effect of the refugee on the national state of America is dependent, therefore, on the manner in which the refugee identifies his cause within an ideological framework which we can comprehend as being good or bad in our national interest, and in a situation of serious violent conflict where the use of our power can be legitimized.

From what has been said here, therefore, it is obvious to me that on the African continent today, this is indeed the Age of the Refugee, armed with the technology of violence in the pursuit of human dignity. Frantz Fanon said it very well:

> History teaches us clearly that the battle against colonialism does not run straight away along the lines of nationalism. For a very long time the native devotes his energies to ending certain definite abuses: forced labor, corporal punishment, inequality in salaries,

limitation to political rights, etc. This fight for democracy against the oppression of mankind will slowly leave the confusion of neo-liberal universalism to emerge, sometimes laboriously, as a claim to nationhood. It so happens that the unpreparedness of the educated classes, the lack of practical links between them and the mass of people, their laziness, and, let it be said, their cowardice at the decisive moment of the struggle will give rise to tragic mishaps.[1]

When considering the problem of the African refugee it seems to me that we cannot seriously ask—is Frantz Fanon right in his assessment of evolutionary change on that continent? But, we can seriously ask if his vision of history can be altered in reality by dealing with the refugee as something other than an institutional hazard in the development process.

COMMENT

ALFRED G. GERTEINY, University of Bridgeport, Connecticut

I wish to congratulate George Metcalfe on his competent and brilliant paper. There is so much in it that is susceptible to discussion, and the time at hand so brief, that justice would not be done to it. I chose, therefore, not to comment directly on its substance but, rather, to provoke some thoughts on a subject in the periphery of this symposium, about which Metcalfe and other speakers have indirectly or unintentionally alluded; that of the psychological refugee, as opposed to the physical, or legally defined refugee.

My crutch is a statement by Metcalfe that "the fundamental imperative to change is economic development", suggesting, of course, that change in Africa, today, is itself an imperative of certain magnitude. In my mind, economic development is but one of the variegated aspects of the problem of change, in fact one of its constituent parts. I wish, therefore, to take the liberty to change the emphasis of the statement less by pettiness than because this seems a prerequisite to the appreciation of my intervention. I would, thus, suggest that the fundamental imperative to economic development—without which the viability of most African states is doomed—is change, and that change, no matter how imperative or, perhaps, because of its imperativeness, is at the basis of Africa's instability, of the painful transitional stage it is experiencing and which begets the refugee.

While appreciating fully the traditional, legal, definition of the term, "refugee" and, indeed, the necessities constituting the definition's rationale, I wish to excise you for the next couple of minutes from the narrow, legalistic definition with which you are familiar, and to lead you into thoughts on the term in its larger and truer African context. For only then one could appreciate fully the extent of the human dilemma of independent Africa—of its tragedy. The 250,000 odd refugees officially classified as such are, indeed, but an infinitesimal fraction of the "wretched" of Africa, the psychological refugees, whose plight I would like you to consider, and whose ranks are formed by all those who, grieved by, even harmed by, the fluidity of things in Africa, have taken refuge from change or, indeed, from tradition without necessarily joining the physical diaspora beyond the national states' borders. With this in mind, Africa appears as a vast repository of refugees, and a greater proportion of Africans, some occupying important positions at the helm of the governments, are psychological refugees groping for, though beyond, help because they are ostensibly unworthy of classification or unwilling to admit to their condition. Their existence, in Africa's political limbo, as it were, has incommensurable effects on, and adds complexities to, the politics of the national state and the psychology of the continent.

A major problem, consistent in its complexities, with which the individual African state has been confronted since independence, is that of promoting planned change and of reacting to unplanned, or random, change which has a dynamism of its own, to make it compatible with the objectives of the State. In either of its aspects, this problem generates unmistakable opposition, though of varying degrees and nature. Thus, there is opposition among the traditionalist segments of the populations to the change promoted by the government, governmental opposition to unofficially initiated change and often coercion in order to impose change. While this may be normal in a politically sophisticated society, in Africa, where political aggregation and national self-consciousness are for the most part limited indeed, it reasonably follows that the modernists—and most of those engaged in the political process are modernists in the African context—constitute a stratum that is just as alien to tradition as the colonial government was, and is, therefore, usually rejected or simply ignored. This mutual alienation of government and governed leads to withdrawal, aggressiveness, passive disobedience, or emigration and, at least for the government, unreasonable coercion, the whole building to a crescendo in a vicious cycle.

In such a climate of hostility and indifference, and of hostile indifference and personal and group withdrawal, one can easily see how the elite could take refuge from what may be called the "tyranny of tradition," and go into personal politics with all the tyranny it usually engenders. Indeed, as "refugees" from the people, they have added to their reasonable understanding of the necessity for change, the emotional fervor and often blindness that characterize so many of the physical refugees, which contribute substantially to, as well as explains, their inflexibility and the authoritarianism of their government.

In the same vein, the traditional segment of the peoples—by far the largest—to whom modernity and change, political frontiers or the lack of them and, indeed, national governments and their actions are sacreligious and offensive forces, without seeking exile abroad, often elect to find refuge in apathy and passive disobedience, a process which considerably slows down change and augments the painful period of transition.

To bring my argument to its essentials, let me conclude that the existence of the official and legally classified physical refugees, and of the larger, unclassified and unnumbered psychological refugees, represents the most outstanding plight of a continent seeking refuge from the problems of transition.

NOTES

1. Frantz Fanon, *The Wretched of the Earth* (New York: Grove Press, 1963), p. 121.

UTILIZATION OF THE EDUCATED REFUGEE FROM SOUTHERN AFRICA

JOSEPH SHORT, African American Institute

One standing rule of the American space exploration effort is that no astronaut should be launched into space without reasonable assurance that he can be returned safely to terra firma. Hence, elaborate precautions are taken—a series of unmanned test flights are run—to ensure that there will be a safe splash-down at the end of the manned flight to follow. In this manner the astronaut's safe return is inseparably linked with, and not to be carelessly sacrificed to, the exploration objectives themselves.

By contrast, as education programs for southern African refugees developed in the first years of this decade, there were few ways, limited resources and little time to simulate the future as the space explorers have been able to do. It was not possible to predict with certainty when and where a refugee, were he to be provided an education outside his homeland, might ultimately splash-down at the end of flight.

The governing premise that inspired the dramatic development of refugee education programs over the past seven years has proven wrong— so far, This, of course, was that political transition in southern Africa was imminent, that, therefore, no time should be lost in training exiles from the area to assume positions of leadership there when majority rule was attained. While this prediction may seem naive in retrospect, few persons can claim to have dissented overtly from this optimism at a time when it was guiding refugee policy. That prediction, it also should be remembered, followed on a wave of independence throughout sub-Saharan Africa. Would majority rule not come to southern Africa as well? The perception of an urgent need for crash programs in southern Africa refugee education also was reinforced by the Congo crisis of the early 1960s. At that time, excluding theologians, the newly independent Congo had but 12 African graduates in its service. Need soon-to-be liberated countries of southern Africa be afflicted by similar manpower shortages?

Guided partly by miscalculation, refugee education programs developed at a quite impressive pace, supported by an array of international donors and administrative organizations. Although these supporting organizations had varying motives, ranging on a spectrum between humanitarianism and political expediency, for the most part they shared the common expectation that refugees educated under their sponsorship would be able to return to their liberated homelands in the near future. Or at least, they were not very inclined to think rigorously and realistically about what the students in their charge might do upon completion of their studies in the event that majority rule did not come as soon as anticipated.

Thus, in the beginning, attention fixed upon getting refugees educated, and quite secondarily if at all, upon how and where refugee students would ultimately use their education. To the extent that human resource considerations, i.e., assessments of national labor needs and employment opportunities were worked into the selection, testing and counselling components of the various programs, they were based largely on subjective projections about needs and opportunities in the refugees' homelands.

Within the last two years we have been compelled by circumstances to reappraise the assumptions that heretofore have guided refugee education policy. Perhaps we have been excessively slow in acknowledging the intractability of white power in southern Africa. We certainly have been too slow in adapting our educational programs to the present reality of hardening political stalemate in southern Africa.

If, as is likely to be the case for some time, present students cannot return to their homelands, what is to be done? Is not the utilization of educated refugees a more compelling and urgent issue than American aid organizations expected it could possibly be seven years ago? Do we not have a responsibility to put our resources to the service of the refugees whom we have educated, to enable them to find secure, though temporary, homes and employment outside their countries of origin? Must not the educated refugees, whatever the political circumstances of the moment, be viewed as valuable human resources, not to be lost altogether to the service of Africa? These and other questions must be weighed and lead to appropriate action, without delay. For at this very moment, and not to make light of their predicament, many educated refugees, and more to come, are now in orbit. They are unable to reenter their own countries, or to find certain asylum in another country; they are unable to *use* the education that they have struggled to get; they are unable to realize the promise of personal fulfillment; they are unable to make the contributions expected of the educated.

At the beginning of this decade one relatively small, though distinguishable group of refugees fleeing white-controlled South Africa, Southwest Africa, Southern Rhodesia, Angola and Mozambique, attracted the interest of aid organizations. These were the "partially" educated refugees, who by quite arbitrary definition, were those with at least a primary education, or all or part of a secondary education. Some of these refugees seeking asylum in border countries were freedom fighters, leaving their countries on instruction of one or another liberation movement. Others were "political" refugees, seeking freedom from political oppression. Still others had exiled themselves in search of a better life, including opportunities for continued education and employment.

The ambition among these exiles for further education, quite fortunately for them, found positive response among a variety of governmental, international and private organizations. Among these were the following: the liberation movements; governments of independent African countries; international and regional intergovernmental organizations, including the United Nations, the Organization of African Unity, and the Economic Commission for Africa; inter-organizational groups, such as the Joint Committee for the High Commission Territories and the International Refugee Council of Zambia (IRCOZ); private organizations primarily concerned with providing educational and training opportunities, e.g., the African-American Institute, Commonwealth Scholarship Scheme, International University Exchange Fund, Board of Missions of the Methodist Church, Otto Benecke Stiftung (Germany), and World University Service; non-African governmental bodies, e.g., Swedish International Development Authority (SIDA), the U. S. State Department; and, finally, a multitude of educational institutions, e.g., Lincoln, Rochester, and Syracuse universities which developed special refugee programs.

One need only to read the list of donors to realize that the motives of the various aid-givers have been quite diverse. It should, at least, be said that aid-givers have frequently tended to pursue their respective courses, with relatively little mutual cooperation. Of course, there have been notable exceptions. For example, several African governments have been exceedingly cooperative with outside organizations seeking to provide educational assistance to refugees. Moreover, over the last two years there has developed a distinct trend to cooperative, co-ordinated effort. Perhaps in the face of repatriation and utilization problems, aid-givers are seeking mutual consolation or at worst, to pass the buck. One would hope, however, that this trend testifies to the mutual realization that utilization of educated refugees, among other refugee problems, is a challenge demanding joint effort.

There have been two major types of refugee education programs, university and secondary. Despite the generally acknowledged need for technical and vocational education programs, there are presently few accomplishments to applaud. Most of the groups just mentioned have supported university education, a few, secondary education. Americans are perhaps more familiar with the university programs, through the presence of refugee students in this country, than with secondary school projects, which for the most part are based in Africa. Secondary education has become a special subject of interest because so many refugees are unprepared for university study.

The Joint Committee in London has long been a pacesetter in secondary education, providing placements and financial assistance to refugees. The Scandanavian countries and several voluntary agencies have aided schools in Botswana, Lesotho and Swaziland, enabling those institutions to enroll South Africans. In the Congo, international donors have acted through the Congo Protestant Relief Service to establish two major secondary schools for Angolans, Sonabata and Fuma, with a combined enrollment of about 275 students. Also the African-

American Institute has developed two secondary schools for southern Africans in Zambia and Tanzania. These schools are presently near capacity enrollment of 550 students.

This brief survey of refugee education activity is only suggestive of the magnitude and scope of the utilization challenge that grows out of educational efforts over seven years. For one thing, the challenge is to facilitate asylum and employment for refugees of varying educational achievement. Some have attained, or will complete, undergraduate and/or graduate studies. Others, for lack of opportunity or capacity, will only complete their secondary education. Some will have technical or vocational education to put to work. Finally, there will be those who have advanced their education, without having formally completed one kind of educational program or another.

PROBLEM OF REFUGEE UTILIZATION: NATURE AND MAGNITUDE

The nature of the utilization problem can be put quite simply. Assuming no political transition in white-controlled southern Africa for the indefinite future, how and where will refugees be able to put their education to work in the most personally satisfying and productive fashion? Estimating exactly how many refugees to whom this question applies is impossible, because there is no single repository of complete statistics collected on a world-wide basis, or for that matter, on a Western-countries basis. A Central Register of refugee student information, now being established under the administration of the International University Exchange Fund in Leiden, Holland, will hopefully fill the void of student statistics. Even current statistics on refugees educated in American universities and colleges are difficult to obtain.

However, to impart a sense of the magnitude of the utilization problem, the relatively accurate statistics compiled recently in the United States are quite suggestive. These were presented to the Workshop on the Training and Utilization of Refugee Students from Southern Africa, sponsored by the African-American Institute and Syracuse University in April 1967. Reported to that Workshop were these figures: "796 African students from southern Africa presently enrolled at U.S. institutions are expected to graduate by 1971, including 72 Angolans, 124 Mozambicans, 288

Rhodesians, 226 South Africans, and 86 Southwest Africans."[1]

These are sobering figures, not, of course, including estimates for students studying on other continents, including approximately 750–1000 secondary students in Africa alone. Moreover, refugee utilization is an immediate challenge. As the Workshop report also indicated, "it is estimated that 197 southern African students will complete U.S. study programs in 1967 . . . 137 students are expected to graduate in 1968."[2] We know, of course, that many though relatively fewer completed their studies before 1967.

UTILIZATION FOR WHAT PURPOSE?

It has been stated that the ultimate objective of refugee education has been to prepare students for nation-building roles in their homelands, once they have achieved majority rule and independence. The one pre-condition for realization of this objective, of course, does not yet exist. Therefore, shorter-term objectives must receive greater emphasis.

At the previously mentioned workshop, Mr. H. Mohammed Sahnoun, then Deputy Secretary General of the OAU, among other African spokesmen, contended that "Refugee students should, first of all, participate in the struggle for freedom."[3] The Workshop itself concluded, ". . . there is only one ultimate solution to the over-all problem (of repatriation and utilization). This is to establish majority governments in the countries of southern Africa."[4] In all sympathy to this point of view, it must be asked precisely how the students should be deployed to participate in the freedom struggle. The answer must come from the liberation movements, from independent African governments and inter-African organizations like the OAU, and from the students themselves. Certainly most sponsoring agencies are prepared to follow African leadership in facilitating student return to the freedom struggle.

Having said this, it must also be asked if participation in the liberation effort necessarily precludes the encouragement of student return to points not directly on the "African battle line." The African response to this question seems to be that it does not. Some have urged that qualified students be encouraged to return to the service of their fellow countrymen in exile in independent Africa, in some cases numbering in the thousands.

For example, refugee settlements are in great need of doctors, social workers, teachers and so on.

Finally, many African leaders share the opinion of Mr. H. E. Lij Endalkachew MaKonnen, Permanent Representative of Ethiopia to the United Nations, that "the freedom movements may not always be in a position to absorb all young refugees all at once."[5] He is joined by many others in the conviction that repatriation to and employment in independent Africa, on a temporary but secure basis, is one of the most promising utilization alternatives of all. As he has so well stated the case:

> On the one hand, the problems and social conditions in these countries are by and large the same as those prevailing in southern Africa itself. This helps to make the experience both interesting and worthwhile. Moreover, the services of these young refugees, if they are rightly trained for the right types of jobs, can be of great benefit to the individual host countries that receive them. In this way, triple benefits are derived—for the refugees, the host country, and the continent as a whole.[6]

In this connection, it is already clear that refugee graduates as a group constitute a new and very promising source of trained manpower for developing Africa. As a particular case in point, the author of Chapter 14, Mr. Mtshali, now completing his doctoral studies under the Southern African Student Program in this country, is returning shortly to Africa to teach at the University of Zambia.

Viewed from the aid-givers perspective, the African spokesmen's emphasis upon utilization of educated refugees *in Africa* finds great receptivity, whether it be for active participation in the freedom struggle, or for service in independent Africa. There is one as yet unmentiond reason why this is the case. The justification for educational assistance to refugees is seriously weakened, to the extent that graduates remain in countries outside Africa. There are less expensive ways of educating Americans, Swedes, Germans and Dutch than to educate refugees who, for all practical purposes, when they remain in these countries, become nationals.

OBSTACLES TO REFUGEE UTILIZATION

It is all too easy to talk glibly of the desirability of refugee return to, and employment in, Africa. There are difficult obstacles to be overcome before there can be assurance that the opportunities to return are commensurate with the numbers of students who have graduated and will graduate in the immediate years to come. Although this presentation has dealt primarily with refugees outside Africa, the settlement and productive use of refugee students in Africa, mostly at secondary level, may be only slightly less problematic, and require similar and equally ambitious schemes, to ensure opportunity for settlement and employment. Nevertheless, comments on the obstacles to the utilization of refugees presently outside Africa are, by and large, applicable to those still there.

First, there are limitations and peculiarities in the manpower absorption capacities of the liberation parties and the independent African countries. Some parties are hard pressed to finance their essential operatives, let alone to absorb large numbers of returning students. One rather promising alternative, already being used to some extent, is when the returning student can be employed in the locale of party activity and provide his services to the party on a voluntary basis.

Each independent African country, of course, has its own manpower needs. This being the case, a premium must be put on preparing students in fields in which there is high labor demand in independent Africa. A brief paper, "The Manpower Situation in Africa in Relation to Educated Refugees", prepared by the ECA for the Conference on the Legal, Economic and Social Aspects of African Refugee Problems, Addis Ababa, 9-18 October 1967 (AFR/Conf. 1967/No. 11) makes several important points on this subject:

> The training of young Africans . . . should be seen in terms . . . of the wider field of manpower requirements of the countries from which they come . . . Education must serve the purpose of creating the type of skills required for economic development . . . If the educational requirements of African refugees are seen in the African context, the same yardsticks to their educational programs should apply even if their training is sponsored by non-African or international institutions and organizations. The same consideration should be borne in mind whether the refugees are returning to their home countries or to other African countries which will agree to grant them residence or asylum.

The ECA paper also lists many high priority development fields in which refugees might expect to find opportunity, e.g., in teaching, accounting, soil conservation or geology. Speaking to the reality that many refugees are nearing completion of their studies or have completed their studies in low priority fields, the ECA asserts:

> Refugees already trained in fields of low priority should be given one or two years of specialized training in some of the priority fields required by African governments in order to reorient them to the employment market and increase their prospects for employment.

The message, of course is quite clear: education of the refugee should from the very outset be designed for the manpower needs of his homeland and of the independent African country in which he may temporarily live.

Second, the students' lack of travel documents as Mr. Schachter has pointed out, is both a major source of their insecurity and an intractible obstacle to their return and employment in Africa. Commonly, students have fled their homelands without passports, and thereafter are plagued with the difficulty of securing visas to travel onwards, without first having a document from the country of their first asylum entitling them to return. Efforts are presently being made to spread responsibility among African countries for granting permanent residence and for issuing travel documents with return clauses. Many students now abroad hold no documents entitling them to return to an African country.

For the independent African countries the issuance of travel documents, with return clauses especially, is often a matter of considerable gravity. This is particularly true for the countries bordering the white redoubt, which it cannot be said too often, have not only carried their own national burdens but also have been remarkably generous to their brothers seeking asylum. Whenever there has been reluctance among these countries to accept refugees for an indefinite period of residence, there are often justifiable reasons, usually too little appreciated by outsiders. For example, some countries like Lesotho and Botswana are simply not able to absorb and employ large numbers of refugees. In other countries, like Zambia and Tanzania, the available employment opportunities may not accord with qualifications of the returning refugee. Under some circumstances, refugees may be seen as competitors for jobs desired by nationals. Or, in political terms, large aggregations of refugees may be seen as a threat to the internal or international security of the asylum country.

Third, many grand designs for utilization of students do not sufficiently take into account the views of the students themselves. Were there majority rule in southern Africa, there can be little doubt that few students would not wish to return home. Under conditions of political stalemate, however, many students believe they will find greater security outside the African continent, whether by extending their studies indefinitely, or by taking employment where opportunities seem more plentiful. Some have lost their political fervor, others had none to begin with. Some have married citizens in their countries of study, others are enticed by the urbanized life and high standards of living found in the developed countries where they study. And some students, having failed to identify certain opportunities to serve in the freedom struggle or to be employed in independent Africa, simply despair and try to make the best of a bad situation, wherever they are.

Finally, relatively too little attention has been given by all parties to education programs to planning and organizing to facilitate the repatriation and utilization of present students. This, and the reorientation of refugee education to square with real manpower needs in Africa, are major and immediate challenges for the aid organizations, liberation parties, African and foreign governments, international and inter-African organizations and educational institutions.

The kind of energy, creativity, and human and financial resources that have brought refugee education programs into existence have now got to be turned upon the difficulties that could well negate much that has gone before.

ORGANIZING TO AID STUDENT
UTILIZATION

This presentation has suggested more issues than solutions. But one issue seems paramount at this moment: whether or not there is the organizational will and capacity to go the extra mile to make refugee education pay off. Presently, aid organizations, political parties and international organizations are only gingerly testing the water, while a veritable tidal wave of graduating students moves in a downward arch. Few have really committed organizational talent and financial resources to help get graduates into useful, satisfying, and self-redeeming employment.

One fact seems quite certain. Many of the seemingly insurmountable obstacles to refugee utilization do give and bend, if only sometimes by inches, when subjected to hard-slugging and painstaking effort. Will the effort be made?

One positive, as yet quite tentative, step in this direction in 1967 came from the Addis Ababa Conference on the Legal, Economic and Social Aspects of African Refugee Problems, held in early October, organized jointly by the ECA, the OAU, the UNHCR and the Dag Hammarskjold Foundation. Twenty-two African governments, representatives from several inter-governmental organizations, and observers from 27 voluntary agencies attended the Conference.

Perhaps the most significant recommendation of the Conference concerning utilization of students was the calling for the establishment of a "Bureau for Placement and Education of African Refugees" within the secretariat of the OAU. This bureau is to have a "Consultative Board", composed of representatives of OAU, ECA, UNHCR, ILO, UNESCO and observers from non-governmental organizations. A "Standing Committee" of the same membership is to help coordinate efforts of non-governmental organizations with those of the Bureau.

The function of the Bureau is the "promotion of the resettlement and the employment of African refugees and to collect and provide information concerning educational, training and employment opportunities."

This Conference *recommendation* has yet to be ratified under OAU constitutional procedures. However, if it is, and more importantly, if the Bureau does become an effective, functioning body, a major organizational gap will be filled. Many have long hoped that organizational leadership in refugee utilization would someday emerge from Africa. How much more promising the prospect of removing the obstacles to student utilization, if Africa takes the problem to heart.

How much more promising, if *all* who have given to education now take this problem of utilization to heart!

COMMENT

DAVID G. SCANLON, Teachers College, Columbia University, New York

First, may I say that I can only hope to highlight a few of the basic ideas and add to what has just been said. It is a fact that, up to the present time, of all the students from other lands who have studied in the United States, more African students have returned to their native continent. Among students from other continents, for example two Asian countries, as many as 90 percent of the students who have come here to study over the last ten years have remained in the United States, or have moved on to Canada. African students traditionally have wanted to return and, therefore, within the situation suggested by Mr. Short, it seems that it is our responsibility to make sure that this return is possible. Coordination of refugees is certainly the number one priority, and in this, one would have to look quite frankly at the different types of refugees: some may be from southern Africa, others may come out of other African countries as the political fortunes change within those countries. An international organization suggested by the Organization of African Unity, the OAU, would certainly do much to make this classification possible and to find the countries in the areas that do have a need for the skills and talents that the returned refugees have. However, a kind of central office that will give a catalog of the skills of the refugees is, perhaps, not enough. Or at least it is not enough unless there is also a coordination of the types of education offered for refugee students in the United States and in England—as there are two of the large centers at the present time—and this raises dangerous problems that most of us in education are constantly facing.

Every African country has a manpower planning scheme. Whether or not this is developed along the lines of the Haribson-Meyers approach to education in economic development, or whether it is simply a series of goals to be achieved within the next five years, there are certainly educational implications for the manpower required. And here the agencies, the universities, the governmental groups that have been involved in providing education face a very difficult problem.

According to the charter of UNESCO, everyone in the world has a right to education. If education is considered a right, then the path is fairly simple. However, having agreed to this, how do we move to the next step? Is it a principle, that one might borrow from economics, of consumer sovereignty? Does everyone have the right to study whatever he wants to study? I think that in the United States, England, Germany, and France, this principle on the surface is fairly well established. Any student can take any course if he can gain entry to the university. However, I would also submit that there are also ways, internally, that the United States government, that England and France, have controlled entrance into specific subject areas. For example, in our own case, federal fellowships and scholarships under the National Defense Education Act obviously offer rather enticing rewards to those who will follow a particular line of study. Therefore, in this case as well, the principle of consumer sovereignty is not fully followed. There are advantages to majoring in subjects that are viewed by governments and by industry as desirable. A shortage of engineers would mean, certainly, as in the past after World War II, federal scholarships for the training of engineers. So we have to look at the principle of consumer sovereignty in, perhaps, a more realistic way.

Second, is education an investment? Mr. Short has viewed education in the process of nation-building as geared completely to economic planning, with the idea that an educated person is more valuable to a country, but we have been reminded by J. Kenneth Galbraith and many others that one of the difficulties is, you cannot count the amount of economic development a good secondary school teacher is doing in a country. It is much easier to look at a dam or a fertilizer factory and yet, based on our own statistics, the works of Schultz and others that can be documented, it seems that education in the long run will produce much more wealth than material improvements such as the dam, or even the fertilizer factory. But viewing education as investment limits the concept of consumer sovereignty. If education is truly viewed as producing something that will increase the productivity of a country, then it demands in effect that individuals be produced who can take part in this economic development; and if this is true, then it means that the number of fellowships and scholarships and the training of students either in the United States or in Africa, are bound up to this principle.

Now, fortunately, those of us in the universities can sit back and study these issues; we don't have to face the political problems involved in any of these decisions. But, considering the refugee problem, it seems that one would have to look, as the Organization of African Unity has done, at the real manpower needs and how refugee students can be used, at least during this present period, in other sections of Africa, assuming that the political problems listed by Mr. Short can be overcome. And, if this is taken as a principle, then certainly the idea of providing secondary school teachers and other workers in the field of education, is one that many countries in Africa could probably profit from at the present time. Considering the qualifications of South African refugee students, for example, one wonders why the United States government or some agencies or foundations could not be persuaded to support a project that would prepare these refugees to teach in African countries, if by the same token we can send several thousand Peace Corps Volunteers to teach in Africa. This project could be confined mainly to English-speaking Africa, because the language problem alone would perhaps bar many southern African refugees from taking an active role in French-speaking Africa.

All this means that governments will have to think more realistically than they have up to the present time. Here is a valuable pool of skills, a pool that can be utilized. We, in fact, should support this in much the same way as we support AID projects, the Peace Corps and other agencies that supply education to Africa. If Mr. Harbison is correct, and as an educator it is always delightful to sit back and have an economist fight your battles for you, if he is correct that education within Africa is the key to growth, then utilizing even the 187 trained, skilled refugees would contribute to the development of Africa. It would be in harmony with the view of education as an investment and, perhaps, would add that necessary measure of insight to the teaching of African affairs in the secondary schools, colleges, and universities of Africa that is very difficult for the outsider to achieve.

NOTES

1. Jane W. Jacqz, *Refugee Students from Southern Africa* (New York: African-American Institute, 1967), p. 7.

2. Ibid., p. 7.

3. Ibid., p. 11.

4. Ibid., p. iii.

5. Ibid., p. 11.

6. Ibid.

AN AFRICAN EVALUATION
OF THE PROBLEM*

APOLLO KIRONDE, African Section, Department of Political
and Security Council Affairs, U.N., New York

Among the many problems that have appeared in the wake of
African independence is that of refugees. Ten years ago, although there had been movements of peoples across territorial
or national boundaries, such migrations were, on the whole, economically motivated and could not be identified as giving rise to
a refugee problem.

For centuries, migrations from one part of the African continent to another was by no means an uncommon feature. The
exodus of people as a result of political events in their own country or in their country of residence which made their stay or return impossible or intolerable, had to wait the turn of the last
decade when the wind of change that swept across the continent
brought about so many stresses and strains in its train that today
there is in Africa a total population of refugees estimated at close
to one million.

It is significant that the refugees have come from both independent countries; e.g., Burundi, Congo (Kinshasha) Sudan,
Rwanda, and from non-independent countries; e.g., South Africa,
South West Africa, Rhodesia and territories under Portuguese administration. There is a common factor in that in both cases the
refugees have left their countries voluntarily or involuntarily as a
result of political events occurring in their own countries. In the
case of non-self-governing countries it is noteworthy that the wind
of change has caused a backlash in the form of a tightening up
of restrictive and oppressive measures on the part of the colonial-
ists, who have grown increasingly apprehensive because of the

---

* The opinions expressed in this paper are not necessarily shared by the
United Nations.

possibility of self-determination in their own colonial territories.

To the general dissatisfaction with the conditions at home may be added another motivation: the belief, rightly or wrongly held, especially among the youthful refugees, that there were greater economic and social opportunities in independent Africa, and that African States, imbued with the spirit of Pan-Africanism, would welcome them with open arms. I must explain that I have described South Africa as a nonindependent country advisedly, for since its constitution ordains that self-determination and citizenship rights are to be enjoyed by one-fifth of the population, to the deliberate exclusion of the vast majority of the inhabitants, it would be quite wrong to ascribe the attributes of a self-governing state to South Africa. It could also be argued that South Africa represents a curious phenomenon which is *sui generis*—a national state which is partly free and partly unfree, and where independence and colonialism exist cheek by jowl in the same state.

To understand the magnitude and impact of the refugee problem, one must realize that all of the countries of asylum fall within the category of the poor nations of the world. None of them has the requisite funds or technical staff to deal with the problem, and yet the influx of refugees needing assistance is so great in some cases that in Congo (Kinshasha) and in Uganda the refugees constitute as much as 2 percent of the population.

I do not in anyway wish to belittle the contribution of the United Nations family and the voluntary agencies in providing technical and financial assistance, but it is obvious that the decision to assume so burdensome a responsibility was independently made by the African governments themselves, and that they have continued to bear the bulk of this responsibility. One hears of the traditional African hospitality, and now and then, of African socialism. Never before in the annals of history have people with so little agreed to share with so many, nor has such an opportunity to be one's brother's keeper ever presented itself on so grand a scale and been so willingly accepted.

A peculiar feature of the African refugee problem, as distinguished from the problem elsewhere in Europe, Asia and the Middle East, is clearly one of timing. The refugee problem in Africa could not have chosen a less opportune moment. The period immediately after independence is marked by intensive and extensive development on all fronts, and the call upon the scarce resources of newly independent states, both in terms of money and trained personnel, is so great that African countries of asylum have had to make enormous sacrifices even to provide the basic necessities of the refugees. The gravity of the problem has been greatly increased by two factors:

1. The maldistribution of the burden in Africa. Of the 36 African countries, only 12 are shouldering the refugee burden comprising nearly one million refugees and of these, over 70 percent of the refugees are in the Congo (Kinshasha) and Uganda.

2. The big world powers have displayed little interest in the overall refugee problem in Africa when compared to the role that they played, and are still playing, in assisting refugees in Europe, the Middle East and in the Far East. This has meant that the assistance offered to African refugees has come from the governments of asylum, from the United Nations High Commissioner for Refugees, and the other members of the United Nations family, and from voluntary agencies like Oxfam, the World Food Program, to mention only a few.

Furthermore, because the magnitude of the African refugee problem has not been generally appreciated, the assistance offered has been minimal and the heroic efforts of African governments, and others who have assisted in the solution of the problem, have gone unsung.

The basic requirements of the refugee on arrival in his country of asylum is food, water, clothing, shelter, medicines, and tools. After these basic needs have been met, it is important, both for economic and moral reasons, that the refugee should be afforded some constructive outlet for his energies and that he should, as soon as possible, attain a measure of self-sufficiency, especially in matters of food. But even after this stage has been reached, it is important to move to yet another stage when the refugee is able to contribute effectively to the life and development of the host country. It is thus clear that from the outset, the refugee poses both an economic and a social problem of considerable dimensions.

There has been, however, a divergence of policies among African countries of asylum. It has been held by some that there is no need to work beyond the initial land settlement stage inasmuch

Children learn to read and write at the Kahunge refugee center.

At the refugee center in Kayongozi refugees begin work on the foundations of a garage and a workshop to be used by all.

Refugees at the dispensary in Bibwe receive free vaccinations.

In the village of Djimbana 40 percent of population are refugees. Milk and vitamins are distributed daily to mothers and children.

as refugees are there temporarily and will soon go back to their respective countries. Others, however, have been more realistic and have sought a more durable, if not a more permanent solution to the problem.

There is a growing realization among countries of asylum that the refugees have, in most cases, come to stay, if not permanently, at least for a very long while, and that self-sufficiency at subsistence level can only be regarded as a temporary stopgap measure. Zonal development and planning is generally accepted as the best method of consolidating the economic and social condition of the refugee settlements as well as integrating them into the economic and social systems of the country. By means of zonal planning and development, the local population is able to share in whatever advantages accrue to the refugees through development projects primarily intended for refugees; and the refugees, on the other hand, by being integrated into the economic and social life of the country of asylum, are able to make a positive and effective contribution to the overall development of the country, for example, by paying taxes levied on the local inhabitants. Moreover, it is only by a policy of integration that friction can be avoided between the refugees and the local people, who often complain that the former are treated better than themselves.

Desirable indeed as zonal development is, it demands for its success comprehensive surveys on a regional or sub-regional level, if the objectives of strengthening all aspects of the rural services needed for the advancement of the region as a whole and the optimal exploitation of its resources are to be achieved. It is thus obvious that zonal planning schemes normally entail considerable expenditure of money and the deployment of suitable administrative and technical resources, to achieve coherent settlement.

The selection of a suitable nongovernmental and independent executive agency or operating partner has been resorted to with advantage by certain countries and has proved useful in supplying the expertise required and in attracting the technical staff paid for under programs financed by international agencies.

The social and economic problems which confront African governments of asylum, indeed, which have to be resolutely faced and solved by Africa as a whole, may broadly be divided into two categories according to the countries of origin or degree of sophistication of the refugee.

The first category comprises refugees who are either capable of taking advantage of further education or who are qualified and are already in a position to make a useful contribution without further training in the independent African States. Those who fall in this category invariably come from southern Africa, i.e., South Africa, South West Africa and Rhodesia. They are often urbanized, relatively sophisticated people, capable of using their resourcefulness to create problems for the countries of asylum.

The second category comprises what is numerically by far the largest number of refugees in Africa. These are refugees with a rural background. Here the main problem is one of settlement and rehabilitation in rural communities. In dealing with this category of refugees there are two possible solutions. They could be voluntarily repatriated if they could be permanently settled in their countries of asylum. It is significant that, while the short-term needs of both categories are being met in an increasingly systematic and rational manner, the long-term problem posed by both categories are generally harder to solve.

The problem of refugees migrating from southern Africa calls for the most urgent solution, both in its short-term and its long-term manifestation. For upwards of ten years, refugees have been coming out of South Africa and other countries in southern Africa. A number of governmental and nongovernmental agencies have been assisting these refugees in various ways. Because of the interest that the United Nations has had in the political situation prevailing in South Africa, South West Africa and in the territories under Portuguese administration, the organization has established three special educational and training programs for these territories. Other governmental and nongovernmental agencies have entered the field at different times.

The first special training program to be established by the United Nations was for South West Africa under a General Assembly resolution adopted in December 1961. In December of the following year the special training program for territories under Portuguese administration was established under a General Assembly resolution. Last, in 1966, the special training program for South Africa was established pursuant to a decision previously taken in June 1965 under a Security Council resolution.

Since then, the three educational and training programs have, for administrative and directional purposes, been integrated and consolidated. The total number of scholarship holders for all the three programs amounts to three hundred sixty now. The United Nations, however, is not the only body interested in the educational progress of southern Africa. Both governmental and non-governmental agencies, and on both sides of the iron curtain, cater to the educational needs of southern African refugees, so that today the number of southern African refugees undergoing training outside the African continent is over 500 in the United States alone, and must be well over 1,000 in Europe and elsewhere.

The problem today is how to relate the crippling shortage of skilled personnel needed for the economic and social development of the continent with the large number of refugees, particularly of southern African origin, who have either completed or are about to complete their training abroad. It is generally conceded that, while it may not be possible for the refugees to return to their respective countries of origin for a long time to come, it would be carrying coals to Newcastle if they were encouraged to stay in their countries of study outside the African continent. The matter of placement of refugees in Africa after completion of their studies, and the issuance of travel documents to facilitate their movement, was discussed in considerable depth at the recent conference in Addis Ababa which dealt with the legal, economic and social aspects of African refugee problems. The Conference concluded that the aid of policy should be to train African refugees in Africa as much as possible. (See Mr. Short's papers for more details on the training of refugees.)

This had to be done to stem the tide of the ever-increasing number of refugees trained outside the African continent who are irretrievably lost to Africa as part of the brain drain which nations the world over are experiencing in favor of the richer and more developed countries. It is obvious that, apart from the seemingly irresistible motivation behind the world-wide brain drain, it is too much to expect exiles, after they have been exposed to the comfortable standards of life in developed countries, to uproot themselves and emigrate back to Africa where conditions would, in the nature of things, be new, unfamiliar, and uncertain.

The Addis Ababa conference very significantly focused attention on the need for mounting educational schemes for refugees in Africa, and for advising students to pursue such disciplines and training courses as would correspond with the manpower requirements of the African continent. To that end, the conference recommended the establishment of a Bureau of Placement and Education of Refugees within the framework of the Organization of African Unity. Its responsibility will be to collect and distribute information concerning educational, training and employment opportunities in Africa, and to promote with the cooperation of member states of the OAU, the resettlement and employment of African refugees. To assist in coordinating the efforts of the various intergovernmental organizations and with the Bureau, a Standing Committee was also recommended which will consist of representatives of OAU, ECA, UNHCR, UNESCO, and ILO. It was further recommended that a Consultative Board, composed or representatives of OAU, ECA, UNHCR, ILO, UNESCO, and observers from nongovernmental organizations interested in the problem, should advise the Bureau on its general policy.

The recommendation by the Addis Ababa conference that refugees should, whenever possible, be trained in Africa, and the setting up within the OAU of a Coordinating Bureau, mark a turning point in the history of the African refugee problem in respect of education and employment, and I should like to underscore, once again, what they set out to achieve:

1. The education and employment of refugees has hitherto been carried out with the best of intentions, but with a coordination of effort among the various agencies and governmental organizations which was conspicuous by its absence.

2. As far as possible, efforts for the training of refugees should be directed to training inside the continent, and only where the educational facilities in Africa were nonexistent or inadequate would refugees be trained outside the continent. It is maintained that in this way, a triple advantage would be scored: the financial resources would be stretched further; African institutions would need, and would have to be strengthened and expanded; and trainees would more readily be settled and assimilated in the countries in which they have received their education, or in neighboring ones.

3. While the policy of education for the sake of education has considerable support among educationists, particularly in the capital intensive countries, it must be accepted as one of the facts of life that it can have little or no relevancy among refugees. Apart from the fact the refugees are being educated at public expense, and that he who pays the piper has an inalienable right to call the tune, the mere status of refugee at once limits the scope of his employment. It is thus essential that, in selecting the disciplines in which the refugee wishes to specialize, special attention should at all times be paid to those fields of study which command the highest priority in relation to the manpower requirements of Africa.

In conclusion, I should like to stress the international character of the problem of refugees wherever they may be found. While African States and the OAU, to which they all subscribe, recognize that African refugees are primarily their responsibility, the involvement of the big powers should go beyond the present fire-engine efforts, to the level where a lasting solution would be jointly sought by all concerned. I mentioned earlier the decision of the Addis Ababa Conference on Refugees to train refugees in Africa, as far as possible. This is a recommendation which has found favor among all the governmental and other agencies engaged in the education of African exiles, and who have already on their hands trained refugees who cannot or will not return to Africa. If the charitable commiseration of those governmental agencies was actuated by genuine humanitarian motives, and not by a desire to win for themselves a sphere of influence in Africa or a place in the sun, then they will go farther and assist in the placement of African refugees in African institutions. This, in turn, will require contributions, both capital and recurrent, to enable African institutions, already bursting at the seams, to expand and strengthen their facilities and to make room for the additional number of students and trainees.

PART II

CASE STUDIES

REFUGEES FROM THE SUDAN

9

MOHAMED AWAD, University of Cairo, U.A.R.

There are now, perhaps, one million refugees in the continent of Africa; people who decided to abandon their home country and move to one or more of the adjacent territories. The states involved in these movements all lie to the south of the Sahara and the impact of their migrations has been felt in the neighboring countries. Although some aspects of this phenomenon are similar in all cases, there are, however, points of difference peculiar to every country concerned. Here, an attempt will be made to explain the problem as it pertains to the Sudan and its people.

The republic of the Sudan is the largest political unit in Africa, and has an area of about one million square miles. Owing, however, to extensive tracts of desert and semidesert, the population is about 13 million. In the middle of the Sudan runs the river Nile, coming partly from the Great Lakes region in the center of Africa, partly from the Highlands of Ethiopia.

For administrative purposes, the land is divided into some nine provinces; the northern six of these are often referred to as the North, and the three southern are referred to as the South. These three southern provinces are known as:

1. *The Upper Nile,* extending up to the 10th parallel of latitude (in the center even to latitude 12).
2. *Equatoria,* further south, bordering on Uganda and Kenya.
3. *Bahr-el Ghazal,* to the southwest, bordering on the Congo-Kinshasa and the Central African Republics.

These three southern provinces embrace the territories involved in the question of refugees. It is from these provinces, especially from the furthest areas, to the southeast and southwest that most of the displaced populations come; their number probably does not much exceed one hundred thousand.

The area of those southern provinces is about one quarter of

115

the whole of the Sudan, and the population does not exceed the same proportion, that is, in the neighborhood of two and one-half millions. The land is a vast plain in the center, but rather hilly to the east, the south and the west. The central districts are liable to become extensive swamps after the summer rainfall, which is rather heavy. They become extremely dry during the early months of the year (January to April).

These swamps have made it well-nigh impossible to penetrate from the north. The only suitable means of communication was to follow the Upper Nile, and avoid losing one's way through the many channels. It had always been extremely difficult to go very far if a sailing boat were employed. This accounts for the fact that no outside expedition had ever been able to sail the waters of the Upper Nile until river steamers were employed in the middle of the Nineteenth Century; then the first expedition penetrated the swampy areas and reached the borderlands of what is now Uganda.

Once isolation was terminated, intercourse with the north, for good or bad, was established. In order to grasp the relationship which developed, even if it failed to develop sufficiently, it is necessary to mention that the first expedition to the south was carried out by the authorities ruling Egypt. Mohamed Ali, the Albanian Viceroy of Egypt, which was itself part of the Ottoman Empire, had ordered the first expedition, after his authority had been established in the Sudan. His successors have sent other expeditions. The kind of relationship which developed between north and south was not always a happy one. The southern people led a very primitive and simple existence. A little primitive and shifting agriculture, extensive cattle herding, and some hunting and fishing, constituted the basis of all the economy. There were very few arts and crafts. Houses consisted, as indeed they often still do, of round huts of mud and wood, with conical roofs thatched with grass. There were usually no textiles. Most tribes used no clothing at all, others covered their bodies with hides. Such economy could not permit of any useful trade between the north and south. Perhaps some produce from the hunt, ivory, some hides and other similar products, could form articles of barter.

The most unfortunate development, however, was that of the slave trade, carried out by a few individuals from the north. This was occurring, from about 1860 onwards, at a time when the whole world was strongly condemning the wretched practice. The Khedive Ismail made an effort to stop the slave trade, and sent several expeditions for the purpose under the leadership of Europeans like Sir Samuel Baker, and General Gordon. There is no need to doubt his motives, but his methods of ruling the Sudan, as well as that of his successors, led to the well-known Revolt of the Al-mahdi, the national Sudanese leader. This occurred in 1881, and its result was the elimination of Egyptian rule and the expulsion of Egyptian forces. This state of affairs continued until 1898, when the Sudan was reconquered by a mixed army of British and Egyptians, under the leadership of Lord Kitchener. Egypt itself was by that time under British occupation, and both Egypt and the Sudan fell under British influence. Nevertheless, the British did not make the Sudan a British Colony, but decided that it should be under a condominium, i.e., under joint partnership of Egypt and England and under both British and Egyptian flags. But there was no hiding the fact that the role of Egypt was that of the sleeping partner. The conduct of all the affairs in the Sudan, both as regards internal administration and external relations, were entirely in British hands.

The establishment of the condominium marks a great landmark in the modern history of the Sudan. It is particularly important because it marked a new policy for the south, a policy which was gradually and deliberately pursued. As soon as the entire land, north and south, was completely pacified in the early years of the 20th century, the Central Government in Khartum, began to draw a plan for an entirely new policy as far as the South was concerned. This policy was based on the idea that the north was completely different from the south, the south being mainly Negroid, while the north is Arab or Arabicised, with Islam as the main religion, while the south was little touched by the Muslim faith.

Perhaps it is useful to make some comment on this idea. We should begin by ignoring ethnic differences. The north, it is true, is basically Caucasoid, but there has been a great deal of admixture, if only through the acquisition of slaves, in the course of a great many centuries, and the wide-spread habit of having many wives, whose children received equal treatment. Again, ethnically speaking, there has been in the south, in several periods of its history, a fairly large absorption of Caucasic blood, which anthropologists like C. G. Seligman, have made abundantly clear in his book on "The Pagan Tribes of the Anglo-Egyptian Sudan."

The long isolation of the south, however, made it culturally and socially different from the north, so that the Sudan, as a whole, is a multicultural country. But in this respect the Sudan is not unique among other multicultured countries, like Ethiopia, Kenya, Uganda, Tanzania, and a host of others both in Africa and other continents. Nor is the north culturally uniform. It contains many elements which can scarcely be described as Arabicised; like the Beja of the Eastern Sudan, the Fur and allied tribes in the West, the Nubians in the North, and the Nuba of Southern Kordofan, and several others, who all constitute together the Northern Sudan. The fact, however, that the south was more different from the north, than the northern districts are different from one another, led the British rulers of the Sudan to try and devise a special policy for the south.

It is perhaps natural that under the circumstances two alternative courses were open before the government. The first is the policy of *integration* which would involve that great efforts should be exerted to educate the southern population, and develop economic as well as cultural relations with the north, even if this meant exposing the south to Islamic and Arabic influences. After all, the north and south are bound to live together in the same political unit, and there should be complete conciliation and harmony among the two sections of the Sudan.

The second course would be a policy of *separation,* as complete as possible, between the north and the south, which meant that the three southern provinces should be separately developed in all economic, cultural, social, spiritual, and indeed, in every kind of activity.

Of the two policies open for them, the British rulers of the Sudan decided emphatically and strongly upon the policy of complete separation. Why was this policy preferred and most rigorously pursued? Perhaps it is useful to quote some passages from official dispatches, and others:

The approved policy is to act upon the fact that the peoples of the Southern Sudan are distinctly African and Negroid, and that our obvious duty to them is therefore to push ahead, as fast as we can, with their economic and educational development on African and Negroid lines, and not upon middle Eastern and Arab lines, of progress, which are suitable for Northern Sudan. The Southern peoples can thus be equipped to stand up for themselves in the future, whether their future lot be eventually cast with the Northern Sudan, or with East Africa (or partly with both).

Another dispatch (January 28, 1930) says:

His Excellency the Governor-General directs that the main features of the approved policy of the government for the administration of the Southern Provinces should be stated in simple terms:

The policy of the government in the Southern Sudan is to build up a series of self-contained racial or tribal units, with the structure and organization based, to whatever extent the requirements of equity and good government permit, upon the indigenous customs, traditional usage and beliefs.[1]

It is the aim of the government to encourage, as far as possible, Greek and Syrian traders rather than the Gellaba (Northern) traders. Permits to the latter should be decreased unobstrusively and progressively.

With regard to the language, the circular says: "Every effort should be made to make English the means of communication among the men themselves to the complete exclusion of Arabic."

As concerns religions, though we are told that the new policy should be based upon the indigenous beliefs, Mr. Murray was more candid when he said in 1929, "England as a Christian country, could not, consistently with her profession of faith, become associated with a policy which deliberately and of set purpose aimed at encouraging the conversion to Islam of a population of more than three million pagans who have neither racial nor other affinities with the Moslem Arabs."

It was therefore essential that not only the Arabic language, but also the Islamic Faith, should be eliminated from the south. In places, like Raga and Kafia Kingi in Bahr-El-Gazal Province, Arab and West African communities professing Islam were established; these communities had to be removed and distributed in different provinces in Northern Sudan.

In order to emphasize this policy of separating the south from the north two important measures were taken.

The first was to make the southern provinces "a closed area" to which Northern Sudanese could not be admitted without a special permit. For this purpose, a special "Closed District Order" was issued in 1922, which stipulated that no person, not a native of those districts, shall be allowed to enter the three Southern Provinces, as well as certain other districts bordering on Ethiopia to the east and French Equatorial Africa to the west. This order, like all other disciplinary measures in the Sudan, was carried out with the utmost rigor.

The second measure which was even more important concerned the question of "education" in the closed districts. The Government of the Sudan decided from the very start to hand over all matters of educating the children of the south to the care of the foreign missions. These were to have a free hand in setting up village schools, intermediate schools, and any institution of technical education which they might be able to set up. From 1927 onwards, they were given a regular annual subvention, which was gradually increased until it practically covered more than 90 percent of the education budgets of all the missions. Their work included conversion to the Christian faith, and in order to help them, an Islamic mission was never allowed in the south, and any Muslim resident was not allowed to preach or say his prayers in a conspicuous place. The missions were to be given every help from the administration to enable them to carry out the government policy of making the south a land professing the Christian faith, with English as its "lingua franca".

Altogether there were six missionary societies operating in the Southern Sudan. These were the Roman Catholic Mission, The Church Missionary Society, the Sudan United Mission (Australian), the American Mission, the African Inland Mission, and the Sudan Interior Mission. To avoid competition, every mission had allotted to it an area or a sphere of action. As a result of their efforts there are about two hundred and fifty thousand converts.

Some Sudan writers have alleged that, in the missionary schools, the history of the slave trade in general until 1949, and in the Sudan in particular, was taught in missionary schools, with illustrated booklets and pamphlets (Bashir M. Said, 1965, p. 90). Assuming this to be true, it can only mean that the missions were carrying out, with excessive zeal, the policy laid down by the Sudan Government, which aimed at separating the south from the north. Anything that could be done to discredit the relationship between the two sections of the country should be attempted. Hostility to the Arabic language, to Arab dress, and Arab names and titles, has been the order of the day; and surely, this could best be enhanced by keeping alive the memory of the age of slavery. It is, thus, not fair to blame the missionary schools for carrying out to the letter the declared policy of the State.

Before we pass to the next point, it is important to bear in mind that for administrative purposes every province was ruled by a governor, and each was divided into a number of districts. Each district had a district commissioner who was always an Englishman, sometimes aided by an assistant district commissioner, who sometimes, but rarely, was a Sudanese. These D.C.s were the most important executive officers in the whole country. Many of them were able men, who fully grasped the policy of their government, and helped to carry it out to the smallest detail. The Sudan was one of the most strictly governed countries.

Now the policy of separating the north from the south was vigorously pursued and maintained from its inception early in the twentieth century until the end of World War II. Then suddenly, in 1946, that policy was completely reversed.

That change was embodied in a letter addressed to all the Governors of all the provinces of the Sudan, as well as to all senior officers and heads of departments, and was written by the Civil Secretary, who, next to the Governor General, occupied the most important post in the land. In his letter, the C.S. says:

> The policy of the Sudan Government regarding the Southern Sudan is to act upon the fact that . . . geography and economics . . . combine to render them inextricably bound for future development, to the main eastern and Arabicised Northern Sudan; and therefore to ensure that they shall, by educational and economic development be equipped to stand up for themselves in the future as socially and economically the equals of their partners of the Northern Sudan, in the Sudan of the future.

As a result of the new policy, steps were taken to remove most of the former restrictions. The northern Sudanese could now travel freely to the south, and the Arabic language could be taught in secondary schools. For higher education, southern students could now go to Gordon College in Khartum, not as previously, only to Makerere College in Kampala. In short, the former policy of separation was cancelled and was replaced by a policy of integration.

This change of policy, though very radical, and not without obvious risks, was nevertheless quite inevitable. The Sudan had rendered valuable help in World War II. The help came mainly from the northern Sudanese, who now were sufficiently advanced to aspire to immediate independence, and they agitated for independence for the whole of the Sudan, north and south. The old idea that the south might be joined to Uganda or Kenya, was not favorably received by either. The resources of the south were such as to arouse little desire for its annexation. It was certainly bound to be a burden on whatever land it joined. It therefore became evident that the unity of the north and the south must now be maintained.

Steps were then taken to introduce the north gradually to some form of representative government. A legislative council was set up in Khartoum, to which a few southern members were nominated. An agreement was reached in 1953, between England and Egypt, which made it possible for the Sudan to choose full independence after a brief interval. This occurred on 19 December, 1955. The Sudan voted for complete independence, and the Sudan became an independent republic as of January 1956.

Now the heat of the atmosphere, engendered by the elections, in the south as well as elsewhere, must have enabled some agitators to commit acts of subversion. Even before the first independent Sudan Government had a real chance of coming to grips with the formidable task of nation-building, it was first met with a mutiny of the Equatorial Army in 1955. The Northerners stationed in the south—army leaders, civil servants, teachers—were bewildered by the brutalities unleashed by the mutiny. The mutiny was eventually suppressed, and most of the mutineers punished. Some of them vanished with their arms and were a source of great unrest, and some of them are still at large in the remote corners of the south or just outside the boundaries.

The mutiny of the army of Equatoria, is the first incident which precipitated the sad events that followed in subsequent years, including the flight of southern Sudanese to neighboring countries. It is, therefore, necessary to fully grasp all aspects of the mutiny and its implications.

The mutiny occurred just a few months before the declaration of independence. The condominium regime was still in existence, and an English Governor General was still in full occupation of his post. It was, however, understood that full independence was imminent, and that very soon a fully united Republic of the Sudan, comprising north and south, would come into existence. The idea of united Sudan must have had a great many opponents in the south, and these have not been content with mere passive opposition. Many people from the north were trying to paint a picture of great prosperity and higher standards of living in the south, but there have been others who could see nothing but evil in the unified Sudan, in which the north would be the dominant partner. Irresponsible agitators would not hesitate to repeat stories of the slave trade, and did all they could to arouse the passions of an easily aroused people.

This is not the first time in the history of the south that sections of it were aroused for hostile acts against their rulers. There was, for instance, the rebellion against Major Stigand in Equatoria, in which he was murdered by a Dinka rebel. Then, there was the case of Captain Ferguson, who tried to make the Nuer carry out some works to which they objected. Ferguson went so far in his attempt to befriend the people that he married a native woman, and did not hesitate to join in their dancing and other festivities. But when he insisted on road building and such drudgery, he was attacked and murdered by the Nuer. The Government inflicted terrible punishments on the Nuer tribe.

Sir Harold Macmichael says in his book on the Anglo-Egyptian Sudan, "The troubles experienced by the Government in the swampy areas of the Upper Nile . . . may be recorded with brevity. The genesis in every case is attributable to a mixture of the *natural mistrust* which was felt by these savages for any government of northern extraction, the incitement of witch-doctors, and the zeal of the young warriors to 'blood' themselves."

Sir Harold was referring to the years preceding the last war.

He might also have added, that hostility towards the north has been deliberately installed over several decads into those very susceptible minds.

In the light of all these facts, it is not surprising that the idea of having people from the north assume authority in the south, should have led to trouble. What made the rebellion unfortunate was that it was carried out by the army of Equatoria, and by hot-headed young men, entrusted with arms and articles of destruction. In a brief space of time, several hundred northerners were killed, and only those who managed to flee to their northern homes in time escaped. Of course a military tribunal was set up, and many of the mutineers were punished, and some kind of order was restored. But a great many began to leave the country and to seek new homes in the adjacent territories. Some left in order to join others to make subsequent inroads into the remote southern districts, and this crowd has sometimes been described as an "invading force". Adequate measures to meet this emergency in all its aspects were soon taken by the new government of the Sudan.

It is hardly necessary to give a detailed description of the different stages by which these waves of emigrants left their homes. The account of their movements will thus be fairly brief.

During the ten years following the mutiny, perhaps a little more than one hundred thousand left the south, though quite a considerable number has since returned. According to the account given by the U.N. High Commissioner for Refugees, there were about 99,000 refugees from the Sudan, divided as follows:

In the Central African Republic	25,000
In the Republic of the Congo (Kinshasa)	30,000
In Uganda	44,000
TOTAL	99,000

Although these figures refer to 1966, they probably are substantially the same at the present moment. They actually refer to the number of persons in different settlements who are being assisted by the HCR, or other collaborating agencies. They do not include the contingent which fled to Kenya, nor do they include individuals and groups who do not receive any assistance from HCR. This would seem to indicate that the real figure is more than one hundred thousand. But, in view of the fact that a large number of people who left their homes have since returned to the Sudan, the approximate number of those still abroad is not likely to exceed one hundred thousand.

Although all the refugees come from the three southern provinces of Sudan, an area of approximately two hundred fifty thousand square miles, few of them came from very far. Most of the refugees came from the districts adjacent to the host countries which received them. They may have sometimes moved to areas with inhabitants with whom they had some ethnical affinities. This is quite clear in the case of those who wandered from the Bahr-el-Gazal in the southwest to the Republic of Central Africa. Both immigrants and their hosts belonged to Zande tribes, and both spoke the same language. And they were settled in an area fairly close to the frontier at Bambouti. Latecomers were settled in the northern area of the Central African Republic.

The second area to which the Sudanese refugees immigrated was northeast of the Congo (Kinshasa). Again the new abode was not very far from the Sudan frontier. Owing to the fact that most of Africa, south of the Sahara, with the exception of Rwanda-Burundi, is mostly underpopulated, it has not been very difficult to accommodate the new immigrants in an area quite adequate for them and their flocks, if they had any. This is particularly the case in the east of the Congo, which has easily accommodated large and increasing numbers from the Sudan, Rwanda, and others. The only difficulty here was the political troubles, which arose in the Lake Kivu region. This, however, did not affect to any great extent those who have come from the Sudan.

The third country in which the Sudanese sought refuge was Uganda, which, because of its geographical position in the center of Africa, has received more refugees than any other. It should be noted that the frontier between Uganda and the Southern Sudan is fairly long, perhaps some three hundred miles. The most western stretch lies between the Congo and the river Nile. The Uganda province adjoining this boundary is called the Western Nile Province. To the east of the Nile, the frontier extends for another 200 miles along broken chains of mountains, which sometimes reach quite a respectable height of 5,000 feet or more.

The highest peak exceeds ten thousand feet, but although this justifies our describing the frontier region as mountainous, there is practically no difficulty in crossing from north to south, or vice-versa. Even with primitive means of transportation, communication across the mountains has been continuous through the history of those districts. Hence, the ethnic affinities between the people south and north of the mountains. The adjoining district east of the Nile is known as Achali, and further east is called Karamoja. To all these districts refugees have come from the Sudan since the mutiny of 1955 and have been coming since, sometimes in small numbers, sometimes in large groups. The peak of this immigration was between 1960 and 1965.

Usually the immigrants brought with them a lot of cattle, sheep, and goats. This was particularly the case with those coming to Uganda. Those who went to the Congo and Central African Republic were agriculturalists, belonging mostly to the Zande and allied races who did not possess any cattle. Those who came to Uganda were given every possible help by the Government. Considering, however, that the expense of settling some forty thousand people was beyond the means of the local authorities, appeal was made to the U.N. High Commission for Refugees, who, in Uganda as elsewhere, gave every possible economic and technical assistance. Not content with the resources available to it, the HCR managed to secure the help of such charitable organizations, as the Catholic Relief Services, International Committee of the Red Cross, World Council of Churches, Oxfam, and a host of others.

From the moment of their arrival, the refugees are helped with emergency food and shelter, and are soon conducted to an area where they can be settled temporarily, until a more permanent one is selected for them. They are then supplied with tools and seed for growing the crops they need for their subsistence, as well as a surplus cash crop. Both the local government and the HCR are exerting all possible efforts to meet all emergencies, and supply all urgent needs of the refugees. In most cases a beginning has already been made in the way of supplying elementary education for the children of refugees.

In concluding this paper, it is necessary that some reference be made to the policy of the Sudan Government with regard to its own citizens, who are now living in the neighboring countries. It is often suggested that there are three alternatives open to refugees: first, voluntary repatriation; second, settling by a homogeneous group in an adequate area allotted to them, and third, integration in the local population, which would naturally be confined to a small group of individuals or families. The Sudan Government is distinctly in favor of the first alternative, namely, voluntary repatriation. This policy has been pursued with great vigor and imagination, since the new democratic regime succeeded the previous military government. On more than one occasion, the Prime Minister of the Sudan Republic has toured the different districts in the south to get personally acquainted with all their problems and their wishes. Many notables and chiefs from the south have been elected to the new Parliament in Khartoum. Public opinion is distinctly in favor of doing everything possible to effect a return of all refugees, if possible. There are some interesting activities carried out by the government for achieving this objective. Some of these should be mentioned.

A.   A special broadcasting station was set up at Juba, the most important city in the south, and fairly close to Uganda. From there, speeches by eminent southern chiefs, are addressed to their fellow tribesmen, giving them every assurance that all their interests and their welfare will be taken into consideration by their government. It is a government which contains several representatives from the south who are cooperating with their compatriots in the north. There are several southern ministers in the Cabinet, who will see to it that the wishes of the people of the south shall be respected.

The speeches from Juba serve the double purpose of checking the flight of refugees on the one hand, and calling upon those who have already left their homes to return to them and live happily with their relatives and their chiefs.

B.   The Sudan Embassy in Kampala has many agents who are contacting the refugees, persuading them to return to their homes. Everything will be done for them to assure their safe return. They are further promised that no punishment will ever be inflicted, and every assistance is given toward their repatriation, including their settlement in new "Peace Villages".

C.   The third measure taken last year was to assure the fullest cooperation between adjacent countries. After all, the refugee question must not be allowed to spoil the good neighborly relations of countries like the Sudan and Uganda. The need was felt in East and Central Africa for a limited conference of heads of states. As a result, a summit conference was called by President Jomo Kenyatta, to which the heads of the governments of the Sudan, Uganda, Congo (Kinshasa), Tanzania, Somalia, Ethiopia, Malawi, Rwanda, and Burundi were invited. They met at the end of March, 1966 to discuss questions of common interest. From the beginning, it was emphasized that the meeting did not aim at creating a new grouping apart from the OAU, but rather helped in strengthening that organization. The agenda was very flexible and informal. Three questions, however, were thoroughly dealt with:

1.   Importance of maintaining good neighborly relations among the eleven countries represented at the conference.
2.   Strengthening African unity.
3.   Liquidation of colonialism in Africa, with special emphasis on Rhodesia.

The first of these items touches, naturally, the question of refugees, and the question seems to have been discussed in great detail. It was apparently decided that no refugee from an African country shall be allowed to stay in another country except on humanitarian grounds. No refugee shall indulge, at the risk of expulsion, in carrying out any agitation against his own country of origin, unless this country is still under colonial rule.

After the Conference at Nairobi, and on his way home, the Prime Minister of the Sudan spent a few days in Uganda conferring with Dr. Milton Obote, the Prime Minister. They must have discussed thoroughly the measures which should be taken in Uganda so that refugees from the Sudan should be helped either to return to their mother country, or settle peacefully in their new homes.

Most Sudan citizens at present are rather optimistic as regards the question of refugees, and are convinced that most obstacles that were preventing a peaceful satisfactory solution are gradually disappearing.

COMMENT

HUGH H. SMYTHE, United States Ambassador to Malta

Questions could be raised about the balanced perspective of the historical presentation of the problem of refugees from the Sudan made by Professor Mohamed Awad. This is especially so in view of material to be found in such reports as *The Nile Turns Red,* by Alexis Mbali Yangu, and *The Black Book of the Sudan: On the Expulsion of the Missionaries from Southern Sudan— an Answer,* as well as other sources. However, I shall confine my remarks to the pertinent proposals to ameliorate the refugee situation set forth by the Government of the Sudan, as mentioned in the paper.

Professor Awad says there are three alternatives open to the refugees: voluntary repatriation, settlement of a homogeneous group in an adequate area allotted to them, and by integration into the local population. He reports that the "Sudan Government is distinctly in favor of the first alternative" and it "has been pursued with great vigor and imagination." I raise the following points in relation to these three proposals:

1. The heavily favored repatriation of citizens through invitation to return, and failure of the program to attract them, raises major questions as to why the refugees do not want to return? Perhaps a satisfactory answer to this query could be helpful in providing a sound approach to make the policy a more useful and practical one. It is obvious, however, in light of the historical factors mentioned by Professor Awad, that political, religious, historical, judicial, humanitarian, and other elements are at work here, and all will have to be carefully considered in working out a mutually acceptable solution.

2. It seems to me that ethno-tribal similarity may tend to slow down the return of refugees once people become settled. Thus, this proposal would simply, on its surface, tend to defeat the purpose in the suggestion by integration into the local population where tribal and ethnic factors are held in common.

3. Ghettoization as a homogeneous group can only exacerbate

the refugee problem, and would appear to be the most unwise program to follow. It is well established that isolation of encysted groups only leads to further conflict and continuing difficulties, but does not offer any permanent solution to problems where groups are in conflict.

Since I am one who feels that anyone who criticizes a program has an obligation to at least make some suggestions that might be used as a beginning in the search to find an answer to difficulties, I make the following suggestions:

1. The present program to lure the refugees back to the Sudan needs to be reviewed and reorganized to make it more attractive, with this being done with every care and concern to make sure that equal justice is done for all parties involved in the problem.

2. Concrete evidence of guarantees of security of person to the refugees will have to be demonstrated concretely by the Government of the Sudan.

3. Complete acceptance of the refugees as full, first-class citizens whose rights and dignity will be respected and protected must be assured.

4. If integration is to take place, then it must be actual integration on an equal basis, and this must be shown to be a fact.

5. A program to eradicate the hate-filled atmosphere between northerners and southerners must be pursued vigorously by the national government.

6. More than tokenism in representation in government must be followed. Southerners must be given an opportunity to participate fully and on an equal basis in the national government; they must be allowed to share on a fair basis in the exercise of power and authority.

7. Allocation of a larger amount of the national budget to constructive development of the south must be followed, with southerners having a full voice in all such programs undertaken by government on all levels.

8. In the educational system, elevation and integration of the history of southerners as an integral part of pre- and post independence must be instituted in the curricula.

9. Utilization of more southerners in all aspects of official Sudanese life should be practiced. This will help them come to

realize a sense of pride, and develop a feeling of equality.

10. The religious differences simply must be overcome or there can be no lasting and satisfactory solution to the refugee problem. Southerners must be accepted for what they are, and they must be given the opportunity to do as they wish as regards following the religion of their choice.

NOTES

1. For all these and other quotations, see Bashir M. Said, *The Sudan* (London, 1965).

REFERENDUM AND DISPLACEMENT OF POPULATION IN FRENCH SOMALILAND, 1967: POLITICAL FACTORS CREATING REFUGEE SITUATIONS IN AFRICA[1]

10

YASSIN EL-AYOUTY, St. John's University, New York

Before entering upon the discussion of political factors creating refugee situations in Africa, using French Somaliland as a case study, it should be pointed out that the French colony at the Horn of Africa now goes by a different name. The term "French Somaliland" has already been declared non-valid by France whose National Assembly adopted in June 1967 a statute for the Territory calling it the "French Territory of the Afars and the Issas."[2] Somalia has challenged this change in name and the U.N. General Assembly has so far not taken cognizance of it. I shall, therefore, keep the old name, for the purposes of this chapter which relates to the referendum or consultation which took place in the Territory on 19 March 1967.

Situated on the eastern coast of Africa, this northern tip of the Horn lies round the Gulf of Tadjourah, at the head of the Gulf of Aden, just outside the Strait of Bab-el-Mandeb. It has an area of approximately 8,900 square miles, most of which is desert. To its north, lies the Eritrian part of Ethiopia, as well as Ethiopia proper, whose frontier extends on the west and south-west of French Somaliland. The Republic of Somalia lies to the southeast. The French Somalia coast extends eight hundred kilometers. Djibouti, the capital and port, comprises almost half of the population, which totals, according to French sources quoted for the year 1967, nearly one hundred and twenty thousand.

However, Somali sources indicate that the population totals one hundred and twenty-five thousand. The difference is critical in political terms. By the French count, the population comprises 46,300 Afars or Danakils who inhabit the north and west, that is to say the parts adjoining Ethiopia. It also comprises almost thirty thousand Issa Somalis inhabiting the south, which adjoins Somalia. Added to the Afars and Issas there are, according to French sources, 3,200 Arabs, 7,600 French from the Metropole, including the military, and 33,000 "foreigners" who are in fact persons of other Somali tribes.

Thirty-four years, from March 1862 to May 1896, separate between the date of the first treaty by which the Danakil chiefs ceded the territory of Obock to France, to the date of issuing a French Government decree officially naming the territory "Cote francaise des Somalis et Dependances." During that period France also concluded treaties with the Somali tribes when the French moved to the southern part of the territory in 1885, where Djibouti was later established.

It might be said that some of the political factors creating the tensions and population displacement in French Somaliland go back to the enmity dating from medieval times between the Somalis and the Ethiopians. In a speech before the United Nations Decolonization Committee, or the Special Committee of 24, on 10 October 1966, the Somali delegate devoted most of his statement to what he described as Ethiopia's expansionist designs on French Somalia. However, without disregarding the ancient historical factors which have made of the Horn of Africa a tension area for the past five hundred years, the political factors at work in 1967 can be discussed in the following terms.

1. The referendum conducted by the French authorities in French Somaliland in March 1967 was an act which heightened the expectations of the Issa Somalis, and their kith and kin in the Republic of Somalia, that independence might be achieved by political means.

2. The fact that France decided to hold the referendum following the hostile demonstrations which President de Gaulle faced in Djibouti in August 1966 created a Guinea-type situation, promising liberation if the organized answer would be "no" to France.

3. The existence of four main political parties, organized largely around either Issa or Danakil tribal affiliations, made the task of identification of opposition and displacing its members a relatively easy colonial task.

4. The existence of political movements outside the Territory engaging in political activity in exile helped, along with Somalia's sympathy and assistance, to raise the specter of infiltration into French Somaliland. This situation gave the French authorities the necessary pretext to expel thousands of persons from the Territory on the grounds of either territorial, security, or non-eligibility for participation in the referendum.[3]

5. Both Somalia and Ethiopia stated clearly, at the U.N. and in Africa, that their respective national interests were directly involved in the result of the referendum. From September 1966 to March 1967, the Somalis insisted on the need for U.N. supervision of the referendum to ensure fairness of consultations. They could not have campaigned harder for the independence of French Somaliland. As for the Ethiopians, the official statements made prior to the referendum were clearly indicative of Addis Ababa's sympathy for continuation of the status quo, which could be maintained only by a "yes" vote. Mogadiscio and Addis Ababa kept on charging each other with expansionist designs. Such charges and counter-charges represent two sets of competing national claims and aspirations. Ethiopia is obviously fearful lest independence for French Somaliland should eventually lead to the territory's merger with Somalia, and to providing a strong impetus to the demands for secession from Ethiopia by the inhabitants of Eritrea and the Agaden. In fact, Agaden is called by Somali irredentists and their sympathizers "Western Somalia." This is while the Somalia Constitution calls for the pursuit of reunification of all Somali territories, through peaceful and legal means. The application of such a constitutional provision automatically extends to French Somaliland and the Agaden. In addition, Ethiopia relies upon the port facilities of Djibouti for more than 50 percent of imports and exports. In fact, the Foreign Minister of Ethiopia once described the railway and port as the lungs of Ethiopia.

6. The U.N., in continuation of its commitment, begun in earnest in 1960, to the cause of independence for colonial coun-

tries and peoples, could not avoid adoption of specific resolutions, one by its General Assembly on 20 December 1966 and one by its Decolonization Committee, on 15 March 1967. These were specific resolutions calling on France to accept U.N. supervision of the referendum.

7. The struggle for independence in both Eritria to the north and Aden to the east, across from the Strait of Bab-el-Mandab, could not but intensify the struggle in Djibouti in 1966 and 1967 and result in greater displacement of population. This is indicated by the following news item published in the *New York Times*: "The whole southeastern corner of Arabia was free of foreign troops tonight—both Yemen and the Republic of South Yemen, whose two republican governments have declared that they will eventually be united into a single nation."[4]

8. Readiness of the Somali Republic to accept displaced persons within its territory was an interesting political feature of the situation, as it seemed to facilitate the task of its French adversaries. In this respect, it should be noted that Somalia maintains open frontiers for all persons of Somali origin. In addition to this policy framework, Somalia provided asylum for the expellees or "displaced persons" for humanitarian reasons. However, when it became apparent that the French administration was using these methods in order to alter the population structure of the Territory in favor of the Afars, Somalia closed its frontier to further deportations across the frontiers.

9. The nomadic character of more than one-third of the population of French Somaliland made the task of verifying the identity of those who were prevented from participation in the referendum, including the displaced persons, harder.

In studying these political factors relating to French Somaliland, the impact of numbers of the population involved in the evaluation of the situation should always be borne in mind. The number of displaced persons is small if compared with the total number of African refugees south of the Sahara. The Somalis estimate the number of displaced persons from French Somaliland to be 10,000, while the French estimate that number at only 3,000. Whether 10,000 or 3,000, our main concern should be the effect of internal and external political factors on displacing Africans, taking the Horn of Africa as a case that microscopes that cause-and-effect relationship.

It is interesting to note that the Somali Delegation to the U.N. used the term "displaced persons" in reference to people from French Somaliland for the first time in December 1966. The French Government had decided on 21 September 1966 that "population of the Territory would be directly consulted . . . by means of a referendum before 1 July 1967." Three days later, the Somali Delegation to the U.N. addressed a circular letter to all U.N. missions in which I counted no less than eighteen references to what Somalia called "the truly indigenous inhabitants" and their wishes "freely expressed." Behind the repetition of these terms lies what I consider the genuine African fear that what had been gained in the U.N. through affirmation of the need to ascertain the popular will of the inhabitants might be lost through manipulation of the application of the right to self-determination. In that respect, the Somalis came to look upon the first referendum held in French Somaliland in 1958 as false consultation. Somalia, and the Somali population of French Somaliland are convinced that the 1958 referendum was rigged and manipulated. Somalia did not consider that the demonstrations that took place on the occasion of General de Gaulle's visit in August 1966 were against the General in person, but rather an expression of dissatisfaction with their colonial status.[5]

The year 1966 did not pass without the General Assembly of the U.N. adopting a resolution in which it urged France "to create a proper political climate for a referendum to be conducted on an entirely free and democratic basis." The Assembly also requested France to consult with the Secretary-General on "making appropriate arrangements for a U.N. presence before, and supervision during, the holding of the referendum."[6] By the time this resolution was adopted, the Somali Republic was already charging that the number of Somalis expelled from French Somaliland to its Territory totaled six thousand.

By 9 March, that is to say ten days before the referendum, the U.N. Special Committee of 24 had decided to take up immediately the question of "the Djibouti Territory"—as Ethiopia insists on calling it. At that meeting of the Committee, Somalia's main complaint was that the question put to the voters avoided "any clear reference to independence." The voters were to vote "yes" or "no" on the following question: "Do you wish the Territory to remain within the framework ("au sein") of the French Republic with the revised Statute of government and administration, the essential elements of which have been brought to your knowledge?"

Somalia asked, where is the text of that Statute? The answer provided by the U.N. Secretariat was that the text had not been made public. But Somalia had other complaints against the way the referendum was being conducted, chief among which was the fact that France had refused to accept U.N. supervision. She also complained of what she considered as French restrictions on the right to vote, among which the requirement that the voter had to prove residence in the Territory for at least three years. Somalia's comment: "These are very iniquitous requirements for a population which is largely nomadic and which is required, by the nature of their country, to make seasonal migrations to outlying districts and to grazing areas beyond the border." Somalia also added charges of repression, brutality, and deportations of Somalis in the Territory suspected of pro-independence sentiment.

In the meantime, the press accounts were bringing news of Somali and Ethiopian army movements in the areas bordering on French Somaliland, threatening to intervene if the vote of 19 March 1967 was for independence. Somalia announced that it would only intervene if Ethiopia sent in its troops, adding that she, nonetheless, wanted a peaceful resolution of the conflict through the application of the right to self-determination.

The *New York Times* of 19 March 1967 described how "Scores of jeering ragamuffins shouted, 'No to France' and 'Good-bye, Monsieur,' after French Somaliland's Governor disclosed at a news conference . . . that French withdrawal after tomorrow's . . . referendum would raise the specter of war in northeast Africa." Moreover, on 15 March 1967, that is to say only four days before the referendum, the U.N. Decolonization Committee adopted a resolution by which it urged France "to ensure that the forthcoming referendum is conducted in a just and democratic manner." It is significant to note that the Ivory Coast cast a negative vote and stated that "some of the people (in the Territory) did desire independence; but others wished to maintain the *status quo*. It was for the people themselves to decide if and when they were to attain independence."[7] The stand taken by the Ivory Coast reflected lack of unanimity among African states with regard to the application of what the U.N.'s Declaration on Independence had termed "the inalienable right" of the people of French Somaliland (Djibouti) to self-determination and independence. This was clearly reflected in the declaration made by the Ethiopian Ambassador to Tanzania, who stated before the U.N. Decolonization Committee during its visit to Dar-es-Salaam following the referendum, that "The important part was that the people of Djibouti had been given a free choice and that in their wisdom had decided for themselves . . . It should not cause disappointment that they did not always conform to cut-and-dried formulas."

Thus, we see that with the passing of the great decolonization period of the early 1960s in Africa, African States are now looking anew into the formula of the automatic choice of independence in the light of their national interests. In fact, the same Ethiopian Ambassador declared that he felt that "the recent experience in Djibouti had clearly indicated France's dedication to and belief in the process of decolonization." This, of course, is a debatable point. The French statistics indicate that the registered voters numbered as follows: Afars, that is to say those favoring the status quo, 22,000; Issas, that is to say those favoring independence, 14,700; Arabs, 1,408; and, metropolitan French, 923. Out of this total of 39,000 voters, 22,500 voted "oui," indicating preference for continuation of French rule, while 14,700, exactly the number of Issas, voted "non." As for the expellees, French sources reveal that out of 33,000 "foreigners," only 5,500 were deported for not possessing identity documents, or for indulging in political activities. This number equals 4.5 percent of the total population.[8] It would be comparable to displacing 9,000,000 people in the U.S. or 30,000,000 Indians.

The violent rioting which rocked Djibouti on 20 March 1967, during which eleven persons were killed; the declaration of a state of emergency; the transportation of one thousand French paratroopers from France; the jamming of what were called "transit camps" by more than four thousand people who were being screened before determining who were to be expelled to Somalia; and Somalia's appeal to the United Nations High Commissioner for Refugees and other agencies for aid to the Somali refugees, were all manifestations of acute international tension.

It is difficult to assess the validity of claims and counter-claims in a situation where a host of political factors, not the least important of which are the deeply held national interests and well recognized strategic considerations, are simultaneously at play. The problem of using human pawns in the game of international politics will undoubtedly continue. One of the points worthy of our consideration is how to alleviate the intensity of this game and regulate its conduct. In such regulation, both the U.N., in its capacity as a universal organization, and the Organization of African Unity (OAU), as a regional organization, have general roles to perform. Unfortunately, it is still the sovereign nation-states, on which the membership of such organizations is based, which are called upon to determine the roles of these bodies in that sensitive sphere.

The extent to which the nation-states might be ready to accept the formulation of a positive role for global or regional organizations to act effectively on political and security problems must depend on a reevaluation of what constitutes "the national interest" within the community of nations.

COMMENT

HERBERT WERLIN, United Nations Institute for Training and Research, Adlai E. Stevenson Fellow

As I see it, the problem of the Horn of Africa is due to a problem on conflicting manifestations and concepts of nationalism. Nationalism, as you know, is a very complicated term, and is even more complicated in Africa because of the fact that the nature of the countries are very new, also nationalism is due mainly to anti-colonialism while the other aspects of nationalism, a sense of common purpose, a sense of patriotism, a sense of common destiny, have not yet really evolved. In the case of Somali, it had

had trouble with both its neighbors, with Ethiopia and with Kenya, and I think that one must ask the nature of this conflict. As I see it, the Somali have sort of an irredentist or a common grouping of all ethnically related peoples. They feel that all Somali people, all who are ethnically related, should be in the same country. Now this is not the view of the neighbors of the Somali. It is not the view of Ethiopia. It is not the view of Kenya, for historical reasons, for situational reasons. In other words, both Ethiopia and Kenya are very heterogeneous countries in a way that Somaliland is not, with the result that they view nationalism and they view their national boundaries in rather different ways. Kenya sees it based upon diplomatic, international agreements or treaties that they have either made or inherited. In the case of Ethiopia, it is a little more complicated. I think that their main desire, their main intent for Djibouti, for example, is an economic matter. This is their chief outlet to the sea and they feel that this is their great need, and that is their claim to this area. Of course, they argue that the majority of the people, the Afars, really do want to be in Ethiopia, but I think that this as well is a very difficult matter to justify one way or another. It is a very complicated situation where you have a group of nomadic people living in this area, one which has never really been properly defined or really established itself culturally. So the question is—How are you going to solve this particular dispute? As I say, Somali emphasizes self-determination. They say that wherever the Somali people are, that land belongs to them. On the other hand, in the case of Kenya, President Kenyatta has said it is all very well for Somali to go back. We will let the Somali go back to their country, but they must leave the land behind them. In the case of Ethiopia, it has another claim, an economic claim to this area. Now the question is, how can these different manifestations and conceptions of nationalism be reconciled. I would suggest that the emphasis must be on trying to get these countries to widen their conception of nationalism in the case of Somali, they must try to secularize and widen their conception to include a variety of people. This may be one approach. Another approach is to Pan Africanize the problem through attempting to create a much larger frame of reference within which cooperation can take place—as, for example, the East African Common Market. I think that these might be studied more as solutions and as a way of reconciling two very conflicting aspirations and conceptions of nationalism.

NOTES

1. The author gratefully acknowledges the benefit he derived from consultations with representatives of Ethopia, France, and Somalia to the United Nations, New York, during the preparation of research for this chapter.

2. It should be recalled here that the close ethnic, linguistic and cultural bonds which have historically existed between the Afars and the Issas have apparently been weakened by intervening political suspicions fostered by the French administration.

3. In 1959, the Liberation Front of the Somalis (FLCS) was established and located in Somalia. It consisted of all political elements from French Somaliland. In 1964, after the FLCS had been reorganized by the OAU, a second "front" was created with the backing of Ethiopia where it is presently located.

4. *The New York Times,* 30 November 1967, p. 2.

5. See the Somali Prime Minister's speech before the United Nations General Assembly on 18 October 1966.

6. General Assembly resolution 2228 (XXI) of 20 December 1966 which in its first two operative paragraphs states that the Assembly: "1. Reaffirms the inalienable right of the people of French Somaliland (Djibouti) to self-determination and independence in accordance with General Assembly resolution 1514 (XV); 2. Calls upon the administering Power to ensure that the right of self-determination shall be freely expressed and exercised by the indigenous inhabitants of the Territory on the basis of universal adult suffrage and with full respect for human rights and fundamental freedoms." See United Nations, *General Assembly, Official Records, Twenty-First Session, Supplement No. 16* (A/6316), p. 72.

7. It is worthy of note that the French Somaliland issue presented a difficult problem to several States Members of the U.N. This was not because of the specific issues relevant to the French Somaliland question per se, but because of the side effects on these States' relations with France itself. This aspect of African international relations deserves to be studied in depth.

8. Calculated on the basis of a total population of 125,000 as estimated by Somali sources.

PORTUGUESE GUINEAN REFUGEES IN SENEGAL*

11

I. WILLIAM ZARTMAN, New York University

West African refugee problems are typically ambiguous, and in their ambiguity pose the basic question of the whole area: When is a refugee a refugee? Populations are highly mobile in the area. The refugee condition, to the extent that it can be so termed, is simply the local answer to ethnically artificial and still largely irrelevant boundaries, or perhaps better, is a traditional fact that modern-type, fine-line boundaries have not altered. In fact, to the contrary, the migration of peoples in West Africa appears to be an enduring phenomenon, perpetuated and accelerated by urbanization and economic modernization.

A typical case—and a convenient one, for which some statistics are readily available—is Ghana. Among Ghana's 7 million people in the early 1960s were (by various sources) some 9 thousand Liberians, 20 thousand Malians, 25 thousand Nigerois, 55 thousand Ivorians, 150 thousand Dahomeyans, 190 thousand Nigerians, 195 thousand Voltaics, and 280 thousand Togolese.[1] Were these people refugees? The vast majority doubtless did not have any "well-founded fear of being persecuted" for anything, as the 1951 Convention and 1967 Protocol require; they were merely seeking better conditions (or fleeing bad conditions, which amounts to roughly the same thing). But if this cause for refugee status is not admitted, then many African "refugees"—elsewhere as well as in West Africa—are not refugees, for many are fleeing rebellious areas or colonial territories, not because of fear of persecution, but simply because conditions are not healthy where they formerly lived.

Or, another case is that of Dahomey-Niger. Statistical tables

*I want to acknowledge the great help of Mr. Robert Waters who compiled sections III and IV of this paper.

143

note that there are 16 thousand refugees from Niger to Dahomey. What the tables do not note is that these refugees, who have indeed fled because of well-founded fears of persecution, are Dahomeyans who went to Niger and have now fled back (home?) to Dahomey. Whose refugees are they then? This is a problem to which this study will return after a discussion of the case in question.

The only notable case of refugees in West Africa[2] involves 55,000 to 65,000 people from Guinea-Bissau (Portuguese Guinea) who have fled to Senegal since 1964. Yet, this one case is typical in many ways of other refugee movements elsewhere throughout the continent. The background of the movement is a nationalist, political struggle, although the active participation of the refugees in political life is doubtful. The major activity in favor of the refugees is carried not by the welcoming population across the border in Senegal, who, somewhat oblivious of international frontiers and national citizenships, is simply receiving large numbers of fellow tribesmen. This basic hospitality is augmented by efforts of the Senegalese government and the United Nations High Commissioner for Refugees (UNHCR).

Before these and other features can be examined, it will be necessary to describe the political setting and struggle for independence in Guinea-Bissau.[3]

I

As in other West African countries, nationalism grew up among those who were partially admitted to the colonial system. Grouped together in the legal category of *assimilados,* 5 thousand Africans and Metis received modern schooling in Guinea and in Portugal, and returned to Guinea to join government or commercial services, whereas others entered the modern economic system as laborers. The rise of nationalist feeling in the early 1950s "coincided with the return to 'Portuguese' Guinea of several Africans who, abroad and particularly in Europe, had closely followed the evolution of colonial policy and the international situation after World War II, and who, along with African students from other Portuguese colonies, had taken the first steps in Portugal on the road of their 'reAfricanization' and of the development of their national conscience."[4]

From the urban and "civilized" population, dissatisfaction and nationalism spread to the over 600,000 Africans in the interior.[5] Among these people, as among the urban Portuguese and *assimilados,* ambiguities arose. Intra-tribal disputes are translated into nationalist-colonialist terms, and many tribal chiefs depend on Portuguese support for continued tenure. Particularly in the Fula regions of the north and southwest, traditional elders have found support from the Portuguese against younger or nationalist rivals. Traditional animosity between the intermingled Diola and Manjak peoples in the north has also been reflected in conflicting views on Portuguese rule, and even in membership in a conflicting nationalist organization by those who do agree to oppose the Portuguese. The Diola-Manjak animosity is exacerbated by centuries of pressure on the Diolas, beginning in the Casamance territory of Senegal, pushing them southward into Manjak territory.[6]

Some of the tribes, on the other hand, have a history of resistance to European penetration. The Portuguese conducted campaigns against coastal groups such as the Bijagos and Balantes as late as the World War I period. These tribes are located in the heavily populated areas of the first and deepest Portuguese penetration. Further in the interior, where there is less European presence, there tends to be proportionately less antagonism to colonial rule.

Although the nationalist activity cannot be interpreted along purely tribal lines,[7] the various tribal reactions to colonial penetration have been important to guerrilla operations, since the nationalist forces tend to live off the land and to rely on local sources of support, arms, and information. The initial outbreaks of guerrilla warfare, and the present areas of strongest nationalist implantation, coincided with the Balante populated areas; other liberated zones, on the other hand, have been established in Manjak (including Pepeis) and Fula-Malinke (Mandingo) regions, mobilizing support against unpopular chiefs.

Economic conditions played an important role in early reform demands as well as in the later spread of the nationalist movement.[8] Portuguese Guinea is an agricultural country, and the local economy is self-sufficient in food. Its largest export crop is peanuts, which during the decade of the 1950s made up fifty to seventy percent of annual exports. The other major crop is rice, an indigenous African variety, lower in yield than the Asian crop, and produced almost exclusively for internal consumption. Not all tribes grow the same products, however; Diolas and Balantes are rice-growers, for example, and Malinkes are not. These commodities are grown by the Africans; seed is distributed during planting season and repayable in kind during harvest. Peanuts are bought by Lebanese or African middlemen, or, to an increasing extent, directly by Portuguese trading companies, who have controlled internal trade by paying cash on delivery in Bissau instead of advancing payment through the middlemen, as was done in the past. The minimum legal price of about seven cents per kilo (about two cents less than in Senegal) is not always respected. Legal bans on usury, practiced by storekeepers who advance food to farmers between harvests, are not always enforced either.

Out of this economic situation, by far the most important factor contributing to the nationalist movement, is the incomplete modernization introduced into the country with the coming of the Portuguese. The imposition of commercial crops, such as peanuts and oil palms, and the incomplete distribution of economic benefits for the Africans as a result of commercial agriculture, created basic dissatisfaction and disruption. These characteristics were even more pronounced among the uprooted urbanized workers, to whom the contrast between participation in modern economic life and the economic, social, and political benefits which they derived from it is much greater than within the agricultural population. Without dissatisfaction and disruption in both town and bush, urban intellectuals could never have been successful in finding support in the primitive countryside. Despite limited Portuguese penetration into the colony, there was enough economic and social disruption of traditional ways to produce a crisis of uneven modernization that fed the nationalist movement.

Thus the sources of nationalism, giving common cause to an unevenly modernized elite and an unevenly dislocated traditional mass, are fourfold: 1) political national consciousness arising from external education and contacts, 2) social national consciousness arising from unequal treatment of skilled and semi-skilled Africans in an urban context, 3) traditional animosity carried over from past opposition to Portuguese penetration and exacerbated by intra- and inter-tribal conflicts, and 4) economic dissatisfaction arising out of disruption by the colonial system without accompanying benefits.

II

Nationalist activity has followed a rather regular progression through successive stages of a liberation struggle, each following the other as a result of natural reactions toward colonial opposition. The African Independence Party of Guinea and Cape Verde Islands (PAIGC) was formed in September 1956, concentrating its efforts among the urban populations, labor and artisans. During 1958, strikes were attempted, with varying success, but a two-weeks' strike begun in late July of the following year in the port of Bissau ended suddenly on 3 August with violent repressive measures. Some 50 strikers were killed, others wounded, and in April 1960, the first wave of arrests against nationalist leaders began.

The "massacre of Pigiguiti quay" made a deep impression on the PAIGC leaders and marked a turning point in the nationalist movement. Convinced that they had made a mistake in concentrating on the urban population, where the government had proven to be strongest, the leaders adopted an eight-point program which aimed principally at shifting the active struggle to the "peasant masses" of the countryside, where the government was weakest and the Portuguese least numerous (point 2), and at working to overcome ethnic and social divisions within the population (point 3), while developing the nationalist organization clandestinely within the cities (point 1); the party also sought to increase its organizational and technical cadres in view of eventual independence (points 4, 7 and 8), and expand its external activity among expatriate Guinean and Cape Verdians (point 6) and in coordination with nationalist organizations in independent Africa, Portuguese Africa and Portugal itself (point 5).[9]

In early August 1961, the PAIGC announced the coming outbreak of direct action, beginning with scattered sabotage, although the first attack on a Portuguese barracks (Tite), took place on 23 January 1962. During the last two weeks of January, a congress of party leaders met in Conakry, where the party seat had been moved, to elaborate statutes and a program.[10] This was the last preliminary step in organizing the nationalist movement, and it appears to have been done after a good deal of initial organization and consideration of party positions had been accomplished, rather than being established as a paper framework in a vacuum.

Three events occurred toward the end of this preparatory period which undoubtedly had some influence on the turn of PAIGC activities. First, starting in August 1961, the Portuguese political police (PIDE) began a new series of arrests among suspected party members. PAIGC claims that over 3,000 members have been jailed since then. Second, on 15 July 1961 rival Guinea groups met in Dakar and constituted a United Liberation Front for Guinea and the Cape Verde Islands (FUL), and two days later, Manjak tribesmen from Senegal, belonging to the major component of the FUL, the Liberation Movement for Guinea and the Cape Verde Islands (MLG) of Francois Mendy, attacked three towns along the northern (Senegalese) border of Portuguese Guinea; after Portugal allegedly violated airspace. Senegal, the same month, became the first African country to break diplomatic relations with Lisbon. Third, two appeals to Portugal in December 1960 and again the next year, containing mainly demands for popularly elected assemblies and negotiations for self-determination, went unanswered; instead, Portugal sent 8,000 troops to the territory, a contingent over three times the size of the Portuguese population there.

The third period of PAIGC activity began on the night of 30 June 1962 with a number of concerted incidents of sabotage designed to isolate the southern part of the country. These attacks were largely aimed at disrupting lines of communications, one of the more developed aspects of the country, thanks to Portuguese investments through the last two Five-Year Plans. The Portuguese returned the attack, searching out PAIGC camps in the bush and seeking to destroy them. Towards the end of 1962, the rebellion broadened into full-scale guerrilla warfare, aimed at destroying the economic and military bases of Portuguese presence and at changing Portuguese thinking on the status of Guinea (as explained in a 6-point PAIGC declaration of 15 February 1963),[11] and also at creating "free zones" within the country.

One such zone was established early in 1963 in the southern triangle between the Geba river and the Guinean border. In

July, a second front was opened in the central region between the Geba and the Cacheu rivers around the PAIGC base area in Oio forest. A year later, two other free zones were carved out of Portuguese territory; the northeast region of Gabu, a Fula peanut-growing area where the tribal chiefs were favorable to the Portuguese, became a new liberated area, and at the other end of the northern border, in the northwest Manjak territory between the Cacheu River and Senegal, another free zone was established. In mid-1965, the southeast region of Boe, between the Corubal River and the Guinean border, was liberated. Thus, isolating the Badora region around Bafata and, more important, the Balante and Manjak (Papeis) regions of Canchungo (Teixeiro Pinto) around the capital, the PAIGC staged attacks as close as 20 miles from Bissau in August 1966. It should be emphasized that within these free zones Portuguese garrisons and fortified hamlets often exist, in variable number from two in Boe (Madina and Beli) to more numerous sites in the south and center. Essentially, liberated areas have become regions where free movement is denied to the Portuguese and enjoyed by the nationalist movement. The PAIGC is thus able to set up alternate organizations and institutions, and the colonial system is forced to withdraw into beleaguered centers, with large regions (some 40 percent of the country) denied to their political control and economic exploitation.

Passage to the fourth stage of nationalist activity was decided upon in the First Party Congress, held in the southern region on 13-17 February 1964.[12] In response to a concerted Portuguese attack on the Como base, and in response to the progress in liberating regions which both required and permitted a more centralized control of military operations by an overall nationalist organization (which was also set up at the Congress), the creation of three types of fighting forces was agreed upon. These were to be guerrilla forces, a militia, and the Armed Revolutionary Forces of the People (FARP). The passage to the military phase of the nationalist struggle allowed armed clashes with larger Portuguese military units, particularly necessary after May when the appointment of General Arnaldo Schulz as combined governor and military commander inaugurated a stronger Portuguese effort at reconquest. By 1965, there were about 16,000 Portuguese troops in the territory (over five times more than the colonial population), and PAIGC fighting forces were claimed to be about 10,000. However, estimates of nationalist forces are naturally ambiguous. It would be nearly impossible to distinguish militants from guerrillas, guerrillas from interior supporters, and supporters from local populations since all four groups overlap. Military command of troops in all three categories is carried out by designated military commanders under national PAIGC control; commanders are responsible for troops, and operations, not for territory, in order to avoid dangers of *"wilayism"*, although political and administrative control of liberated zones remains in the hands of zonal leaders.

In addition to PAIGC activity, minor incursions along the Senegalese border in 1966 and 1967 were made by guerrillas adhering to FLING, an outgrowth of FUL-MLG taken over by Benjamin Pinto-Bull.[13]

III

The bulk of refugees from Portuguese Guinea flee into neighboring Senegal. Various estimates place their number somewhere between 55,000 and 65,000. This group can by no means be considered a nationalistic bloc dedicated to liberating their homeland. Their attitude toward the independence struggle is largely passive; they are neither Portuguese nor Guinean nationalists. Rather, they are simple peasant people who no longer desire to live amidst violence and shooting. Villagers in the truest sense of the word, they have little if any contact with modern society. Few know how to read or write. Hardly any have ever been to a hospital, or have seen a doctor. In many ways, despite their uprooting, life is better in Senegal than it was in Guinea-Bissau.

The exodus of refugees from Portuguese Guinea follows a fairly precise migratory route northward into the Senegalese province of Casamance, between Guinea-Bissau and Gambia. There seem to be few digressions from this path.[14] The reason for a vast movement following a single route seems fairly obvious. Refugees are easily assimilated into the Casamance border villages since the inhabitants belong to the same tribes as they do— Diolas, Manjaks, Balantes, Malinkes, and Fulas, reading from west to east. Along this border, population density ranges from 10 to 35 per square kilometer on the Senegalese side, but less than 10 on the Guinea-Bissau side, except in Diola regions at the Atlantic, and Fula-Malinke regions in the middle and at the eastern end. It is from among the Balantes, Malinkes and Fulas that most refugees appear to come. Thus, the inhabitants speak the same language, lead the same communal life, and sometimes even have shared the same fields which lay across the border.[15] The affinity between the inhabitants and the refugees has proved so strong that, in many cases, the local population has shared everything with the refugees including lodging, tools, seeds, and food stocks.

Since there has always been movement and migration within the frontier region—the border between the two countries is a fiction to the local inhabitants—the refugee concept itself may be called into question. It is more likely to assume that the villagers are simply moving to a more peaceful section of the same tribal area. At any rate, migrating to Senegal is relatively easy for most villagers since the same environment awaits them. Additional incentive to move is provided by an intensive, U.N.-affiliated refugee relief program that has been in operation in Senegal since 1964. The very favorable conditions that exist for refugees in Senegal is perhaps an important factor in accounting for the large numbers leaving Portuguese Guinea.

What began as a mere trickle has now reached flood tide proportions. In 1960, only a small number of refugees were reported in Senegal, although many more may have existed than reported.[16] Their number increased gradually until 1964, but they passed largely unnoticed since they were absorbed by the population and were out of the circuits of official attention. Suddenly, in May 1964—at approximately the same time the rebels switched their tactics from guerrilla warfare to military operations, and began establishing liberated zones in the north of the country— a heavy influx of refugees began to swell the ranks of the earlier arrivals. Since then, both causes have continued to produce the effect of a growing refugee migration.

Beyond this simple cause, however, nationalist activity on either side of the border, and its effect on the refugees, leaves much to be surmised. The region from which the refugees comes includes FLING supporters (Manjaks), PAIGC supporters (Balantes), Portuguese supporters (Malinkes and Fulas), and dissidents from each ethnic group who may express their personal dissatisfaction, subethnic rivalries, or opposition to the chiefs by siding against the party associated with the main ethnic body. PAIGC and FLING have sanctuaries, camps, or supply bases on the Senegalese side, although the former's guerillas tend to attack from the interior northward and the latter from Senegal southward. The 1961 attack of the MLG Manjaks on the local Diolas produced one border skirmish.[17] In April 1963, the same process was repeated, but this time the Diolas counted PAIGC supporters among them and they retaliated against the Manjaks. When the local chief, who appears to be a Diola of PAIGC sympathies, decided to move from Portuguese Bunhague to Senegalese Bouniak and his people followed him, the Portuguese bombed the Senegalese town.[18] In 1965, PAIGC members, FLING members, and Senegalese policemen were involved in a shooting incident in Ziguinchor.[19] Renewed border incursions by Portuguese troops into Senegal in March and September 1967 appear to be in response to increased PAIGC northern activity and possibly also to the revival of FLING attacks across the border.[20] The problem of sorting out political activists from refugees fleeing violence in these incidents is difficult, but it does appear that the two categories are distinct and that the bulk of the refugees (in the mass sense) have not yet been won over to nationalist consciousness. PAIGC leaders and sympathizers have both stated that—apart from such groups as the Balantes—the problem of politicizing the peasantry in general is a major one, and that they are simply not interested in people who flee rather than staying to resist.[21]

By mid-summer 1964, a critical point had been reached when the number of refugees in Casamance had risen to thirty thousand. Because of the overcrowding in the frontier areas, it was increasingly difficult to provide refugees with arable land. As is normal during the rainy season, there was a food shortage throughout Casamance and the Senegalese government turned to the UNHCR for help.

The refugee relief program that has emerged is characteristic of relief programs throughout Africa. Senegal, as the host country, and the United Nations, representing the world community, work closely together in administering the program. As host countries everywhere, Senegal bears the brunt of administering the program and contributes substantially to its support. The UNHCR also provides financial support and is the principal agent in obtaining assistance for the program from countries and agencies throughout the world. As elsewhere, the United States Government, the League of Red Cross Societies, and the Catholic Relief Services have given assistance.

Administration of the program is largely the responsibility of the Comité National chargé du programme d'assistance en faveur des réfugiés au Sénégal. All measures on behalf of refugees are coordinated by the National Committee with which the UNHCR representative in Dakar maintains close contact. The National Committee also makes arrangements with operational partners, e.g., with the Catholic Relief Services in regard to food distribution.

Since neither repatriation nor emigration is desired by refugees, the program concentrates on local settlement. During the initial

TABLE I
Rural Settlement of Refugees in Casamance
Estimates of 1966 Expenditure in US Dollars

| ITEM | TOTAL COST | TO BE FINANCED BY | | |
		Senegal Government	UNHCR	Other international sources
1. Food (including storage, transport and distribution)	527,781		64,923	462,857
2. Health (including building of additional facilities, personnel and vehicles)	305,061	135,714	70,408	98,939
3. Village Settlement and Agriculture				
(a) 1,435 family schemes	243,755	185,980	53,694	
(b) 2,165 family schemes	277,592	224,082	53,510	4,082
4. Contingency Reserve	17,465	—	17,465	—
TOTAL	1,371,654	545,776	260,000	565,878

stages basic necessities such as food, shelter, and medical services are supplied. Then emphasis switches to the program's long term goal of making the refugees self-sustaining. Arable land, tools, seeds, wells, and farming instruction are thus provided. In 1966,

the cost of the program amounted to CFA frs 336,055,175
(U.S. $1,371,654), of which Senegal contributed CMA frs
133,715,000 (U.S. $545,776).[22]

IV

The program that has evolved in Senegal since 1964 is a fairly
complete application of the UNHCR's relief formula for refugees.[23]
It can be divided into three categories: food distribution, medical
services, and rural settlement.

FOOD DISTRIBUTION

During 1964 the distribution of food rations was given top
priority. The High Commissioner allocated $60,000 from his
emergency fund to cover the transportation costs of flour donated
by the United States. The food was rushed from Dakar to
distribution points inland and dispensed by village chiefs and
district commissioners.

During 1965 there was an influx of 20,000 refugees, raising
the total to 50,000. Since these refugees were concentrated in the
Casamance, food shortage was still a major problem, especially
during the pre-harvest "soudure" which normally lasts two months.
Famine was averted only by renewed food shipments of 3,200
tons from the United States. $104,081 was allotted for food trans-
portation costs from the $117,501 food budget approved by the
Executive Committee of the UNHCR at its thirteenth session.

Some fifteen thousand new arrivals were fed for a period of
ten months until the 1966 autumn harvest. Afterwards, food was
distributed to refugees who had not reaped their harvest. Some
two thousand tons of food donated by the United States was
distributed to the new refugees, as well as to earlier arrivals who
were not yet self-supporting. $57,000 of the UNHCR program
for Senegal was allocated for the inland transportation of food.

MEDICAL SERVICES

Catholic Relief Services and the Sengalese Red Cross provided
medical aid in 1964. A health service distributed anti-malaria
drugs and launched several vaccination campaigns. It was not until
1965 that the medical assistance program got under way in full
force. From 15 February to 15 August two nurses of the French

Red Cross operated a mobile medical unit in Kolda and Sedhiou, giving smallpox vaccinations to refugees and Senegalese living in the bush. In the latter part of 1965, the League of Red Cross Societies obtained the services of three nurses (one Canadian, one French, and one Swiss) to continue the mobile unit after the first two nurses had departed. In addition, the High Commissioner purchased two Land-Rovers for the unit from the League of Red Cross Societies for a twelve-month period at a cost of $10,500. Also, two hospital vans and two used Land-Rovers donated by the United States and the United Kingdom were reconditioned and brought to the Casamance. The Government of Senegal paid the wages of drivers and auxiliary personnel. The vehicles made the mobile unit more effective since sick people did not have to wait until the dry season to be treated in dispensaries hundreds of kilometres away. The second unit has proved so successful that the Senegalese Government has decided to maintain the service. Making daily visits to the most remote villages, it traveled more than 30,000 kilometers to 50 different villages in 1965. As a result, more than 15,000 persons were protected against malaria and bilharzi.

Beginning in 1965, medical supplies were donated directly to the Senegalese government by OXFAM, the French and British governments, and the African Institute of New York. The French government also provided equipment for polyclinics. In October 1965, the UNHCR spent $2,248 to replenish drugs and medicine stocks. Three health and social welfare centers were built in Kolda during this year to serve as a base for the mobile teams. Two social and medical centers were established at Tanaff and Missira. Newly arrived refugees are screened in these centers in order to detect communicable diseases and prevent epidemics. The centers also have facilities for first-aid courses and child welfare. Two veterinary clinics for cattle were opened at Tanaff and Tambouna and six more are planned.

Medical services continued to be improved in 1966. Vaccination of refugees was continued on a larger scale since three mobile health units were now in operation. The hospital at Zinguichor and the Noma hypnosery were extended to accommodate refugees at a total cost of $43,000. A new village for lepers was constructed at a cost of $4,000. A request by the Senegalese Red

Cross to the League of Red Cross Societies was also made, and the League has increased its aid in 1967.[24]

SETTLEMENT PROGRAM

During 1964 farm tools, seeds and fertilizers were distributed. The sinking of wells was also begun to augment the water supply. In 1965, the Senegalese government began its resettlement program by moving refugees away from the overcrowded border area. It began organizing the transfer of 20,000 refugees from the departments of Sedhiou (15,000) and Kolda (6,000) to settlements further inland. Projects were also worked out for the transfer and settlement of 1,435 families (8,600 persons) from the rural districts of Diattacounda and Tanaff to the districts of Diende, Boukiling, and Marassoum and from the border villages in the district of Dabo to the area of Sare Lao.

The government is making four hectares of land available to each family it transfers and giving them food, clothing, blankets, tools, seeds, and fertilizers. It is providing for their transportation, digging wells in the new camps and installing veterinary services for cattle.

Although many thousands of refugees have been transferred under the program, many did not wish to leave their friends and relatives in the border area. They fled into the bush and fields when the police came to ask them to leave.

The resettlement project is difficult and complex and is therefore under constant review. It is continually revised as circumstances change. But, it is believed that the refugees will become self-sustaining in the hinterlands where there is available room for cash crop cultivation and little threat of Portuguese retaliation.

As part of the resettlement program, the drilling of fifty water wells was begun in November 1965. The wells and boreholes were completed for the most part in 1966. A limited program of bridge and road construction was launched after the rainy season in 1965 in order to provide an outlet for the new settlement's agricultural production. In 1965, the rice cultivation project at Diatouma was intensified. Under the supervision of an agricultural team sent by the Republic of China, the project is aimed at convincing local people that modern methods of cultivation will increase the rice harvest twenty-fold. At first, efforts to break down tradition met with unexpected difficulties. The first sixty families to work on the project refused to consider rice a cash crop since traditionally it is stored in village dwellings as a sign of respectability. However, a rich yield has been obtained three times a year and the arrival in late 1965 of specialized equipment for the project has since increased production.

Seventeen small bridges were constructed in 1966 at a cost of $13,750. The sinking of forty-two wells cost $13,000. Contributions for cattle veterinary care and the rice cultivation project were $2,250 and $4,000 respectively. A contribution of $3,700 was made for the purchase of school materials for primary schools. Many more thousands of refugees were transfered to the hinterlands under the resettlement program. A unique feature of the 1966 program is the Senegalese government's plan to set up a counseling service for refugees in Dakar. $10,500 was approved by the UNHCR for the service at its sixteenth session. The counseling service may serve as an example to other African states since the movement of unemployed refugees into large cities is by no means confined to Senegal. However, some refugees from Portuguese Guinea who live in Dakar received scholarships and education in Senegalese schools and the University of Dakar.

RELIEF PROGRAM

The 1967 relief program has proved so successful that authorities suspect that many Senegalese are posing as refugees in order to benefit from its services. In order to prevent hostility, the 1967 program has been extended to provide some assistance to the local Senegalese population. So effective was the 1966 program that its allocations were reduced and its monies committed towards expenditures for the first half of 1967, mainly for capital investment—e.g., the extension of the hospital and hypnosery. Also refugees being resettled in the remote regions have been well received by the local population with which they may not have any tribal affiliations. Twenty thousand new arrivals are being integrated into the population. Food for the new arrivals is continuing to be provided by the United States government under bilateral agreements with the government of Senegal. The twenty thousand remaining refugees in Casamance are expected to be self-supporting by the end of 1967. Twenty thousand new arrivals are expected in Senegal in 1968.

V

At the beginning of this study, it was suggested that the refugees from Guinea-Bissau in Senegal were typical of African refugees in general, in many ways.[25] Most notably, in Guinea-Bissau and Senegal, as elsewhere in Africa, the very notion of refugees is up for debate. While a refugee can be considered to be a person who flees persecution or catastrophe in his homeland (and the influx into Senegal certainly fits this much of the description), it is also generally assumed that his movement is temporary, his new home is alien, and his national consciousness is highly developed— perhaps even more so because of his flight. None of these elements seems to obtain in this case, nor are they likely to be found in a number of other cases in Africa.

Thus, the case at hand appears to be as much a migration as a refugee problem. Suffering from the violence of the liberation struggle, and from competing attempts of both sides to control or commit them, they pack up and move elsewhere among their own people. The brunt of their care is borne by their kinfolk. The border they cross is not a demarcation of nationality, patriotism, allegiance, or identification, but simply a line (albeit clearly perceived) between deprivation and sanctuary. The fact that they are taken care of, and that local efforts at integration are reinforced by vigorous assistance from the host government of Senegal backed by international agencies, only increases the attractiveness of the migration. It was estimated that 40,000 had reached the local Senegalese standard of living by 1966 and that the remaining 20,000 would do so the next year. It is easily predictable that the migration will not level off at sixty thousand under those circumstances. Although it will become more and more difficult to integrate increasing numbers of Casamance or resettle them elsewhere nearby, the success of the program in Senegal is an added inducement for further migration from Guinea-Bissau.

Under such conditions, how temporary can the migration be expected to be? Given the lack of nationalist sentiment now apparent and the divergence of economic conditions, it would not be surprising if the refugees never returned. However, in this assessment, not all factors have been—or can now be—considered. One future variable concerns the amount of politization accomplished while in Senegal. Unlike some other African refugee situations, nationalist movements are not called on by the host government to screen the refugees. But, both nationalist movements are present in the area, and may be expected to work on the refugees.

Another factor is the balance of population pressure in the Casamance. Sixty thousand people have entered the underdeveloped, heavily populated Casamance area. Other than being rice- rather than peanut-growers (i.e., producing needed food rather than a glutted-market product), they bring with them no particular skills. Their presence has attracted Senegalese public works efforts, which in turn must be extended to local populations to avoid dissatisfaction. Casamance as a whole has probably benefited from their presence, but how many more can the region absorb?

Although refugees create problems and involve individual misfortune on the mass level, there may also be concomittant benefits. A tenth of the population of Guinea-Bissau has moved out and is probably better off because of it. The migration has probably not been disadvantageous to the Guinean nationalist movement, and it removes a burden of care that the movement would have to bear in the liberated zones. It has also spurred greater attention to the Casamance region, although any dramatic claims of results would be exaggerated. However, the presence of a large, new population in an underdeveloped region with an important agricultural potentiality could provide a useful impetus to government-sponsored rural development—such as *animation rurale*—since the new population is already dependent on government aid and is well integrated with the old population.[26] The apparent ill wind that blows in the refugees may yet be a wind of change that turns some wheels of progress.

NOTES

1. Figures drawn from the Ghana census of 1960 as presented in *Notes d'information,* no. 101 (Paris: Banque centrale des etats de l'Afrique de l'ouest, December 1963). For a discussion of the political role of "exiles"

and "expatriates" in Western Africa, see these references in Zartman, *International Relations in the New Africa*. (Englewood Cliffs: Prentice-Hall, 1966), p. 171.

2. Of course this may not be true either if the alleged 5 million refugees in Nigeria are included: they are certainly persecuted, but less certainly international.

3. For fuller discussions of Portuguese Guinean nationalism, from which sections I and II of this paper are drawn, see Zartman, "Africa's Quiet War", IX *Africa Report*, (February 1964): 2:8-12; Zartman, "Guinea: The Quiet War Goes On," XII *Africa Report*, (November 1967), 8:67-72; Zartman, "Nationalism in Portuguese Guinea," paper presented to the annual meeting of the African Studies Association, October 1966; and Zartman, "The Content of Portuguese Guinean Nationalism," paper presented before the Conference on Brazil and Portuguese African, UCLA, February 1968. The best treatment of the whole issue is General Chaliand, *Lutte armee en Afrique* (Paris: Maspero, 1967).

4. PAIGC, *Development de la Lutte de Liberation Nationale* (n.d. [1963], n.p.), p.1.

5. For a detailed, if critical, report of the government situation, see *Le Peuple de la Guine "Portuguese" devant l'ONU* (PAIGC), (mimeographed), n.d. [ca. 1961], pp. 56-64. Also see series of mimeographed reports submitted by the PAIGC before the Afro-Asian Jurists Conference, Conakry, 15-22 October, 1962: *L'Emigration et le travail force, La Situation politique, Partis politiques et syndicats, La Lutte de liberation nationale, situation Judiciare,* and *Notre peuple, le gouvernement protugais, et l'ONU.*

6. See L. V. Thomas, *Les Diola* (Dakar: IFAN, 1958) 2 vols.

7. The much-touted dangers of tribalism and Cape Verdian domination have generally proven to be overcome, even according to PAIGC rivals; interviews with Henry Labery, August 2, 1965, and with Benjamin Pinto Bull, August 1, 1965.

8. In addition to general sources, see *Le Peuple de la Guine . . .* , pp. 30-50. For a brief review, see VIII *Africa Report*, (November 1963) 10:35.

9. *Le Peuple de la Guine . . .* , p. 59.

10. *PAIGC Statuts et Programme* (n.p., n.d. [1962]).

11. *Le Peuple de la Guine . . .* , p. 59.

12. On the party congress, see Cabral, *Le Development de la Lutte de Liberation Nationale en Guinea "Portuguese" et any Ales du Cap Vert evs 1964* (mimeo, PAIGC), pp. 2-6.

13. See *Le Monde* March 15 and September 21, 1967 for example. Also see *Bombolom, Bulletin d'Information du FLING* (Dakar: 1967), vol. 1.

14. A few refugees migrate to Gambia and to Guinea (Conakry) but their numbers are insignificant. Along the entire Guinea (eastern) border of Guinea-Bissau, population density on both sides is less than 5 people per square kilometer, except for the first 20 miles from the Atlantic (at the extreme southern end) and even there it does not exceed 10 per km. Thus,

despite the fighting in this sector, there are simply fewer people to seek refuge. PAIGC political groups abound in Guinea (Conakry), however. A few refugees in Senegal find their way to Dakar. Some of these are un-employed, but others are adopted in the Portuguese Guinean and Cape Verdian community installed there for more than half a century as laborers, or in higher employment. Some, too, are politically active in the Dakar officers of the PAIGC and FLING. The number of current refugees from Guinea-Bissau in Dakar in 1967 was 1500.

15. See UNHCR document A/AC96/325, p. 40. Border tribes and densities are found in J. Richard-Molard, *Carte Ethno-demographique de l'ouest africain, feuille,* no. 1 (Dakar: IFAN, 1952).

16. A most interesting typewritten report by a visiting group from CIMADE, the international Protestant welfare organization, written in 1962, estimates the number of refugees in the area at the time as 50,000. While the group does not appear to have used any reliable way of counting, the vast difference between this figure and the U.N. figures of 6,000 for 1964 (i.e., before the influx started) indicates how much speculation is involved in any discussion of this nature. Among other interesting observations, the report noted that at that time, refugees frequently returned to their fields or dwellings on the other side of the border to retrieve things at night.

17. Interviews in Dakar and Conakry.

18. Interviews in Dakar. Also U.N. document S/PV. 1028 (November 1963).

19. Interviews in Dakar. Also U.N. Security Council debate, see *Le Monde* May 13-21, 1965.

20. Interviews in Dakar, see also supra, n.13.

21. Gerard Chaliand, *Guinee "portugaise" et Cap Vert en lutte pour leur independence* (Paris: Maspero, 1964) 25, Amilcar Cabral, "La Structure sociale de la Guinee . . . ," *Revolution africaine* (24 June, 1966) 178:18-19.

22. U.N. document A/AC96/301 add. 1, p. 12.

23. The following material is drawn from UNHCR sources, notably A/AC96/301, pp. 7-11 and A/AC96/325, p. 40.

24. Medical care is given by Senegalese hospitals to wounded nationalists from Guinea-Bissau.

25. For further discussions on African refugee problems, see Sven Hamrell, ed., *Refugee Problems in Africa* (Uppsala: The Scandinavian Institute of African Studies, 1967).

26. I am grateful to David Hapgood for this suggestion. A brief report on *animation rurale* in the refugee region is Mansor Mbaye, *L'Organisation de la vie rurale en Casamance, Senegal "An 2" par lui-meme* (special supplement to *Development et Civilisations* [Paris 1962]), pp. 45-49.

REFUGEES FROM SOUTHERN AFRICA 12

Z. K. MATTHEWS,* Former Ambassador of Botswana
to the U.S., and Permanent Representative to the U.N.

Interest in the refugee problem in Africa is indicated by the
many recent conferences on refugee problems in the Continent:
1. International Seminar held in Uppsala, Sweden, 26-28 April
    1966 under the auspices of the Scandinavian Institute of
    African Studies.
2. International Seminar on Refugee Students in Africa held
    in New York in April 1967 under the auspices of the
    African-American Institute.
3. Conference on Refugee Problems in Africa held in Addis
    Ababa, Ethiopia in October 1967 under the auspices of
    the Economic Commission for Africa, the UNHCR, the
    DAU and the Dag Hammarskjold Memorial Foundation.

The countries which may be said to fall within the region of
southern Africa include the following:

South Africa—independent since 1931
South West Africa—Mandated Territory till October 1966
Lesotho—independent since 1966
Botswana—independent since 1966
Swaziland—independent since 1968
Rhodesia—unilateral independence since 1965
Malawi—independent since 1964
Mozambique—Portuguese Colony
Angola—Portuguese Colony
Zambia—independent since 1963

All these are countries from which labor is drawn for the Wit-
watersrand industrial complex which comprises gold mining, coal
mining, the iron and steel industry, etc., as well as the farms

* Deceased.

163

which provide the area with food supplies. Mozambique supplies 100,000 men for the gold mines per annum; Malawi 80,000; Botswana 32,000; Lesotho 200,000, and the rest lesser numbers.

The countries in the region are generally referred to as "white man's countries" because their climates, unlike the climate of, say, the Western African countries, formerly regarded as "white man's graves," are suitable for white settlement. The result is that during the last three hundred years the population of white settlers in this part of Africa has grown to about four million, as against the African population of about thirty million. The white settlers in this region have no intention of leaving and they are therefore determined to retain this area as one ruled and dominated by whites. The following African states have achieved independence in the region: Zambi (1963), Malawi (1964), Botswana (1966), Lesotho (1966), Swaziland (1968), and are ruled by African governments.

The remaining territories, in varying degrees, follow the policy of apartheid or separate development of which South Africa is the chief exponent. Rhodesian policy is but a pale reflection of South African policy, and the Portuguese policy of regarding Mozambique and Angola as provinces of Portugal is but a thinly disguised form of apartheid. The Africans in the so-called white countries have never accepted the policy of white domination of their countries. They have fought against it in various ways throughout the history of the settlement of these territories. They continue to do so today. The white rulers have done, and are doing, all in their power to suppress the African movements for the liberation of these territories from white domination. This suppression has taken the form of banning African political organizations, detaining or arresting their leaders, placing the territories under emergency laws which deny the people freedom of assembly or association, limiting or controlling their education and economic opportunities, and generally denying them an effective share in the government of the country. It is out of these circumstances that the refugee situation in southern Africa has developed.

The number of refugees in southern Africa varies from country to country. The largest number of refugees are Angolan refugees in the Democratic Republic of the Congo, estimated at over three hundred thousand. The next largest number are Mozam-biquan refugees in Tanzania estimated at about 20,000 and in Malawi at about 3,000. The number of refugees in countries further south is much smaller. In Botswana the number is generally about 200, in Lesotho about 100, and in Swaziland slightly more than 100. The reception accorded to them in the different countries to which they may go varies.

In the former High Commission Territories of Lesotho, Botswana and Swaziland—all countries adjacent to or surrounded by South African territory—they are granted asylum, provided they do not engage in local politics or use the country of asylum as a base of operations against South Africa. Permanent settle-ment in these areas is, however, not possible except for a few, owing to the poor prospects for employment or educational opportunities. Refugees in the former High Commission Terri-tories are, therefore, always anxious to leave the countries further north. To do so, they have to run the risk again of crossing South African territory, with the possibility of being arrested enroute.

In Zambia, the next country which they can enter without fear of molestation or forced repatriation, they find that in accordance with government policy they are not allowed to settle, but must produce travel documents and written assurances that some coun-try further north is prepared to grant them asylum. In other words, in Zambia they are regarded as persons in transit to some other country. No employment opportunities are open to them unless they are in possession of valid travel documents, a condition which no refugee can fulfill.

Tanzania is the country which has been most hospitable to South African refugees. Not only have they been granted asylum, but the Government has, within the limits of available resources, been willing to provide them with financial assistance. It must be pointed out, however, that Tanzania is primarily interested in South African refugees who fall into the category of "freedom fighters." Such refugees must be vouched for by one or other of the South African political parties based in Tanzania as genuine "freedom fighters". If a refugee is not a "freedom fighter", or ceases to be one by reason of resignation or expulsion from the party under which he was registered, he is liable to be declared a prohibited immigrant and deported from the country or repatriated to his country of origin. It would appear that the political parties can use the threat of prohibited immigrant status as a disciplinary measure to build up the strength of the resistance movement, or to swell the ranks of those undergoing training in military camps.

By agreement between the government of the countries concerned, once an individual is declared a prohibited immigrant in one of the East African territories of Tanzania, Kenya, Uganda, and Zambia, he is regarded as a prohibited immigrant in all of them. The plight of such prohibited immigrants can well be imagined.

One of the recent developments in the refugee field is the increasing interest of the United Nations in setting in motion practical measures for assisting South African nationals. As is well known, the South African question has occupied the attention of the United Nations Organization ever since its inception.

Endless debates have been held on the question of the policy of apartheid followed by the Government of South Africa, and condemnatory resolutions of various kinds have been adopted and presented to the South African government for its consideration. All these resolutions have been rejected by the South African Government on the ground that they represent interference in the domestic affairs of a Member State which is beyond the jurisdiction of the United Nations in terms of its own Charter (Article 2[7]). In the meantime, the South African Government has pursued its policy of apartheid with utmost vigor, both by means of legislation and administrative action, and the action it has taken against critics of the regime in the light of the powers it has assumed, has resulted in bannings, house arrest, long-term imprisonment, and even death sentences. Condemnation and protest, representation and appeal, threats of boycott and economic sanctions—all have proved of no avail in bringing about a change of policy.

In 1964 the United Nations appointed a Committee of Experts to study the South African question and to make recommendations. Among the recommendations made by the Committee of Experts was one which called for the establishment of a United Nations Education and Training Program for South Africans. The program is intended "to enable as many South Africans as possible to qualify as lawyers, engineers, agronomists, public administrators, teachers at all levels, and skilled workers, as well as training in such fields as labor, education, business, and industrial management, so that they may play a full part as quickly as possible in the political, economic, and social advance of their country, in accordance with the purposes and principles of the United Nations Charter."

In the meantime, the General Assembly has established a United Nations Trust Fund for South Africa which is used for grants to voluntary organizations, governments of host countries of refugees from South Africa, and other appropriate bodies. A Committee of Trustees of the Fund has been appointed which consists of the representatives of:

Sweden— Sverker C. Astrom, Chairman
Nigeria—J. C. Iyalla, Vice-Chairman
Pakistan—Ahmed Ali
Chile—Javier Illanes
Morocco—Day Ould Sidi Baba

The Trust Fund is to be used for grants for the following purposes:

(a) Legal assistance to persons charged under discriminatory and repressive legislation in South Africa.

(b) Relief for dependents of persons persecuted by the Government of South Africa for acts arising from opposition to the policies of apartheid.

(c) Education of prisoners, their children and other dependents.

(d) Relief for refugees from South Africa.

Consultations have been held with various voluntary agencies, including the World Council of Churches, to find out to what extent, if any, they will be able to cooperate with the Committee of the Trust Fund in the implementation of its program.

As the Committee puts it "This operation is not intended to resolve the political and social problems with which other United Nations organs are concerned. Its purpose is to meet a limited, albeit urgent and clear, need of a humanitarian character. If it does, in addition, help people in South Africa to view their problems with less bitterness, it will be considerably worthwhile."

In considering the needs of these refugees, account must be taken of their requirements while in transit and their requirements when they reach their destination. While they are in transit, the following measures are necessary:

1. Providing relief for the refugees while they are in the former High Commission Territories and to assist in the matter of finding employment for those who are compelled to remain there, in farm settlement, market gardening schemes, etc. Reliable contacts through whom such assistance can be channeled are available.

2. Helping with transport for refugees en route from the High Commission Territories to the north, i.e., to Zambia and beyond. It is estimated that it costs 5 pounds or 6 pounds per head to remove refugees from Francistown to Lusaka by road and rail.

3. Establishing a reception center or centers in Francistown, Botswana (the usual point of exit from the Republic) and in Zambia.

4. Finding employment in Zambia or elsewhere for refugees who cannot be given further education.

5. Selecting refugees for further education and establishing a coordinated network of educational opportunities, mainly in Africa, but also overseas.

In Dar-es-Salaam itself, the urgent needs of the refugees are, as follows:

1. Rent for those occupying premises outside the refugee camp provided by the Tanzanian Government for a limited number.

2. Feeding. The Tanzanian Government used to give each recognized refugee an allowance of twenty-one shillings per week to enable him to feed himself, but has now discontinued this form of assistance.

3. Clothing. (Each refugee generally arrives with only the clothes he has on).

4. Children's clothing—for children from one to sixteen years of age who at present number 30.

5. School fees for children of school age.

6. Educational facilities for those who have not yet attained an educational standard entitling them to university entrance.

7. Finding scholarships for those who are able to enter universities or other institutions of vocational training in Africa or elsewhere.
8. Medicaments—antimalaria tablets, aspirins, etc., for the whole group.
9. Providing employment for those with professional qualifications, and any others for whom vacancies can be found in the limited economy of Tanzania.
10. Pastoral care for all the refugees.

The refugee problem in southern Africa differs from the refugee problem in other parts of Africa. In the latter, i.e., other parts of Africa, the refugee problem arises out of internal upheavals or disputes between Africans due to inter-tribal conflicts as in Rwanda and Burundi between the Wa-Hutu and the Wa-Tutsi, or different cultural or religious backgrounds as between the Northern Sudanese and the Southern Sudanese, or the dominant Hausa and the Ibo in Nigeria. In southern Africa, the refugee situation arises out of the problem of white minority rule over black majorities. This applies in South Africa, Southwest Africa and the Portuguese colonies of Mozambique and Angola. Another characteristic feature of the refugee situation in southern Africa is that, except for Angola and Mozambique, we are concerned here not with the kind of mass exodus which has occurred in countries like Rwanda or the Sudan, or even Angola, but with small groups or with individuals who for fear of arrest or detention or some other form of persecution, have decided to leave their country.

Mention must also be made of the wide distribution of southern African refugees compared with refugees from other areas who tend to be found in one or two countries of asylum. Apart from those in the United States, United Kingdom, and other parts of Europe, Southern African refugees are to be found in significant numbers in Lesotho, Swaziland, Botswana, Zambia, Tanzania, Ethiopia, with isolated groups in Kenya, Congo (Kinshasa), and Nigeria.

Finally, refugees from southern Africa consist not only of Africans, but include whites who for their sympathy with African suffering or with the cause of African liberation, have fallen foul of the authorities in countries such as the Republic of South

Africa or Rhodesia. Some have left of their own accord, while others who happened to be nationals of countries such as the United Kingdom or the United States, have been deported.

Another problem presented by refugees from southern Africa, especially from South Africa, is that they have no prospect of a return to their country of origin in the foreseeable future, unless they are prepared to face imprisonment for illegal departure from the country. In the case of the Republic of South Africa, the penalty for unlawful departure from the country may involve two years imprisonment. This creates problems with possible countries of asylum which, while on humanitarian grounds may be willing to accord refugees asylum, do not look with favor upon the permanent settlement of such refugees. Having regard for the difficulty of providing employment opportunities for their own nationals, they are not anxious to be burdened with finding employment for foreigners, especially where such foreigners are better qualified for employment than their own nationals.

The crisis in the affairs of Southern Rhodesia which was precipitated by the Unilateral Declaration of Independence by Ian Smith and his followers on 11 November 1965 continues. As is well known, the Unilateral Declaration of Independence was followed by the declaration of a State of Emergency in the country. The Emergency Regulations have given the Minister of Law and Order even more extensive powers than he had before. A considerable number of people have been detained under the Emergency Regulations. This means that:

    they do not have recourse to the courts;
    they cannot secure normal legal aid;
    habeas corpus is eliminated;
    they live in overcrowded quarters;
    they are not given an opportunity even to see their relatives;
    their whereabouts are seldom reported to their next of kin;
    they invariably lose their jobs;
    their families suffer;
    there are firm rumors to the effect that in detention "spare diet"
        is meted out to those who do not "cooperate", and that
        beating is resorted to in order to extract evidence.

There is no means of discovering the exact number, and the

publication of information or pictures of restrictees is a punishable offence.

Since UDI, the freedom of restrictees has been curtailed. Instead of being allowed to roam over a large area at will, as they could hitherto, they are now confined to a small area which is surrounded with barbed wire and which is guarded day and night by armed troops.

Further, they are no longer allowed to live in the huts which they built for themselves, but all occupy the galvanized iron barns provided by the government. Worse still, they are not allowed visitors as in days gone by. To gain access to the camps, an application in writing has to be submitted to the authority and the reason for desiring to make the visit stated. No minister of religion has been allowed in the Gonagudzingwa Camp since May 1965.

Censorship of news in the press and over the air continues. The BBC has established a station in Botswana for the special purpose of broadcasting to Rhodesia. It is now a punishable offense to listen in public to news from outside stations. Some of the local newspapers continue to defy the censorship regulations which forbid them to leave any blank spaces or to publish the notice which says that "all material in this edition has been subject to Government censorship." No government action has been taken against them so far.

Deportation orders have been issued against alleged critics of the regime. These have included press representatives both local and foreign church leaders, and others. Among those who have been affected by these orders can be mentioned the late Bishop Pike of the Episcopal Church in California, U.S.A.; the Rev. and Mrs. Donald Abbott of the American Board Mission in Rhodesia (after fifteen years service in the country); Mr. Brian Porter, a teacher who had come to the country to join his bride-to-be; volunteer workers from Amnesty International who had hoped to assist with the distribution of relief to the needy.

The problems of southern Africa, arising out of the policies followed by the white administering powers in the area, have been the subject of numerous resolutions in the United Nations over the years. While the basic issues of the fundamental rights and freedoms and self-determination for the majority of the inhabitants of this area have not yet been satisfactorily solved, there are certain practical steps which have been taken by the U.N., to bring aid to the victims of these policies. I refer, in particular, to the training and education programs which have been set in motion for Africans from these areas. These include:

1. The special training program for Southwest Africans, established in 1961.
2. The special training program for Africans from Portuguese Territories, established in 1962.
3. The special education and training program for South Africans abroad, established in 1964.
4. The U.N. Trust Fund for South Africa, established in 1965, whose mandate is somewhat under that of the three programs mentioned above.

In 1966, the General Assembly passed Resolution 2235(xxi) deciding to consolidate the three special training programs referred to, and set up an Advisory Committee on the Consolidation and Integration of these programs for southern Africa. The consolidation of programs is intended to ensure increased efficiency, and to promote further development and expansion.

The Advisory Committee has already held a number of meetings. Since the inception of the three programs, 46 member States have contributed either study grants or funds in supplementation of the relevant resolutions of the U.N., and about 800 persons have received assistance to pursue their education in other countries.

THE CONGO

13

EDOUARD BUSTIN, Boston University

As often happens when Africa is discussed these days, the subject of the Congo inevitably turns up and draws passionate responses in the same way a lightning rod draws electricity. The reason for this phenomenon is obvious enough. Most of the problems that beset newly independent nations somehow seem to acquire unprecedented dimensions in the Congo, and conflicts which may remain latent in other parts of the continent frequently reach their crisis point in that country. As a result, the Congo has acquired an unenviable reputation as a sort of showcase in reverse, a miasmic political hothouse, where the tribulations of an emerging state inevitably assume larger-than-life proportions. What few observers seem to recognize, however, is the fact that the Congo is not so much a monstrous exception as the fast-ripening product of conditions that prevail over most of the continent: the first of many army coups in sub-Saharan Africa occurred in the Congo and the "Congolization" of Nigeria is now a dramatic reality. The analysis of this process is unfortunately distorted by the injection of emotional biases, whatever their source, into a rational discussion of the problem; the result is that the Congo is often viewed as a source of glee by white supremacists, or as a source of embarrassment by African nationalists—neither attitude being objectively justified in my opinion—to the detriment of a genuine understanding of the real causes of the Congo's problems.

The problem of refugees is no exception to this pattern. The Congo is indeed of exemplary significance for the understanding of the African refugee problem, not only because of the magnitude of the numbers of individuals involved in involuntary migrations since 1960, but also (or perhaps, primarily) because the Congo offers examples of almost every single type of situation

173

likely to generate such involuntary migrations, whether by individuals, or groups.

Most Congolese refugees never left the Congo at all, but simply migrated from one area where they felt their safety was in jeopardy to another where it might be assured. Yet, despite the fact that their exodus was caused by local, rather than national, conditions there is no need to introduce a differentiation that would be largely artificial between those who did or did not leave the country: first, because those who did were, for the most part, living in border areas and African political boundaries are frequently seen as irrelevant by frontier tribes; and second, because both types of refugees were reacting to conditions internal to the Congo. On the other hand, for every man who leaves the Congo there is one who enters it to seek refuge for a variety of reasons. This second group is extremely heterogeneous in terms of their motivations, though not necessarily in the sense of being alien to the Congolese people. For convenience's sake, rather than for any particular epistemological reason, these two categories of refugees will be studied separately.

CONGOLESE REFUGEES

In a sense, all Congolese who have fled their homes since 1960 are "political refugees", to the extent that their exodus has been caused by man-made, rather than natural, calamity. Most of them, however, are "political refugees" only to the same extent as European Jews fleeing from Nazi terror: the political dimension of their predicament is supplied not by their beliefs or behavior, but by the manipulation of human emotions for political ends. As is usual the world over, only a small percentage have gone into exile (voluntarily or not) as a result of actions deliberately conceived by them to gain political power. The bulk of the refugees have been the victims of inter-group tensions in which ethnic, rather than ideological, factors have played the most important part.

The Lulua-BaLuba Conflict

"Tribalism" is one of the most elusive and over-worked concepts applied to Africa. Ethnic consciousness operates at different levels and ranges in its scope and significance from the blindest form of parochialism to a set of reactions collectively dignified under the term "nationalism". Tribalism in Africa—at least as a factor affecting political behavior—is not, contrary to superficial assumptions, a legacy of traditional Africa, but rather a by-product of urbanization and social change. Even when its roots predate the colonial age, it is often of relatively recent origin and has usually gained a new dimension as a result of the colonial situation.

A good example of this type of conflict is the Lulua-BaLuba dispute. It was not until the 1870s that a segment of the Kasai BaLuba, settled in the Lulua valley under the chieftainship of one Mukenge Kalamba, came to regard themselves as a distinct group. In the 1800s, large numbers of Luba who had been forced to flee from Cokwe incursions asked for permission to settle in the Lulua valley. These early refugees retained their separate identity and held land only by sufferance. Under Belgian rule, the Kasai BaLuba, whose traditional institutions had been disrupted as a result of the unsettled conditions prevailing in that part of Africa during the late 19th century, were more easily attracted by the opportunities for change introduced by the Europeans. They, accordingly, accepted Western education and salaried employment with more alacrity than most of their neighbors. Furthermore, the development of transportation coupled with their lack of a stable heartland made them more receptive to the attraction of employment in faraway places. The Kasai Luba were soon to be found in sizeable numbers in all major towns between Leopoldville and Elisabethville, and particularly in the Kasai provincial capital of Luluabourg—itself built on lands belonging to the Lulua.

Administratively, the Belgians contributed to the problem when they refused to recognize the Lulua area as a separate native administration unit under a Lulua paramount chief and, instead, organized separate units for the BaLuba living on Lulua lands under Luba "chiefs" who had no traditional status. This was done in the late 1920s and brought no immediate reaction from the Lulua inasmuch as land was still relatively plentiful in the area at the time. Characteristically, it was when they began to seek employment in the urban centers (especially in Luluabourg) that the Lulua began to realize that the best jobs were invariably occupied by the Luba, and to feel threatened by their once-despised neighbors and "guests".

The results of this situation are well known, and there is no time to launch into a more detailed discussion of the Lulua-Luba conflict. Two important factors need to be mentioned here, however. First of all, the dimensions of the Lulua-Luba conflict in the Luluabourg area became complicated toward the beginning of 1959, by the increasingly restless political atmosphere which characterized this period. A number of educated BaLuba living in the capital, who had been instrumental in the early attempts to set up a nationalist movement in the Congo, became actively involved in the defense of Luba interests in Kasai. The best known and most active of these was Albert Kalonji. From this moment on, the conflict became hopelessly embroiled in national politics, and vice-versa. The split in the ranks of the Mouvement National Congolais, most dynamic of Congolese political formations, pitted Kalonji against Lumumba but the former soon turned his wing of the party into a political vehicle of the Kasai BaLuba. As a result, Lumumba's attempt to isolate his rival led him to seek the alliance of the Lulua and other Kasai ethnic groups. This only reinforced the BaLuba's sense of isolation. The rest of the story is well known.

A second consideration is that the sudden acceleration in the pace of political developments in the Congo after January 1959 undoubtedly resulted in a stiffening of the Lulua-Luba tension and in a feeling on both sides that, since they could not trust each other's future intentions, some sort of settlement had to be negotiated as soon as possible. An agreement signed between twenty-five Kasai chiefs in January 1960, but later repudiated by the non-traditional Luba leaders, provided for the evacuation of the BaLuba from Lulua lands. At that time, the exodus of the BaLuba toward southeastern Kasai had already begun and by the end of January, the number of displaced persons of Luba origin was already estimated at between 35,000 and 50,000 persons.

Anti-Luba riots broke out in Luluabourg in the spring and only increased the flux. By the time of the general elections, the BaLuba's sense of bitterness and frustrations had reached such dimensions as to make it impossible for them to cooperate with other ethnic groups in the provincial government of Kasai. Kalonji's failure to become the rallying point of anti-Lumumba forces only increased his determination to go it alone, if necessary. For a while, it appeared as though the BaLuba might be placated by the setting up of a separate province in Southeastern Kasai, but when Katanga seceded, the temptation to follow suit was too strong to resist and the "Autonomous State of South Kasai" was proclaimed in August 1960.

The political aspects of this whole episode (which saw, among other things, the ritual installation of Albert Kalonji as *Mulopwe* of the BaLuba, as well as several other bizarre developments) need not be elaborated upon. Kalonji's alliance with Tshombe made his fledging state the victim of Prime Minister Lumumba's attempt to maintain national unity by force: Congolese Army troops invaded South Kasai and massacred large numbers of Ba-Luba. In turn, the BaLuba themselves were to assert a harsh rule over the minority groups in the southeastern Kasai area, particularly the Kaniok. Yet, when the Congo was divided into twenty-one provinces (as against six at the time of independence), South Kasai was one of them and even today when most of the old provinces have been restored by President Mobutu, the particularism of two major ethnic groups (the BaKongo and the Ba-Luba) has been partly deferred to, so that lower Congo and eastern Kasai remain separate provinces.

The Katanga Secession
Many of the factors which account for the animosity felt toward the Kasai BaLuba also apply in the context of the Katanga copperbelt, where the immigrants from Kasai (an overwhelming majority of them being BaLuba) were resented for their ability to succeed in a changing urban-industrial environment. The initial political cleavage was between the immigrants and the self-styled "authentic Katongese," i.e., members of ethnic groups indigenous to Katanga—a term which normally encompasses the Lunda, Cokwe, Tabwa, etc., but also the Katange branch of the BaLuba. In fact, under the loose and somewhat inappropriate term of Ba-Luba, a number of tribes of central and northwestern Katanga are commonly covered. These various tribes, however, have widely different backgrounds and had never in the past acted as a single force. As to their relationship with the Kasai BaLuba, it

ranged from indifference to concern (mostly positive but some of it diffident or even hostile).

It was against this backdrop that a Katangese regional party, the CONAKAT, was organized in 1959, with the more or less occult backing of white settler interest. Originally, the party appealed to all "autochthonous Katangese" groups, but the Katanga BaLuba (by far the most important single ethnic group in Katange, though certainly not the most homogeneous) soon became alienated from the CONAKAT, partly as a result of what they felt to be the unduly large influence exercised by South Katange groups (particularly the BaYeke and the Lunda), and partly because the CONAKAT's opposition to Kasai immigrants increasingly took the form of an anti-Luba campaign by which the Katanga BaLuba (though indigenous) felt indirectly threatened. The offshoot of this situation was, first of all, a split within the ranks of CONAKAT then, as the 1960 elections drew near, an actual reversal of alliances which saw the Kasai immigrants and the bulk of the Katange Luba (plus the Cokwe) join forces against the CONAKAT's brand of parochialism. This realignment of forces was complicated by the affiliation at the national level of this anti-CONAKAT alliance (known as the *Cartel Katangais*) with Lumumba's strongly unitarist party, the MNC.

When the CONAKAT captured the Katanga provincial government and declared a secession, the *Cartel* (representing roughly one-half of the Katanga electorate) strenuously opposed this policy and its members were persecuted by the Tshombe regime. This resistance took many forms: in the north most of the BaLuba and related groups went into open rebellion against the secessionist government and were the victims of ruthless military operations in which white mercenaries were employed for the first time. In the urban centers of the south, the BaLuba were the targets of veritable pogroms by the backers of the Tshombe regime. One of the most notorious effects of this situation was the more or less improvised organization of a BaLuba refugee camp under U.N. protection on the outskirts of Elizabethville. The whole episode became the subject of much acrimonious controversy between local U.N. authorities and the Katanga regime, with the latter accusing the international organization of deliberately setting up this human powder keg at the heart of the secessionist capital.

The Katanga secession resulted in the displacement of a large number of persons. Some of these were political refugees in the usual sense of the term. To the extent that they managed to avoid assassination or imprisonment, opposition party members were forced to rebuild their lives outside of Katanga. A few of these politicians, who had been elected at the national level, or were skillfull enough to launch a fresh political career, became part of the national political establishment. Others, however, never succeeded in this readaption and fell by the wayside, whether dropping into oblivion, becoming embroiled in shady activities or simply returning to their previous line of work. The fate of the majority of the refugees was less enviable. Families were torn asunder, their members dispersed in opposite regions of the Congo when they were not actually massacred. Those comparatively fortunate refugees who were shipped back to South Kasai came after the early waves of refugees from the Luluabourg area and found no land to cultivate in the heavily overpopulated BaLuba province, thus adding to the already critical shortages in that region. When the Katanga secession was over, however, a number of these refugees made their way back to the industrial centers of Katanga where many BaLuba are again living today.

The Lumumbist Uprisings

The circumstances surrounding the fall of Prime Minister Lumumba and the first intervention by the military on the political scene created a sequel of violent reactions which, in turn, resulted in the uprooting of thousands of Congolese. The first group of refugees were the members of Lumumba's political entourage who decided to withdraw to Stanleyville (now Kisangani), the core of the solidly Lumumbist northeast, even though several of them (such as Antoine Gizenga, Lumumba's Vice-Premier and heir apparent) did not originate from this area. Their attempt to set up a rival government in exile was radically different by its motivations from Kantaga's secessionist aims. Gizenga and his followers were always ardent supporters of Congolese national unity and their political claims extended to the whole country, not just to the areas which had cast their votes for Lumumba's party.

Nevertheless, from the viewpoint of the Kasa-Vubu government in Leopoldville, theirs was a divisive movement which threatened, in fact, the central government's control of a substantial portion of the country in very much the same way as the Katanga secession. The Stanleyville dissidence was finally reduced more or less peacefully by a shrewd combination of economic pressure (including a blockade of the river traffic) and political concessions which had the effect of persuading a number of Lumumbist politicians to participate in the formation of a government of national reconciliation headed by Cyrille Adoula. But, while the Lumumbist political elite—or at least its moderate wing—was thus being mollified into participating in a coalition dominated by their erstwhile opponents, a different kind of discontent was simmering at the village level in many parts of the Congo. Much of this latent protest had its roots in pre-independence conditions, but the lack of any tangible improvement in the peasants' lot (which in many cases underwent an actual regression) contrasting with all too visible rise in the fortunes of many politicians after independence, set off a violent reaction in many parts of the country. In many cases, such dissatisfaction could be, and was, exploited by political radicals, but these never were the true source of the insurgents' dynamism.

There is, of course, no place here for a more penetrating analysis of the motivations of these village rebels, but it is important to realize that, despite their more or less synchronic appearance in various parts of the Congo, beginning in late 1963, these movements remained, by and large, disconnected and relatively isolated. Premier Adoula's inability to deal with the challenge of the rebellion eventually cost him his job and, in a sense, paved the way for the reentry of former secessionist leader Tshombe on the national political scene. As Prime Minister, Tshombe lost no time in calling for the expert assistance of those white mercenaries who had been a mainstay of his Katanga regime. Congolese army units, spearheaded by mercenary commandos, rapidly restored central government control over the major urban centers in the rebel areas (though not without some bitter fighting as in the case of Stanleyville where the U.S. and Belgian "rescue mission" was certainly not devoid of any military significance), but they largely failed in their attempts to control the rural countryside despite the extensive terror which they deliberately spread in the path of their incursions.

As a result of this type of campaigning, thousands of villagers took to the bush and there is accordingly no way to determine with any degree of certainty how many Congolese fled their homes, how far they went, and how long they stayed away. Generally speaking, one may venture to say that, as the rebellion lost its momentum, most of the peasantry eventually returned to their villages. However, one of the objectives pursued by the military was the sealing off of the Congo's eastern boundaries in an attempt to check the infiltration of supplies for the rebels. As a result, several frontier tribes found themselves in the theatre of operations and a sizeable number of these tribesmen fled to safety in neighboring Uganda, Rwanda, and Burundi where some of them have remained.

As for the opposition leaders, many of them had left the country in the early stages of the rebellion and attempted—without much success—to direct it from a distance. In fact, these political refugees represented a rather motley group and never once were they able to reconcile their differences and to form a united front. Some evaded arrest in the capital by seeking asylum in neighboring Brazzaville where they organized a National Liberation Council. Others set up headquarters in Stanleyville until that city was captured. Others still operated from various points in East Africa and attempted to organize the supply of arms to the rebels, while a few were based in Cairo. Only the leader of the Kwilu movement, Pierre Mulele, stayed among his followers throughout the rebellion and disappeared when the movement finally collapsed. Few of these politicians seem to have exercised any deep influence on the "Simba" or "Muleist" rebel troops.

The Tshombist Uprisings

After the end of the Katanga secession, only a very small number of political leaders went into exile; in fact, the only notable politician to leave the country at all was Moise Tshombe, who did so under no immediate threat of arrest or physical harm, but primarily as a precaution against future reprisals, and used the pretext of ill health to dilute the political significance of his departure. Certainly, there was no effort by Tshombe and his immediate entourage at the time to cast themselves in the role of political exiles, even if their self-imposed absence from the Congo was in fact motivated by Tshombe's political ambitions, as later became clear. However, while Katanga officials were allowed for the most part to pursue their official careers (though, obviously, in a different framework), units of the Katanga *gendarmerie* along with some of their white mercenary officers crossed the Congolese border into Angola where they were apparently allowed to maintain some degree of military preparedness in view of the day when their services might again be needed.

It has been suggested, though no real evidence is available, that temporary employment was found for these men by the Portuguese authorities as a counter-guerrilla force used against the Angola nationalists. In any case, the fact that many of these gendarmes belong to ethnic groups straddling the Congo-Angola border (notably Mr. Tshombe's own tribe, the Lunda) undoubtedly made it easier for many of them to adjust to their position as semi-exiles. Those who had not quietly returned to the Congo by mid-1964 did so when their former leader, Moise Tshombe, came back to the Congo as Premier and Katangese units were extensively used in the campaigns against the rebels in the East. Indeed, when Tshombe fell from power in October 1964 most troops originating from Katanga were stationed in the northeast and since it would have been unwise for the new regime to send them back to Katanga, they remained there until the summer of 1966, at which time they mutinied for the first time at Kisangani (formerly Stanleyville).

This first mutiny, which involved some, but not all, mercenaries, finally collapsed in September and only minimal reprisals were taken at the time against the Katangese troops. Their leader, Colonel Tshimpola, was eventually tried and executed, but the Katanga contingent itself was not disbanded and remained stationed in the northeast. During 1966-1967, however, the Mobutu regime became embroiled in a protracted dispute with Belgian interest groups—notably the behemoth of the Congo mining industry, *Union Miniere*—and a fresh conspiracy aimed at bringing Tshombe back to power began unfolding in the spring of 1967. Tshombe's plans were dealt a major blow when he was delivered by a member of his entourage into the hands of the Algerian authorities. This unforeseen development apparently precipitated the outbreak of a second mutiny by the Katangese units and white mercenary commandos stationed at Kisangani (July 5). Simultaneously, insurrection flared out of a smaller scale in the two eastern towns of Kindu and Bukavu.

The 1967 mutiny, however, was not a mere repetition of the incidents of the previous summer. Within eight days of the outbreak, the mutineers, led by a Belgian adventurer named Jean Schramme, were forced by the Congolese National Army to withdraw from Kisangani and began a long south-eastward trek across Maniema, regrouping first at Punia, then marching on to the Congo-Rwanda border. They then captured the border city of Bukavu (August 9) and holed up there for what turned out to be a protracted siege. Being assured of an easy escape by virtue of their control of the three bridges leading into Rwanda, they managed to pin down more than half of the Congolese Army, thus unmanning central government posts in other parts of the country in anticipation of a second attack by other pro-Tshombe forces striking from Angola.

A combination of factors (including strong diplomatic pressure from the United States upon Portugal) delayed the opening of this second front, and by the time a small Tshombist commando entered Katanga from Angola, the Bukavu mutineers were being forced to withdraw into Rwanda where they were immediately disarmed and interned. The diversionary strike in Katanga, in turn, was easily disposed of and there only remained the thorny diplomatic problem of what to do with the black and white mutineers.

In September, when it had appeared that the insurgents could hold off Congolese army pressure from their Bukavu stronghold, the Organization of African Unity, meeting in Kinshasa, had approved the principle of an internationally supervised withdrawal of the mutineers into Rwanda, to be followed by their evacuation to Europe (in the case of the white mercenaries) and to Zambia (where the Katangese soldiers and their families would be resettled). The International Red Cross Committee offered to arrange for this operation, but negotiations bogged down when one side, then the other, came to feel that time was on its side. Finally, the insurgents were driven from Bukavu by force of arms and the

Congo decided to oppose the evacuation scheme and to demand the extradition of the leaders of the mutiny.

After further consultations with other African states, however, the 950 Katangese mutineers (along with their 1,576 dependents) were offered an amnesty which they accepted and they were, accordingly, in the process of being repatriated at the time of this writing. As for the white mercenaries—whose fate is, in any case, of no concern to this symposium—the Secretary General of the OAU suggested that they would be released if their respective governments agreed to compensate the Congo for the extensive destruction caused by their murderous rashness. It seems, however, that the prospect of hundreds of additional Congolese refugees having to be relocated in some other part of the continent as a result of the latest Tshombist uprising will not materialize.

AFRICAN REFUGEES IN THE CONGO

As mentioned earlier, the Congo has a two-dimensional refugee problem. Although estimates concerning the number of refugees are frequently unreliable, it is safe to assume that the number of Africans who entered the Congo in search of security approximately equals that of the Congolese who left their country for the same reason. Unfortunately, the arithmetics of the refugee problem are not simply those that apply to other human migrations. There is no sense in which the influx of refugees from neighboring countries "compensates" for the exile of Congolese from their homeland, except perhaps in the narrowest statistical sense. In every other respect, this influx adds to the problems faced by the Kinshasa Government, and the same can of course be said of the other African governments, so that the refugee problem is of a nature that has almost wholly negative consequences.

Virtually every country situated on the Congo's periphery (as well as a few that are not) has refugees now living in the Congo. The reasons which caused these men to leave their respective countries are extremely diverse, but their reasons for seeking refuge in the Congo are almost always identical: physical proximity rather than ideological affinity with the Congolese regime appears to be the dominant factor. Most of the refugees who moved to the Congo belong to ethnic groups which straddle political boundaries. Such is the case of the BaKongo, Cokwe, Azande or Banyarwanda.

Refugees from Portuguese Africa[1]

Since becoming independent, the Congo, by virtue of its location, has become a pole of attraction for Angola nationalists struggling against Portuguese rule. Indeed, the first armed movement to develop in Portuguese Africa originated in the BaKongo area of northwestern Angola. The followers of Holden Roberto who harrassed Portuguese forces in the early 1960s and who organized the Revolutionary Government of Angola in Exile (GRAE) belonged, almost to a man, to the BaKongo group and were allowed some freedom of movement as well as training facilities in the Lower-Congo area (where, in any case, many of them had lived and worked at various times of their lives prior to 1960). With the gradual restoration of Portuguese control in the northwest, however, new focal points of unrest have begun to appear in eastern Angola and, accordingly, there has been in recent months an increasing flow of Cokwe refugees into southeastern Congo (particularly into Catanga).

The Congo's own position toward Angola nationalists has wavered in accordance with its domestic political vicissitudes. The Adoula government openly favored Holden Roberto's GRAE over the more militant MLPA (Popular Movement for the Liberation of Angola), but as GRAE suffered the effects of Portugal's counter-guerrilla campaign, as well as those of its own internal dissensions, official expressions of support from Kinshasa grew more cautious. Irrespective of GRAE's effectiveness, Congolese official support for the Angola nationalists does create serious problems, since Portugal has many ways to retaliate against an overly hostile Congo. One such method is to stop traffic on the Benguela railway which represents the major export route for Katanga minerals.[2] However, since the railway is controlled by non-Portuguese interests, interference with rail traffic has been sporadic, and has always been officially attributed to rebel activities. Another type of pressure (which was actually threatened by Portugal at one point) would be for Portugal to interfere with navigation in the Congo estuary, the southern bank of which is controlled by Portugal). Yet a third, more occult and possibly more effective, form of blackmail is for Portugal to allow subversive activities against the Congo to be organized on Angola soil.

The facilities offered to Tshombe, both during and after the Katanga secession, belong to this type of action. Indeed, when Tshombe became Prime Minister of the Congo in 1964, political activities by Angola refugees in the Congo were drastically curbed, presumably as the result of a tacit *quid pro quo* for services rendered to his cause by the Portuguese authorities. Since Tshombe's ouster, Angola has again been used as a sanctuary by forces favoring his return, while Lisbon has served as a rallying point for white mercenaries. In contrast with the refugees from Angola, the number of refugees from Portuguese East Africa (Mozambique) in the Congo is quite small. Virtually all of them are concentrated in the Katanga copperbelt and essentially represent a spillover from Zambia. According to a 1966 report by the East Katanga Department of the Interior, most refugees from Portuguese Africa (whether from Angola or Mozambique) have "neither food nor lodging; they are not registered or identified; they pay no taxes and generally subsist on expedients." Moreover, while the Angola refugees have a spokesman who occasionally manages to wrest some financial support out of the Congolese authorities, those from Mozambique, having nothing in common with the Angolans, are left to their own devices.

Refugees from the Sudan[3]

Uganda, rather than the Congo, has been the major concentration point of refugees from the southern Sudan and the roots of the north-south conflict in the Sudan obviously fall outside the scope of this chapter. The political repercussions of this problem, however, are worth mentioning in at least one respect. To the extent that Khartoum occasionally appeared to support radical nationalists in the eastern Congo, the Kinshasa authorities have found themselves in the position of exploiting the racial dimension of the north-south conflict. This became particularly apparent under Tshombe who was the target of violent attacks by the Arab states (particularly the UAR), and who reacted (in part, maybe, because of the anti-Arab bias of his right-wing European entourage) by mounting an extensive, though somewhat naive, anti-Arab campaign throughout the Congo.

One of the aspects of this campaign was the support extended to southern Sudan rebels who were being depicted in the press as the victims of "Arab (or Muslim) imperialism." Tshombe apparently considered using these refugees in the struggle against radical nationalist rebels in the Eastern Congo and it is notable that the Lumumbist uprisings never successfully extended into Azande areas. The major effect of the southern Sudan situation on the internal affairs of the Congo, however, was that equipment destined for the Congolese guerrillas often seemed to have been intercepted by the southern Sudanese rebels, thus seriously reducing the effectiveness of that particular supply route.

Refugees from Rwanda and Burundi

The bulk of these refugees is represented by members of the Tusi caste of Rwanda who lost power to the Hutu majority in the 1960 revolution. An unusual aspect of the 1960 Huto uprising was that it took place while Belgium was still in charge of the trust territory, and it has been suggested that the Belgians' decision to shift their support from the traditional ruling class to the Huto populace was instrumental in the launching of the revolution. Whatever the case may be, the Tusi attempted to retain control by adopting a radical nationalistic stance. As a result, the Tusi aristocrats, paradoxically, found support for their cause among Communist nations, and they also encountered sympathy in the eastern Congo at times when radical nationalists were in control of that area. Thus it was that Tusi refugees occasionally fought side by side with the Lumumbist rebels against the Congolese National Army, which explains why Tshombe (and later, Mobutu) attempted to have them resettled in Tanzania. Burundi, on the other hand, where the Tusi have by and large kept the upper hand, has supplied fewer refugees to the Congo. Those Burundi nationals who fled their country after the unsuccessful 1965 Huto uprising took refuge for the most part in Hutu-ruled Rwanda rather than in the Congo.

Refugees from Zambia

Refugees from Zambia represent a rather special and highly localized phenomenon. These are members of the so-called "Lumpa" sect (i.e., followers of prophetess Alice Lenshina) whose refusal to fall in step with the Zambian civil authorities led to their persecution in their own country. Since most of them belong to ethnic groups situated astride the Congo-Zambia boundary, some three thousand five hundred of them have taken refuge in the Sakania border area of Katanga province. Even in their case, however, political undertones have complicated the situation. The Lumpa were suspected by Zambia's ruling party of being either favorable to, or instigated by, the opposition. On the other hand, clashes between the Zambian authorities and the sect took place at the time when Tshombe was Prime Minister in the Congo. For this reason, the refugees were suspected of shifting their allegiance to Tshombe, who, in turn, had been on excellent terms with Zambian opposition leader Harry Nkumbula during the Katanga secession.

After Tshombe lost power, both President Mobutu and President Kaunda of Zambia were anxious to extirpate what they viewed as a potentially dangerous situation by persuading the refugees to return to Zambia. The Lumpa, however, were reluctant to be repatriated and, at the time of this writing, the problem has not been entirely solved, despite the concurrence of views between the Kinshasa and Lusaka authorities. These refugees do not seem to pose a major welfare problem, however, since they have found land to farm and have been able to grow their own crops. The fact that they are not complete strangers in this border area undoubtedly makes their integration easier, but the sudden character of their influx posed a serious health and sanitation problem for a while, as indicated by the high death rate among the refugees during the first months following their arrival.

*   *   *

Refugee problems can be handled by international organizations, but such an approach can only be a substitute for bilateral or multilateral agreements between the countries concerned, where such negotiations are possible. Agreements of this type, while probably more satisfactory on a long-term basis, nevertheless raise serious problems. Refugees may become mere pawns in a diplomatic power game and even an agreement between governments does not guarantee that the refugees' own views and interests will be given adequate consideration (as illustrated by the Lumpa problem).

As far as the Congo is concerned, the very possibility of negotiating the problem of refugees with neighboring countries was, for a long time, compromised by the diplomatic isolation of the Kinshasa authorities. This was particularly true under Tshombe whose relations with the rest of Africa were generally detestable. One of the major achievements of the Mobutu regime, on the other hand, has been the improvement of the Congo's relations with all of its neighbors except Portugal. One of the first manifestations of this new spirit was the April 1966 East and Central African summit conference (also called the "Good Neighbors' Conference") where for the first time, a general solution of accumulated refugee problems was discussed. Since that time, contacts have remained good between the Congo and its neighbors, and the gradual elimination of the refugee problem is now well under way. On a smaller scale, refugee problems were also discussed at the 1967 Goma conference where the Congo acted as a mediator between Rwanda and Burundi. The normalization of relations between these three territories formerly under Belgian rule would go a long way toward insuring not only that refugees will no longer be manipulated for political purposes, but also that the human dimension of their tragedy will be given proper recognition.

NOTES

1. For detailed discussion of the case of Portuguese Guinean refugees, see chap. 11.

2. Such a measure also affects Zambia which has been trying to ship its mineral production through Congo and Angola in order to avoid dealing with white-ruled Rhodesia. The political drawbacks of this solution played a considerable part in Zambia's decision to attempt the construction of a new rail line to Dar-es-Salaam (the so-called "Tan-Zam" route).

3. For discussion of the case of these refugees, see chap. 9.

SOME POLITICAL IMPLICATIONS OF THE REFUGEE PROBLEM IN SOUTH WEST AFRICA

14

BENEDICT V. MTSHALI, University of Zambia

It is impossible to discuss any refugees without first discussing the political conditions which determine—indeed produce—this phenomenon. In this paper, the term *refugees* means "persons who have fled from political oppression and who cannot return (to their fatherland) for political reasons, without fear of reprisal; these refugees may never have been affiliated with a particular liberation movement.[1]

Since the history of South West Africa from German imperial rule to the League of Nations right up to the United Nations has been extensively written[2], this paper will concentrate on recent developments.

Following the electoral victory of the Nationalist Party in 1948, the policy of apartheid has been applied to this territory with increasing rigor as if it were South Africa's fifth province. It must be noted that, in practice, Pretoria does so treat this territory but in international law, South West Africa has a status different from that of a province. The League of Nations asked South Africa to exercise a mandate so as to promote the material and moral welfare of the inhabitants.

The African people fail to see how the policy of apartheid can benefit them. It has been roundly condemned many times. Perhaps the most incisive criticism came from the Netherlands, a country which, for historical reasons, South Africa wants on her side. The Dutch columnist, H. J. Neuman wrote in *De Tijd-Maasbode* (Amsterdam) 11 November 1963 that "The Bantus are simply forced by the Government (of South Africa) to be satisfied in the manner which best suits the Whites."[3] But as in the case of their South African counterparts, the Africans of South West Africa have opposed apartheid. For their opposition, they have been arrested, banned and forced to flee from their country. Here we see one cause of a certain type of refugee, the political, namely the direct harsh reaction of South Africa to political opposition from activists. Another cause has been the overall political climate which, because of apartheid, cannot be tolerated by some South West Africans. They, therefore, leave their country to obtain education and enjoy a better life elsewhere.

The last five years have witnessed the rise of a special type of political refugee—the fighting militant or *freedom* fighter. This is the man who under the auspices of his political organization, for example the South West African People's Organization (SWAPO), leaves his country to undergo military training to prepare himself for liberating his fatherland by arms.

As a result of the rejection of the case against South Africa's exercise of her mandate by the International Court of Justice on 18 July 1966, there has been an increase both in the number and in the activities of such militants. The outcome of this case convinced the Africans that, in the words of *The Jerusalem Post Weekly* (22 July 1966), "the remedy for grievances that may exist over the administration of South West Africa should be sought through political rather than legal action." But in its edition of 23 July 1966, *De Groeve Amsterdammer* (Amsterdam) reported a new phase in Africa: "Right now the African countries feel especially deeply, that political and diplomatic means of pressure are insufficient to wrest justice. It would not be surprising if many Africans no longer saw any alternative other than a guerilla struggle."[4]

Perhaps unwittingly, this Dutch publication accurately reflected the views of the South West African Political Organization. After the Court's decision a SWAPO official said in Dar es Salaam, "We have no alternative but to rise in arms and bring about our own liberation."[5] A month later, the South African Parliament was told of armed clashes in South West Africa between the security forces and the so-called "Terrorist Infiltrators."[6] Since then, the call to arms has been reechoed in many African capitals. For example, Kenya's ruling party, the Kenya African National Union, urged "free Africa [to] give our brothers the weapons to wage their struggle." It also quoted Jomo Kanyatta's words that "the tree of liberty had to be watered with blood."[7]

How does the increase in the number and the activity of militants affect the refugees and South Africa's relations with Africa and the rest of the world?

Regarding refugees, political organizations from South West Africa, especially SWAPO, are having their men trained outside and inside South West Africa. In other words, they are being militarized. Some are then sent back home, e.g., through Angola into Ovamboland, to train others or to engage the South African forces, or to do both. The international circles now know of the existence of SWAPO's guerilla units in South West Africa. Thirty-six of their members have been arrested and put on trial in South Africa on charges of terrorism.[8] It should be mentioned here that SWAPO seems to regard its men outside the country not as refugees. The policy is that, far from having run away, they are subject to assignment in South West Africa. This policy tallies with that of the African National Congress (ANC) of South Africa.[9]

The effects on South Africa's relations with Africa fall into two categories (1) relations with Rhodesia and the Portuguese colonies of Angola and Mozambique (Professor Gwendolen Carter calls this white-dominated part of Africa the White Redoubt);[10] and (2) relations with independent Africa.

1. *Relations with White Redoubt*: The outbreak of guerrilla warfare has strengthened the ties between South Africa and the Portuguese-controlled Angola. The security and the intelligence forces of both countries cooperate in fighting the guerrillas in Ovamboland.[11] This cooperation is in the interest of both countries, since both are being attacked by guerrillas on various flanks.

2. *Relations with independent Africa*: Because of geography, Botswana is the most directly involved of all the African states. Before Botswana's independence, South West African refugees tried to go through Bechuanaland. The South African police tried to stop them. In this regard, the most famous case is that of the physician, Dr. Kenneth Abrahams, who was abducted in Bechuanaland and spirited to Cape Town.[12]

But the so-called Maun Affair is more important since it concerned the United Nations' right to visit a territory under its jurisdiction. In 1961, the Committee on South Africa left New York to gather testimony from South West African refugees in the town of Maun in Bechuanaland. South Africa threatened to arrest the members of the committee if they entered without visas (which Pretoria had earlier denied the committee).

South African troops were then deployed along the border with Bechuanaland. At this point, Britain sought an understanding from the committee that it would not enter the territory through Bechuanaland without Pretoria's permission. When the committee refused to give this understanding, London withdrew the visas it had issued for entry into Bechuanaland, and the committee turned back in Rhodesia. Clearly in this incident, South Africa exerted influence on Britain, whereas in the Abraham's case Britain did so. In both cases, though, Bechuanaland was intimately involved in affairs concerning refugees from South West Africa.

Since attaining independence, Botswana has been under South African pressure to hand over people accused of criminal offences, while they claim to be refugees. Botswana's economic dependence on the Republic leaves her open to all sorts of pressures. How she will react to all these has yet to be seen. However, it seems likely that in some cases she will take action to meet South African demands or to appear to be doing so. For example, the 1967 Report of the Committee of 24 records the case (see paragraph 47) of eight SWAPO members who were declared prohibited immigrants on 14 November 1966 after reports that armed Africans had been arrested in Botswana on their way to Ovamboland.

I think South Africa's reaction to independent Africa will take two directions:

1. In the case of African states, politically independent but economically dependent on her, South Africa will have a strong bargaining position. She will try to force these states to be hostile to South West Africa's political refugees, or to be neutral—all this in return for economic assistance which these states sorely need.

2. South Africa can safely ignore, as posing no immediate threat to her security, those states not economically dependent on her. For one thing, their borders are far from hers; moreover,

militarily they have yet to prove in deed their abhorrence of apartheid by launching an attack. In the South African view, the failure of the African states to act in the case of relatively weak Rhodesia (i.e., relative to South Africa), creates a credibility gap between their words and deeds.[13]

South Africa has even gone one step further. She has warned these states, in case they become a serious threat, that she can launch a preemptive military strike against them—like Israel against the Arab states in June 1967. *The Johannesburg Sunday Times* of 11 June 1967, reported that the South African Minister of Labor, Mr. M. Viljoen, had said that the Arab-Israeli conflict had "not only brought the Arab states to a reevaluation of their position; it also ought to make some of the most loudmouthed African leaders, who continually threatened attacks on South Africa, think again."

Fully aware of South Africa's economic and military power, the African states may, therefore, not take any overt steps to help the South West Africans. Even providing passages to refugees or armed units may prove politically embarrassing.

To give the impression that the African states alone can be influenced by South Africa would be grossly misleading. Those Western countries plying a profitable trade with the Republic have been reluctant to act either individually, or within the context of the United Nations, on the major South West African question—namely depriving South Africa of her grip on the territory. If this could be settled, the refugee question would, of course, disappear. But these states have also been strong on words, but short on action.

However, one should add that some of them are active in promoting the educational welfare of political refugees through scholarship programs operating in Africa and elsewhere. These may very well be an attempt on their part to quiet the compunctions of their consciences for their identification, in South West African nationalist opinion, with apartheid. These programs may also be an example of enlightened self-interest. In case of a nationalist victory, the sponsors could argue that they too contributed toward change.

Since the South African authorities know of this educational aid to political refugees, it would not be surprising if, as the struggle gains in momentum, they exert pressure on the sponsors to stop engaging in such "hostile" activities. In other words, it is likely that South Africa's friends in the U.S.A. will pressure the State Department to stop programs like those of the African-American Institute.[14] Until the start of the recent guerrilla activity, South Africa has been slightly irritated, not seriously worried, by Western aid to political refugees, especially students.

Consideration of pressures on the U.S.A. leads me to an evaluation of effective United Nations action on South West Africa since the U.S.A. role would be crucial—indeed, decisive. She is the major financial supporter of the U.N. and is the other pole in this bipolar international system.

What are the chances of such action? South African policy-makers realize that South West Africa is their Achilles Heel—the first area where a successful breakthrough can be made against apartheid. Hence their determination to retain control at all costs.

U.N. action has a slim chance of success, I think. First of all, South Africa enjoys the advantage of geographical nearness, whereas any U.N. force would, I think, have to use one of the African states as a base. Would this not invite a preemptive strike by South Africa? Such a possibility is not remote, considering South Africa's recent warning. Some U.N. members, opposed to force, may bring up this convenient point and thus thwart U.N. action without appearing to be openly opposed to such action.

Second, there are Western fears that military action would exacerbate racial tension and spark off a wave of violence in southern Africa. South Africa's allies in maintaining the status quo—Rhodesia and Portugal—would not stand idly by if she considered herself attacked. Of course, she herself actively helps them as can be seen in the case of her forces fighting in Rhodesia. Moreover, *The Observer* of 26 November 1967 reported a government official as having said that the increasing guerrilla activity in southern Africa justified South Africa's sending troops to help Portugal defend her possessions in Angola and Mozambique.

My third reason for doubting is that the fear of a Communist takeover in southern Africa is still exploited for propaganda reasons. Thomas P. Melady has quoted the widely-respected columnist, Colin Legum, as saying that, disillusioned with the

West, the nationalists have had to turn to the Communists for support.[15] I think that this is a valid assessment. But, instead of correcting this situation, some Western policy-makers may decide, for fear of Communism, to help the so-called Unholy Trinity of Vorster, Smith, and Salazar.

To summarize this section: I see no chance in the near future of meaningful U.N. action on the major South West African question from which the refugee phenomenon arises. (The latter can hardly be solved without first tackling the former.) In my view, the future of the U.N. may very well be decided by the South West African question, just as that of the League of Nations was sealed by Ethiopia.

Lack of U.N. action will have other consequences. It will, I think, accelerate the growth of two trends. First of all, the *White Redoubt* will openly defy international opinion. South Africa's invasion in 1967 of the British territory of Rhodesia (if I may perpetuate this fiction) is a case in point. One need not be wedded to the doctrine of *realpolitik* in order to argue that this defiance is in line with South Africa's basic urge in foreign policy. She is in the paradoxical position of being the most developed and most powerful state on the African continent. Yet, she is unable to exert any substantial and positive influence in Africa, while elsewhere other major powers do so. Thus, whenever she has a chance to fulfill her policy needs, she will act. She will flex her muscles and expand her influence. After all, did Machiavelli not say that expansion is the mark of a healthy state? She will, thus, retain South West Africa and help (if not control) Rhodesia and Portugal. For the present rulers, southern Africa is a field of activity for their boundless energy: their *lebensraum*. Regrettably, but realistically, one has to include within South Africa's sphere of influence, Botswana and Lesotho, two states which, while unable to resist South Africa's economic might, nevertheless oppose her apartheid policies on ideological grounds. But, are they unique? I leave the question of answers to other participants. But, my view is that South Africa's economic expansionism will extend to other African states who will have to choose between ideological opposition and their national interests.[16] One need not be wedded to Marx in order to point out the crucial importance of economic factors in determining the national interest.

The second trend will, I think, be the following: increased co-operation in the Unholy Trinity will result in increased coopera-tion, to meet a common danger, among liberation movements from South Africa and South West Africa. I restrict myself to South West Africa although readers of the supposedly confidential pub-lication *Africa 1965, 1966* will know that there are other coali-tions among the liberation movements of southern Africa.[17] To return to South West Africa, SWAPO, the only political organiza-tion recognized by the Organization of African Unity, is on friendly terms with the African National Congress of South Africa (ANC), because the latter favorably mentions the former in its official publication *Sechaba*. This line-up of African nationalists ranged against White security forces may well indicate the start of that confrontation which President Kaunda has sought to avert—that is, a racial war in southern Africa. South West Africa could be, and ought to be, one area where this confrontation can be averted through decisive international action, provided, of course, that the major powers seriously want to act. If they do, the phenomenon of the political refugee will eventually disappear.

While many of us regard international action as desirable in solving the problem of South West Africa, practical considera-tions incline me to the view that the major drive must come from the nationalists of South West Africa. This drive makes force inevitable.

In short, the problem of the refugee from South West Africa has to be solved primarily by the nationalists. Their problem be-ing political, and in the final analysis, military, it requires no bold venture into prophecy to say that ultimately they will resort more and more to political and military means to help themselves.

NOTES

1. Jane W. Jacqz, *Refugee Students from Southern Africa,* Report of a Workshop on the Training and Utilization of Refugee Students from South-ern Africa sponsored by the African-American Institute and Syracuse Uni-versity at Lubin House, New York City, April 18-19, 1967 (New York: African-American Institute, 1967), p. 4.

2. For a brief account see, for example, Gwendolen M. Carter, *The Politics of Inequality: South Africa Since 1948* (London: Thames & Hudson), chap. 15; and International Commission of Jurists, *South Africa and the Rule of*

Law (Geneva: International Commission of Jurists, 1960), chap. 11.

3. "De Bantoes worden door de regering eenvoudig gedwongen om gelukkig te zijn op de manier die de blanken bet beste past." (This translation and others from the Dutch are mine).

4. "De Afrikaanse landen envaren op bet ogenblik bjzonder scherp dat politieke en diplomatieke pressie-middelen ontoeveikend zjn om rechtvaardigbeid of te dwingen. Het zon niet verwonderlijk zijn wanneer veel Afrikanen geen andere mogelijkheid meer zagen dan de guerrillastnjd." In *The Observer* (London), July 4, 1966.

5. *The Times* (London), July 22, 1966.

6. *The Guardian* (London), August 27, 1966.

7. *Kenya Digest* (London), no. 61, August 3, 1966, p. 2. The African National Congress of South Africa also wholeheartedly supported an armed struggle by the people of South Africa "to regain their lost dignity and realise their aspirations." See editorial in *Spotlight on South Africa,* October 7, 1966.

8. *New York Times,* November 17, 1967.

9. See Jacqz, op. cit., p. 4.

10. See her article, "Rhodesia-Embattled Frontier of Africa's White Redoubt," *Northwestern Review,* vol. 1, no. 2, February 1966.

11. U.N. General Assembly, *Report of the Special Committee on the Situation with regard to the Implementation of the Declaration on the Granting of Independence to Colonial Countries and Peoples,* chap. 5, "South West Africa," A/6700/Add. 2, 31 October 1967, paragraph 46. (This committee is also known by the less cumbersome name The Committee of Twenty-four.)

12. See *The Daily Telegraph* and *The Times* (London), August 28, 1963. Abrahams was later released and returned to Bechuanaland.

13. For some views on this, see B. V. Mtshali's *Rhodesia—Background to Conflict* (New York; Hawthorn, 1967).

14. For these, see Jane W. Jacqz, op. cit., p. 34.

15. See his article on Rhodesia in *The Long Island Catholic,* November 24, 1967.

16. For views on ideology and the national interest in African diplomacy see William Zartman in Vernon McKay, ed., *African Diplomacy* (New York: Praeger, 1966).

17. The ANC tends to line up with SWAPO, ZAPU (Rhodesia), FRELIMO (Mozambique), MPLA (Angola). The line-up with ZAPA was officially stated, in a joint statement issued in Lusaka on August 19, 1967, which *inter alia* said: "We wish to declare here that the fighting that is presently going on in the Wankie area is indeed being carried out by a combined force of Z.A.P.U. and A.N.C." For more evidence, see *The New York Times,* October 5, 1967, for Lawrence Fellows' report "Confrontation is Sharpening in Southern Africa."

PART III

ASPECTS OF NATIONAL AND INTERNATIONAL AID

THE U.S. STATE DEPARTMENT'S ATTITUDE TOWARD THE PROBLEM OF REFUGEES

15

JAMES WINE, Special Assistant to the Secretary of State for Refugee and Migration Affairs

Any serious discussion of the refugee problem cannot be confined to a mere updating of statistics pinpointing as expertly as possible the location of the uprooted, displaced, dispossessed, and homeless in the various countries of their dispersion. It must, of necessity, be part of a broadly-based discussion of the problem which should be troubling all thinking men and women—namely, the need for a clear understanding of the new dynamics of our times and what each individual's response to it should be.

When we speak of the refugee problem today, we are no longer referring to a strictly European phenomenon resulting from the great upheavals of two World Wars. Today, we are faced for the first time with a new and universal concept of the refugee problem. The World Refugee Report, an annual survey of the U. S. Committee for Refugees, shows refugees divided among the various continents as follows (in round figures): Asia, 7,300,000; Middle East, 1,300,000; Latin America, 1,300,000; Africa, 1,000,000; and Europe, 243,000. Furthermore, we are faced with the alarming fact that while affluence increased in the developed nations, the margin between life and death for refugees in underdeveloped areas, such as Africa, continues to narrow with each passing day.

The major shift in focus of the refugee problem is the direct and natural result of two other shifts of foci which have taken place in the last few years. Idological tensions have lessened in the developed world while the role of idology is still important in the lesser developed countries where problems can still be seen in simplistic and almost absolute terms. As idological tensions have decreased, so has conflict among the developed nations. The focus of violence has shifted. Conflicts are between developed nations and less developed nations; and, increasingly, instability in the underdeveloped world is itself a source of global tensions. The refugee problem, given these new conditions, can only increase in the next few years.

It is important for us to reject the notion that we are faced with the traditional European refugee problem only restaged in a new, and more exotic, setting. The refugee problem today is intrinsically a new phenomenon requiring new approaches and providing us with a new and difficult challenge.

While the United States—both in her public and private sectors—has been traditionally in the forefront of those actively concerned with refugees, there are increasingly ominous indications of a trend to avoid becoming involved with the problems of others. As the refugee problem continues to grow, we have become less sensitive and less aware of the human needs involved. To an extent, this is attributable to what some describe as an increasing Kafkaesque posture by government and to world circumstances, causing reshuffling of national priorities.

Furthermore, each crisis always summons to the fore different crises managers, most of whom will differ somewhat in humanitarian outlook. This can otherwise be explained in general terms by our insufficient knowledge, understanding, and awareness prevailing in many troubled areas of Africa, Asia, the Middle East, and Latin America. It was fairly easy for the average American to comprehend more fully the problem of the European refugee as he was bound to them by a commonality of race, culture, and religion. Many Americans still maintain strong ethnic ties with their countries of ancestral origin. How different it is in the case of the African or Palestinian refugee, so foreign to us in speech, religion, and way of life. We are faced with a serious and perhaps insoluable problem of communications as their problems are often in terms which are intellectually incapable of comprehending. Few Americans have more than a superficial knowledge of the remote and exotic lands, such as Shangugu (Rwanda) or Hyangcha (Nepal), in which the number of refugees is increasing daily. The net result of this lack of communication is our tragic failure to see the modern-day refugee problem as a human equation.

This failure is a part of a more fundamental and more tragic failure, for our attitudes—or our nonattitudes—toward the pressing human problems around the world are a projection of the way we view ourselves and our own society. I must now speak to, and of, the American scene. We are, in a sense, the "old world" in that experience is now passing from America to the other developed countries, and not from Europe to America as was once the case. Most of the countries around the globe are struggling to make the transition from a basically agricultural society to a predominately industrial one, and will undergo many of the same tensions and dislocations which were experienced by the developed countries as well as a vastly improved standard of living. To complicate matters further, while some countries continue the slow process of industrialization and others have yet to begin, the United States has quickly progressed to what may be called a "post-industrial era". This rapid shift has resulted in a search for a redefinition of the meaning of life—a crisis of identity and values. Social problems in the United States today are concerned with such things as the intelligent use of leisure, the multiple effects of automation, the achievement of psychic well-being, and the growing alienation of the younger generation. The gap between our basic concerns and those of the overwhelming majority of the world's people is widening at an ever-increasing pace, despite the many efforts being made to bridge it. The gap does not only exist between nations—there is a large schism in our own country as well.

Our concern for that part of our society which is still struggling with the problems of industrialization—those who for one reason or another do not share our affluence has been less than profound. "There are still very few but the poor who feel for the poor." Too many still value some lives more than others. Not long ago there was a particularly shocking and brutal murder. But one had the gnawing feeling that the public found it so because it happened to a young person who had had "everything." Would our outrage have been as great if it had been a child of the ghetto?

Indeed—a crisis of identity, values, and priorities. We must begin to ask ourselves the right questions—and in the right way. Not "how do we control riots?" but *"why* are there riots?" Not "how do we solve the hippie problem?" but "why are there hippies, and what can they tell us about our society?" Not "what can *we* do about our attitudes, our priorities, our value structure?" but "what can *I* do, what do I know about myself and the meaning of life in relation to others, what can I do to increase my capacity for love, understanding and commitment?" When a society is faced with serious internal contradictions, the result is distrust, misunderstanding, conflict, and tension.

We are, to recapitulate, faced with three different levels of crisis—one, the crisis of purpose and meaning in our own highly advanced technically oriented society; two, the crisis of comprehending and dealing resolutely with the residue of grave unresolved problems and contradictions at home; and last but not least, the crisis of being able to understand the totally different problems of other people living on distant shores. These various levels of crisis are totally interrelated and cannot be resolved independently of one another. The challenge of making this a world of peace and meaningful and creative prosperity for all will not be easily achieved, but must, nonetheless, be faced—or we must be prepared for continued conflict, violence, and anarchy.

When written in Chinese, the world "crisis" is composed of two characters—one represents danger and one represents opportunity. Periods of crisis have historically provided people with the necessity for choice—the need for creative and original thinking to solve persistent as well as new problems. We are facing a real crisis today, the crisis of post-industrialization, which has never been faced by any society in the past, and therefore has no precedents. Basically then, we must understand ourselves in human terms in order to understand the human problems of others. If we fail to preserve humanism at home by helping the less fortunate in our own country, there is little likelihood that we would be overly concerned with the pressing problems of existence daily facing our fellow human beings abroad.

The amazing, and in ways miraculous, technological revolution which has taken place during this century in the highly developed countries, especially the United States, has created new and perplexing dilemmas. Concurrently, however, it provides us with novel and powerful tools with which to deal with the problems that seemed insoluable just a few years ago. The horizon is almost limitless today if man learns to harness these recently acquired techniques to attack the causes of human need and suffering.

There have been revolutionary developments not only in the physical sciences, but in the social sciences as well. We are better equipped today than ever before to understand why people act as they do, and to assist people in the full utilization of their God-given attributes and abilities.

These new approaches must be applied liberally to improve the refugee situation. So many people blanch when they hear references to "Systems" approaches because of its cold mechanized sound. On the contrary, one of the consequences of this more effective research is the increased awareness of the total social environment of refugees. In short, we can see the refugee as a part of his human setting and not just as an isolated and unrelated statistic. This modern research approach can be used to determine what conditions created the refugee, what are the individual desires and aspirations of the refugee, and they can help us determine what would be the most effective action on their behalf. Man has finally discovered that the refugee can easily be converted from an unwanted burden and liability to a powerful resource for development, so desperately yearned for by the underdeveloped countries. Perhaps the key to resolving the refugee problem in the underdeveloped world is in teaching the host countries how best to utilize refugees in the development of their economies, to the mutual benefit of all concerned.

To summarize briefly then, let me repeat that we are living at a time of crisis and challenge. We must not be frightened or shirk our responsibility to come to terms with both new and old problems, but, rather, meet the challenge full on and make our era one of intense creativity. As conditions continue to change at an ever quickening rate, we must learn to think always in dynamic terms rather than revert to the safety of static pat answers which were unsuccessful in the past. It has been said that we "are in an interregnum between old value systems that have not worked and new ones not yet born, an empty period which could be borne more patiently were it not for the great and unique dangers that beset mankind." If our world is to progress we must attempt to rethink basic issues, reshape our environment, and create a real breakthrough in mutual understanding. Only when we honestly understand the true nature of our own humanness can we begin to appreciate the human situation of others, and the universality of man. We must be prepared to share in the human predicament of our fellowman, be he our closest neighbor or a stranger oceans and environments away. Not only must we share in his human predicament, we must become *involved* with his predicament. We must have a clearer understanding of the problem as a whole. The voluntary agencies are certainly involved with the predicament of refugees. We have said that even as the refugee problem continues to grow, the American public has become less sensitive and less aware of the human needs involved. The voluntary agencies must take special care and pains to avoid this loss of sensitivity as their burden increases—to think of refugees only in terms of numbers, location, and tons of grain, is not to think about refugees at all. There is also a role and an opportunity for private enterprise to attack the conditions that cause refugees—especially in the less developed world where economic development is the elusive key to the future well-being of her people. Private enterprise could do much to introduce the creative aspects of our modern technology and business management. The government through its various agencies is also involved—planning, financing, and, hopefully, helping to coordinate the total effort (see the Appendix at the end of this chapter). We have said that there are various approaches to the solution of a refugee problem—sociological, systematic, academic, mechanical—these utilize the resources of our universities, scientific laboratories, church and secular organizations, business, and our government.

But there is yet another resource—the most important of all—our individual commitment and involvement. These problems cannot be solved *en masse,* they cannot be delegated. In this case our Government is not representative—it cannot fulfill our personal responsibility. Nor can membership in various church or secular organizations fulfill our personal responsibility. Too many would like to believe that that is enough, too many could be described, as was Burke, by these words of Thomas Paine: "(Burke) is not affected by the reality of distress touching his heart, but by the showy resemblance of striking his imagination. He pities the plumage, but forgets the dying bird." Each of us has a different "dying bird" that we have forgotten, but they all have a common factor—a thread which links them together—the absence of true humanitarian attitudes, a demise of humanitarian concern.

Whether we speak of refugees, or crime in the streets, or riots in our cities—the problem lies with our attitudes. Because of this common denominator, it doesn't matter which problem we as individuals attack, for they are all really a part of the same larger problem. I know perfectly well that not everyone will become personally or actively involved with refugees. That is not the need—the need is that we each make a commitment on the personal plane of our lives. From that initial commitment, concern and sympathetic understanding of other problems will flow. This is your challenge as well as ours. Both the older and younger generations must attempt through a better utilization of old tools, and armed with the sophisticated techniques of our age, to resolve mankind's perennial problems. When man truly understands himself, only then can he begin to help others.

ADDENDUM

United States Government Assistance to African Refugees

ASSISTANCE TO THE UNHCR

During fiscal year 1967 the United States contributed $400,000 to the United Nations High Commissioner for Refugees, which constituted approximately 13 percent of total government contributions; the High Commissioner allocates more than 50 percent of his budget to assist refugees in sub-Sahara Africa. It is anticipated that the U. S. contribution in fiscal year 1968 will be increased. During the same period, the United States Government contributed $50,000 to the budget of the International Committee of the Red Cross which plays an active role in Africa.

FOOD ASSISTANCE

Over the past ten years, the United States Government has supplied more than $50 million in United States commodities to feed hungry refugees; United States commodity assistance to African refugees has averaged out at over $2 million per year over the last five years. The Food for Peace commodity programs for refugees are administered through United States voluntary agencies, international agencies such as the World Food Program, and under government-to-government agreements.

EDUCATIONAL ASSISTANCE

Since 1961, the United States Government has actively supported the education of African refugees. In fiscal year 1967 the government spent about $3 million on two programs administered by the private African-American Institute. One program, sponsored by the United States Agency for International Development (AID), supported two secondary schools in East Africa for refugees from the minority-ruled areas of southern Africa. The other program, financed by the Bureau of Educational and Cultural Affairs of the Department of State, provided scholarships for 479 refugees from southern Africa to study in the United States. The United States also contributed to the United Nations pilot Education and Training Program for South Africans and has included in the 1968 foreign aid act a further contribution to the program.

THE PROBLEMS
OF REFUGEES

16

SADRUDDIN AGA KHAN, U.N. High Commissioner
for Refugees

The problems of refugees with which I am most concerned at present are essentially those in Africa, and before entering into a discussion of what we have been able to do to resolve some of these problems, I would like to tell you something about the Office—what it is, what its terms of reference are, and how it began to become involved in the African refugee situations.

The Office was established in 1951, to deal principally with what was the main problem at that time, i.e., the accumulation of refugees of the Second World War in Europe. The International Refugee Organization, which was a large agency concentrating essentially on the solution to the refugee problem through their resettlement in other countries, was just in the process of winding up its activities. I do not have to tell you of the very generous welcome that was extended here in the United States to these refugees, many of whom came from refugee camps in Europe. The Office of the High Commissioner was called upon at that time to extend its international protection to the refugees who had not yet been resettled through the International Refugee Organization. This protection meant that, in fact, the High Commissioner replaced to a certain extent, the governments whose protection the refugees no longer enjoyed. The refugee, unlike any other alien, does not have an embassy or a consulate to represent him, so that when he has left his country to seek asylum in another country, he is of course in need of some sort of protection in order that he may enjoy a proper legal status, including the right to education, the right to work, and some form of social security, and where he can obtain a travel document if he needs to travel.

209

It was soon realized that just granting refugees international protection did not constitute a solution to their problems. Many were still in camps. They needed homes, they needed a new start in life—a way to become, or at least to start becoming, self-supporting, and so legal protection had to be combined with some material assistance. It was thanks to the efforts of the first United Nations High Commissioner for Refugees, Dr. G. J. van Heuven Goedhart, that a limited program of material assistance was initiated, and thanks largely to the generosity of the private organizations and, essentially, to the Ford Foundation, that a pilot program from the local integration of nonsettled European refugees could be launched, mainly in European countries with a camp population. Shortly after this pilot program was initiated the UNHCR Annual Programs for Material Assistance were started.

Now, after many years of effort, a solution to the problems of refugees in Europe is in sight. This has been made possible through the very generous response of the international community, and of countries of immigration such as Australia, Canada, New Zealand, the Scandinavian countries, and the United States, and through the fact that for some years now, the economic situation in Europe has been such that jobs have become available for nonsettled refugees.

In Europe today, we are, in the main, caring for handicapped refugees who, because of long years spent in camps, have suffered so much, both mentally and physically, that they are no longer able, without assistance, to integrate into society, and so need individual care and attention. We must be ready to face new problems in Europe, should they arise, but I would express the hope that the present political détente in Europe will have an effect on the refugee problems on that continent which, I trust, will be solved in the near future.

In the meantime, as I have said, there are still some nonsettled refugees requiring assistance in Europe, most of them handicapped. They are for the most part in Germany, Austria, and Italy. There is also still an influx of new arrivals in Western Europe, who are seeking asylum or who want to emigrate overseas. A problem still exists of Cubans who wish to join their relatives in the United States and who, instead of going directly to the U. S.

from Cuba, travel to Spain, where they may have to stay for some time until they get their visas for the U.S.A. But these problems are dealt with successfully as they arise, through the current program of my Office. We have thus been able to avoid the accumulation of human misery such as was found in the camps in the postwar years. One of the consequences of the recent war in the Middle East was the increase of arrivals of refugees in Europe. Several minority groups who had been living in the Middle East for many years were uprooted as a result of the war, and some arrived in Europe having no government to protect them, and so formed a new problem. We are hoping that in this case also, resettlement or integration will be accomplished very quickly, so that the people will not be forced to spend idle months in camps while awaiting the opportunity to start a new life.

However, the refugee problem is not concentrated in one area of the world. It is an endemic problem closely linked with political upheavals and instability; today, it is to be found essentially in Africa. There are still problems in Latin America, where there are refugees who need the same care and attention as those I mentioned in Europe. There are also problems in Asia, such as those of the Chinese refugees in Macao and Hong Kong. We have programs for the relief and settlement of Tibetan refugees in India and Nepal—sixty thousand of them. As I have said, however, the largest problem today is in Africa, where there are some eighty thousand refugees.

What has bought about this refugee situation in Africa? The problems have been discussed by many of the previous speakers who are participating in this symposium. You have heard about the instability due to the former colonial administrations in Africa. You have also heard of border disputes and tensions. I think, generally speaking, that they can be ascribed to three main causes.

First of all, there is the struggle of people to attain independence in areas where for many years there was, or still is, colonial administration, and where sections of the population are still attempting to achieve independence, sometimes with force. This creates a great deal of instability in areas where the fighting takes place, and many people have thus been uprooted in Angola, Mozambique, Portuguese New Guinea, and also in areas where there are white minority governments, such as South Africa and Rhodesia.

The second main cause may also be linked with the achievement of independence, which, in many areas in Africa, has created upheavals that are sometimes the result of ethnic and tribal divergencies. In Rwanda, there was a tremendous constitutional change when a feudal traditional monarch who had been ruling for years, was overthrown and replaced by the tribal majority, the Basutos, bringing about armed conflict and much bloodshed, so that many refugees fled. The problems of the Sudan, about which my distinguished friend, Mr. Awad, has told you, are linked with past history. Mainly for racial reasons, there is a pressing problem resulting from the confrontation between north and south, which has led to the flight of some of the population of the southern Sudan into neighboring territories, and particularly into Uganda.

The third cause is civil war. Such a war took place in the Democratic Republic of the Congo, where for many reasons, including ideological reasons, a whole area of the eastern part of the country rebelled against the central government at Kinshasa, and as a result, many people fled the country.

What then is the role of my Office? First of all, we have been called upon to face emergencies because, when large groups of refugees arrive in a host country, economic and social problems are created. And, here I would like to say that the African governments and people have always shown a tremendous spirit of solidarity and understanding in welcoming thousands of refugees, sharing whatever they could share with them in terms of food and lodgings, and also giving them land on which they could ultimately settle.

In meeting these emergencies, my Office plays essentially a catalytic role by calling on assistance from voluntary agencies such as the Red Cross and on other U.N. agencies, as for example, the World Food Program, which has supplied millions of dollars for food, and which relies to a great extent on the United States for this type of aid. The refugees need rations of this kind when they arrive, since they are always completely destitute. At this emergency stage, there is also a need to distribute clothing and sometimes medical supplies. Then, very quickly, we try to begin the settlement phase for the refugees.

This means that land has to be found, if possible far away from the borders, so that the refugees do not become an additional source of friction and tension. And on this land, we try to establish rural communities by helping the refugees to sow seeds and collect their crops, to build villages and schools and, where possible, to provide them with all the facilities they need to bring their standard of living as quickly as possible to the level of that of the local population.

This means that we face a great many problems. In some countries like Burundi where there are sixty thousand refugees, it is extremely difficult for a government already faced with many problems, to take care of the refugees. There, when we had reached a stage where settlement could be consolidated, we started a pilot project, based on the close relationship between the solution of the problems of refugees and the development of the area concerned. Now, in cooperation with the United Nations Development Program and with the ILO, FAO, UNESCO, and a few other members of the U.N. system, we have decided to put into operation a zonal integration plan whereby the refugees will be able to contribute fully to the economic and social development of the area where they have been welcomed.

This is also being done in the Central African Republic, where the Government recently requested the U.N. Development Program to plan a global zonal development program for an area where refugees from the Sudan are being settled. The same method is being followed in the eastern province of the Congo for the Rwandese refugees.

Needless to say, we still feel that the best solution to any refugee problem, including those in Africa, lies in voluntary repatriation. But, unfortunately, the social and political instability which still prevail in the countries from where many refugees came does not allow repatriation to take place.

Therefore, if we cannot facilitate the voluntary return of refugees, we have found that it is essential to settle them quickly, to avoid the type of stagnation which we had in Europe in the camps, to avoid the type of situation that exists in the Middle East today, where, as you know, over a million people are uprooted, of whom a large number is still living in camps. I would like to say here

Watutsi refugees wait near Goma to be taken to the
Bibwe center.

A refugee carpenter at Mbamba Bay, a UNHCR settlement on the shores of
Lake Malawi, busies himself making a bed for his home.

Mozambiquan refugee children attend classes in a school at Mbamba Bay, a UNHCR-sponsored settlement of four thousand.

Watutsi refugees at the resettlement center in Bibwe, created with UNHCR help, build their own houses with grass and bamboo.

that my Office is not responsible for the Palestine refugees. This is the concern of the United Nations Relief and Works Agency which has its headquarters in Beirut in the Lebanon, and which has quite a different approach and different terms of reference from those of UNHCR.

It is clear that if you allow a refugee situation to become stagnant, if you have large groups of unsettled people who are without work, who cannot look after themselves and become self-supporting, who are the victims of political unrest, and sometimes of political agitation, this results in instability and great human suffering among the refugees.

So, let us avoid in Africa what could not be avoided elsewhere, and through the effective techniques which my Office can apply, let us try to settle the refugees quickly and convert what might at first be considered as a burden, into an economic asset to the new community.

This is completely in line with the objectives of the United Nations to maintain peace and stability and improve friendly relations between States. It is also in keeping with the present efforts of the United Nations to promote to the fullest extent the utilization of human resources, particularly in developing areas.

At this juncture perhaps I might say a few words concerning the nature of the African refugee problem. It has been suggested that it mainly differs from other refugee problems in the sense that when refugees in Africa flee from one country to another, they often find themselves among their fellow tribesmen, and so are made welcome from the start. It is hard to generalize about this. I think, however, that integration has been much more spontaneous in Africa than in Europe, where the concept of nationality is more developed. A refugee crossing the border to another European country finds himself a foreigner, an alien. He speaks a different language and his professional qualifications are different. In Africa, on the other hand, many of the people are farmers whose standards of living are very similar in different countries. Also, since the borders in Africa were arbitrarily established by colonial powers, the ethnic groups are often the same on both sides of a frontier, with the result that a refugee arriving in Uganda or the Congo, may well find that the people along the border are able to speak his language and, on the whole, are related ethnically to him. The same is true of Sudanese refugees entering the Central African Republic and Tanzania. This has made our job much easier. A marked difference, on the other hand, again imposed in a way by the former colonial administration, is the fact that the Rwandese, for example, are educated in French. A Rwandese refugee arriving in Uganda, where the language is English, would have to contend with this, even though the local dialect may be the same.

Our work would never have been possible without the co-operation and unstinting support which we have received, not only from the United Nations and all the members of the U.N. System, which are dealing with economic and social development, but also from the vast network of voluntary agencies with which we have worked closely for so many years. The nongovernmental agencies have also been helping us enormously in Africa, not only by acting as our operational partners in many situations, but also by helping us to receive the necessary funds from private sources which we need to finance our work.

It is a sad reflection that the small program which I am administering, and which varies from $4,500,000 to $5,000,000 per year, could not so far be wholly financed by government contributions. It is sad indeed that this very small amount, which represents the basic minimum need of refugees all over the world every year—this small nucleus around which everything else that is done for refugees is built—is not wholly financed by governments. At the present time, governments finance only approximately 60 percent of this voluntary program which means that we have to continue to rely on the generosity and assistance of the public in general, and of course, to do this we have to spread information about the African refugee situation in countries like the United States. This is one of the reasons why I am so grateful to all of you who have participated in the symposium for the study in depth which you have been able to carry out.

I would like to dwell a little longer on this question of the size of the UNCHR Program and on the problems involved in its financing. The whole of my Office is, as I explained, marginal and catalytic, so that once refugees in a given country have become self-supporting, assistance activities on the part of UNHCR are limited to international protection, until such time as they have acquired the nationality of their country of residence and cease to be refugees. The size of the material assistance program is based partly on the requests received from governments for assistance to refugees on their territory, and partly on what my Office may reasonably expect to receive in terms of financial contributions to these programs. The latter are submitted to the thirty governments' Executive Committee of my program, which usually adopts our proposals without too many changes. By so doing, however, they are not committed to give UNHCR the funds required for the carrying out of the program, and they usually leave it to the High Commissioner to collect the necessary funds. The contribution of most governments is worked out by their respective treasuries on an annual basis and, as you may be aware, it is very difficult to get the treasuries to increase their appropriation. In most cases, steps to this effect must be taken a long time ahead.

At this juncture, approximately two-thirds of the UNHCR programs are financed through governmental contributions. The balance must be obtained through fund raising among private sources, such as voluntary agencies, individual persons, or, as was the case in October 1966, through a general fund-raising campaign. Only a small part of the proceeds of such campaigns, however, is handed to the High Commissioner for his annual program. Most of the funds are spent by the voluntary agencies which have participated in the fund raising and may wish to use the money for other refugees who do not come within the competence of UNHCR, such as the Palestine refugees or the refugees in Vietnam. The first group is the concern of the United Nations Relief and Works Agency, whereas the second are people inside their own country, and for that reason are not the concern of UNHCR. Even when the funds concerned are earmarked for assistance to refugees coming within the purview of UNHCR, it stands to reason that the voluntary agencies, acting upon the wishes of their constituents, wish to spend the money they collect on important programs of their own choice, rather than to fill the financial gap in the program of an intergovernmental agency like UNHCR, which, they feel, should be financed from governmental funds.

If my Office had more funds available, it would be able to concentrate more on seeking permanent solutions to the problems of refugees instead of having to devote a considerable part of its efforts to fund raising. It would also be able to do more to consolidate the settlement of refugees in Africa. In other words, it would be able to carry out the job more rapidly and more effectively. The minimum required would be that the 40 percent gap between the financial target and the amount of contributions received from governments be filled by additional governmental contributions.

There are, of course, several aspects of the refugee problem in Africa. One of them is the problem of African refugees in the great urban centers on the continent of Africa, in cities like Cairo, Dakar, Dar-es-Salaam, or Bujumbura in Burundi. In such places, there are more and more individual refugees who are seeking opportunities to settle down, to find jobs, or to further their education, unlike the other refugees who can be settled on land as farmers and can cultivate their own crops.

This is a problem of great concern to us, and one which I know you share, since I have seen that a great deal of your time during this symposium has been devoted to education. I would like to say in this connection that, as a start, the twenty-two African governments who took part in the recent Conference on the Legal, Economic and Social Aspects of African Refugee Problems, which was held in Addis Ababa, decided to establish an Employment and Placement Bureau which would be based in Addis Ababa under the auspices of the Organization of African Unity. Any refugees who wish to study, who want jobs, who have vocational skills, would thus be able to register their qualifications, which would be checked and maintained in a central filing system so that all the governments in Africa could somehow share this burden and seek ways of absorbing that category of refugees also.

A great many refugees have obtained, and will continue to obtain, scholarships for education abroad, but there is a problem here which I think deserves to be underlined. It is a fact that many of these refugees, like other Africans who obtain scholarships abroad, do not return to their countries. We have heard frequently about the problem of the "brain drain". There is today the problem of a potential brain drain in Africa of which we have to be aware and which we cannot afford to ignore. If we are to promote the secondary or higher education of African refugees, I think it is important that they should contribute to the development of their countries in the future, and that one day they should go back to help their countries after independence has been achieved in the areas where this is not yet the case. I believe, therefore, that the Addis Ababa Placement Bureau might play a very important role in Africa and help to prevent the paradox of Africans finding very good jobs in Europe or in the United States, while there is still a need for experts from Europe and the developed countries to go to Africa to help the Africans. This we must avoid, and we can at least ensure that refugees can obtain education on the continent of Africa, so that they are not forced to go to other countries and then not return.

In conclusion, I want to stress the importance of multilateral channels of assistance in Africa. It has been found that African countries are not willing to accept bilateral aid for assistance to refugees. This aid may be thought to have political implications; it may not always be acceptable from the point of view of the countries of origin of the refugees, who might consider it as a hostile act. On the other hand, the help channeled through the United Nations and the Office of the High Commissioner has always been accepted. It has been found that by coordinating this relief, and by promoting settlement of the refugees, it proved possible not only to remove the sources of human misery but also the sources of tension, because both the countries of origin and the countries of asylum have found UNHCR aid acceptable— they have welcomed it, and this, whenever discussed, has usually been unanimously agreed.

Before concluding, I would like to revert to the basic question of international protection and give you a little more information in respect of the issue of travel documents, and also of the 1951 Convention and of the Protocol relating to the status of refugees. The Office of the High Commissioner for Refugees does not issue passports, as this is a fundamental right of a sovereign state. Before the World War II, refugees could obtain what has come to be known as "Nansen passports". Since the entering into force of the 1951 Convention relating to the status of refugees, that document has been replaced by a travel document issued in accordance with the terms of that Convention and recognized by governments which have signed the Convention. Sometimes my Office may act in an advisory capacity, when a decision has to be made as to whether the man is a refugee or not. The 1951 Convention applied only to persons who had become refugees due to events occurring prior to 1951, so that in fact, there was a discrimination in status between these persons—mostly Europeans—and those who became refugees as a result of events taking place after 1951—mostly Africans and Asians. This has been eliminated through the signing of a Protocol to the 1951 Convention which is referred to as the 1967 Protocol. This had been opened for signature by the Secretary-General and has now come into force. Its provisions broadened the scope of the Convention to cover new groups of refugees. Governments which sign this Protocol will issue Convention travel documents also to the persons recognized as refugees under the terms of the Protocol. In the meantime, governments may issue refugees with ordinary travel documents, or passports of convenience, as has already been done on many occasions in the past.

Let me just add a few words concerning the crucial question of the protection of refugees under the terms of the 1967 Protocol. This legal instrument has, of course, only just come into force, but I trust that governments will soon apply its provisions. In addition, however, many countries have internal legislation of long standing and maintain a humanitarian tradition whereby asylum-seekers are not forced to return to their countries of origin. There are other instruments than the Protocol on which this attitude can be based, such as, for instance, the Charter of the United Nations and the Declaration of Human Rights, which would prevent forceful repatriation. My Office can intervene in cases where we believe that the persons concerned are bona fide refugees, not of course, if they are common criminals—we cannot protect them from justice. But if these people have a well-founded fear of persecution, we can certainly intervene, and can ask the countries to observe humanitarian principles and to allow the refugees to remain at least until a country of permanent settlement can be found for them.

Recently, the Third Committee of the General Assembly completed its consideration of the item on refugees. During the discussions, we heard approximately sixty speakers from Africa.

Their support for our humanitarian work was unanimous, which is a source of encouragement to me. I should like to express the hope, in conclusion, that with the understanding of our work which you have shown, and the general approval of my Office's efforts to solve the African refugee problem which now exists, we shall be able to continue to serve the aims of the United Nations, i.e., to help maintain peace and stability, and to assist countries, especially in Africa, to achieve further economic and social development in peace.

APPENDIXES

APPENDIX I

CONVENTION RELATING TO THE STATUS OF REFUGEES*

PREAMBLE

The High Contracting Parties,

Considering that the Charter of the United Nations and the Universal Declaration of Human Rights approved on 10 December 1948 by the General Assembly have affirmed the principle that human beings shall enjoy fundamental rights and freedoms without discrimination,

Considering that the United Nations has, on various occasions, manifested its profound concern for refugees and endeavoured to assure refugees the widest possible exercise of these fundamental rights and freedoms,

Considering that it is desirable to revise and consolidate previous international agreements relating to the status of refugees and to extend the scope of and the protection accorded by such instruments by means of a new agreement,

Considering that the grant of asylum may place unduly heavy burdens on certain countries, and that a satisfactory solution of a problem of which the United Nations has recognized the international scope and nature cannot therefore be achieved without international co-operation,

Expressing the wish that all States, recognizing the social and humanitarian nature of the problem of refugees, will do everything within their power to prevent this problem from becoming a cause of tension between States,

Noting that the United Nations High Commissioner for Refugees is charged with the task of supervising international conventions providing for the protection of refugees, and recognizing that the effective co-ordination of measures taken to deal with this problem

*Published by the Office of the U.N. High Commissioner for Refugees, 1966. HCR/INF/29/Rev. 1.

will depend upon the co-operation of States with the High Commissioner,

Have agreed as follows:

CHAPTER I: GENERAL PROVISIONS

Article 1

DEFINITION OF THE TERM "REFUGEE"

A. For the purposes of the present Convention, the term "refugee" shall apply to any person who:

(1) Has been considered a refugee under the Arrangements of 12 May 1962 and 30 June 1928 or under the Conventions of 28 October 1933 and 10 February 1938, the Protocol of 14 September 1939 or the Constitution of the International Refugee Organization;

Decisions of non-eligibility taken by the International Refugee Organization during the period of its activities shall not prevent the status of refugee being accorded to persons who fulfil the conditions of paragraph 2 of this section;

(2) As a result of events occurring before 1 January 1951 and owing to well-founded fear of being persecuted for reasons of race, religion, nationality, membership of a particular social group or political opinion, is outside the country of his nationality and is unable or, owing to such fear, is unwilling to avail himself of the protection of that country; or who, not having a nationality and being outside the country of his former habitual residence as a result of such events, is unable or, owing to such fear, is unwilling to return to it.

In the case of a person who has more than one nationality, the term "the country of his nationality" shall mean each of the countries of which he is a national, and a person shall not be deemed to be lacking the protection of the country of his nationality if, without any valid reason based on well-founded fear, he has not availed himself of the protection of one of the countries of which he is a national.

B. (1) For the purposes of this Convention, the words "events occurring before 1 January 1951" in Article 1, Section A, shall be understood to mean either

(a) "events occurring in Europe before 1 January 1951"; or

(b) "events occurring in Europe or elsewhere before 1 January 1951"; and each Contracting State shall make a declaration at the time of signature, ratification or accession, specifying which of these meanings it applies for the purpose of its obligations under this Convention.

(2) Any Contracting State which has adopted alternative (a) may at any time extend its obligations by adopting alternative (b) by means of a notification addressed to the Secretary-General of the United Nations.

C. This Convention shall cease to apply to any person falling under the terms of section A if:

(1) He has voluntarily re-availed himself of the protection of the country of his nationality; or

(2) Having lost his nationality, he has voluntarily re-acquired it; or

(3) He has acquired a new nationality, and enjoys the protection of the country of his new nationality; or

(4) He has voluntarily re-established himself in the country which he left or outside which he remained owing to fear of persecution; or

(5) He can no longer, because the circumstances in connexion with which he has been recognized as a refugee have ceased to exist, continue to refuse to avail himself of the protection of the country of his nationality;

Provided that this paragraph shall not apply to a refugee falling under section A (1) of this Article who is able to invoke compelling reasons arising out of previous persecution for refusing to avail himself of the protection of the country of nationality;

(6) Being a person who has no nationality he is, because the circumstances in connexion with which he has been recognized as a refugee have ceased to exist, able to return to the country of his former habitual residence;

Provided that this paragraph shall not apply to a refugee falling under section A (1) of this Article who is able to invoke compelling reasons arising out of previous persecution for refusing to return to the country of his former habitual residence.

D. This Convention shall not apply to persons who are at present receiving from organs or agencies of the United Nations other than the United Nations High Commissioner for Refugees protection or assistance.

When such protection or assistance has ceased for any reason, without the position of such persons being definitely settled in accordance with the relevant resolutions adopted by the General Assembly of the United Nations, these persons shall *ipso facto* be entitled to the benefits of this Convention.

E. This Convention shall not apply to a person who is recognized by the competent authorities of the country in which he has taken residence as having the rights and obligations which are attached to the possession of the nationality of that country.

F. The provisions of this Convention shall not apply to any person with respect to whom there are serious reasons for considering that:

(a) he has committed a crime against peace, a war crime, or a crime against humanity, as defined in the international instruments drawn up to make provision in respect of such crimes;

(b) he has committed a serious non-political crime outside the country of refuge prior to his admission to that country as a refugee;

(c) he has been guilty of acts contrary to the purposes and principles of the United Nations.

Article 2

GENERAL OBLIGATIONS

Every refugee has duties to the country in which he finds himself, which require in particular that he conform to its laws and regulations as to measures taken for the maintenance of public order.

Article 3

NON-DISCRIMINATION

The Contracting States shall apply the provisions of this Convention to refugees without discrimination as to race, religion or country of origin.

Article 4

RELIGION

The Contracting States shall accord to refugees within their territories treatment at least as favourable as that accorded to their nationals and respect to freedom to practise their religion and freedom as regards the religious education of their children.

Article 5

RIGHTS GRANTED APART FROM THIS CONVENTION

Nothing in this Convention shall be deemed to impair any rights and benefits granted by a Contracting State to refugees apart from this Convention.

Article 6

THE TERM "IN THE SAME CIRCUMSTANCES"

For the purpose of this Convention, the term "in the same circumstances" implies that any requirements (including requirements as to length and conditions of sojourn or residence) which the particular individual would have to fulfil for the enjoyment of the right in question, if he were not a refugee, must be fulfilled by him, with the exception of requirements which by their nature a refugee is incapable of fulfilling.

Article 7

EXEMPTION FROM RECIPROCITY

1. Except where this convention contains more favourable provisions, a Contracting State shall accord to refugees the same treatment as is accorded to aliens generally.

2. After a period of three years' residence, all refugees shall enjoy exemption from legislative reciprocity in the territory of the Contracting States.

3. Each Contracting State shall continue to accord to refugees the rights and benefits to which they were already entitled, in the absence of reciprocity, at the date of entry into force of this Convention for that State.

4. The Contracting States shall consider favourably the possibility of according to refugees, in the absence of reciprocity, rights

and benefits beyond those to which they are entitled according to paragraphs 2 and 3, and to extending exemption from reciprocity to refugees who do not fulfil the conditions provided for in paragraphs 2 and 3.

5. The provisions of paragraphs 2 and 3 apply both to the rights and benefits referred to in articles 13, 18, 19, 21 and 22 of this Convention and to rights and benefits for which this Convention does not provide.

Article 8

EXEMPTION FROM EXCEPTIONAL MEASURES

With regard to exceptional measures which may be taken against the person, property or interests of nationals of a foreign State, the Contracting States shall not apply such measures to a refugee who is formally a national of the said State solely on account of such nationality. Contracting States which, under their legislation, are prevented from applying the general principle expressed in this article, shall, in appropriate cases, grant exemptions in favour of such refugees.

Article 9

PROVISIONAL MEASURES

Nothing in this Convention shall prevent a Contracting State, in time of war or other grave and exceptional circumstances, from taking provisional measures which it considers to be essential to the national security in the case of a particular person, pending a determination by the Contracting State that that person is in fact a refugee and that the continuance of such measures is necessary in his case in the interests of national security.

Article 10

CONTINUITY OF RESIDENCE

1. Where a refugee has been forcibly displaced during the Second World War and removed to the territory of a Contracting State, and is resident there, the period of such enforced sojourn shall be considered to have been lawful residence within that territory.

2. Where a refugee has been forcibly displaced during the Sec-

ond World War from the territory of a Contracting State and has, prior to the date of entry into force of this Convention, returned there for the purpose of taking up residence, the period of residence before and after such enforced displacement shall be regarded as one uninterrupted period for any purposes for which uninterrupted residence is required.

Article 11

REFUGEE SEAMEN

In the case of refugees regularly serving as crew members on board a ship flying the flag of a Contracting State, that State shall give sympathetic consideration to their establishment on its territory and the issue of travel documents to them or their temporary admission to its territory particularly with a view to facilitating their establishment in another country.

CHAPTER II: JURIDICAL STATUS

Article 12

PERSONAL STATUS

1. The personal status of a refugee shall be governed by the law of the country of his domicile or, if he has no domicile, by the law of the country of his residence.

2. Rights previously acquired by a refugee and dependent on personal status, more particularly rights attaching to marriage, shall be respected by a Contracting State, subject to compliance, if this be necessary, with the formalities required by the law of that State, provided that the right in question is one which would have been recognized by the law of that State had he not become a refugee.

Article 13

MOVABLE AND IMMOVABLE PROPERTY

The Contracting States shall accord to a refugee treatment as favourable as possible and, in any event, not less favourable than that accorded to aliens generally in the same circumstances, as regards the acquisition of movable and immovable property and other rights pertaining thereto, and to leases and other contracts relating to movable and immovable property.

Article 14

ARTISTIC RIGHTS AND INDUSTRIAL PROPERTY

In respect of the protection of industrial property, such as inventions, designs or models, trade marks, trade names, and of rights in literary, artistic and scientific works, a refugee shall be accorded in the country in which he has his habitual residence the same protection as is accorded to nationals of that country. In the territory of any other Contracting State, he shall be accorded the same protection as is accorded in that territory to nationals of the country in which he has his habitual residence.

Article 15

RIGHT OF ASSOCIATION

As regards non-political and non-profit-making associations and trade unions the Contracting States shall accord to refugees lawfully staying in their territory the most favourable treatment accorded to nationals of a foreign country, in the same circumstances.

Article 16

ACCESS TO COURTS

1. A refugee shall have free access to the courts of law on the territory of all Contracting States.

2. A refugee shall enjoy in the Contracting State in which he has his habitual residence the same treatment as a national in matters pertaining to access to the Courts, including legal assistance and exemption from *cautio judicatum solvi*.

3. A refugee shall be accorded in the matters referred to in paragraph 2 in countries other than that in which he has his habitual residence the treatment granted to a national of the country of his habitual residence.

CHAPTER III: GAINFUL EMPLOYMENT

Article 17

WAGE-EARNING EMPLOYMENT

1. The Contracting State shall accord to refugees lawfully staying in their territory the most favourable treatment accorded to nationals of a foreign country in the same circumstances, as regards the right to engage in wage-earning employment.

2. In any case, restrictive measures imposed on aliens or the employment of aliens for the protection of the national labour market shall not be applied to a refugee who was already exempt from them at the date of entry into force of this Convention for the Contracting State concerned, or who fulfils one of the following conditions:

(a) He has completed three years' residence in the country;

(b) He has a spouse possessing the nationality of the country of residence. A refugee may not invoke the benefits of this provision if he has abandoned his spouse;

(c) He has one or more children possessing the nationality of the country of residence.

3. The Contracting States shall give sympathetic consideration to assimilating the rights of all refugees with regard to wage-earning employment to those of nationals, and in particular of those refugees who have entered their territory pursuant to programmes of labour recruitment or under immigration schemes.

Article 18

SELF-EMPLOYMENT

The Contracting States shall accord to a refugee lawfully in their territory treatment as favourable as possible and, in any event, not less favourable than that accorded to aliens generally in the same circumstances, as regards the right to engage on his own account in agriculture, industry, handicrafts and commerce and to establish commercial and industrial companies.

Article 19

LIBERAL PROFESSIONS

1. Each Contracting State shall accord to refugees lawfully

staying in their territory who hold diplomas recognized by the competent authorities of that State, and who are desirous of practising a liberal profession, treatment as favourable as possible and, in any event, not less favourable than that accorded to aliens generally in the same circumstances.

2. The Contracting States shall use their best endeavours consistently with their laws and constitutions to secure the settlement of such refugees in the territories, other than the metropolitan territory, for whose international relations they are responsible.

CHAPTER IV: WELFARE

Article 20

RATIONING

Where a rationing system exists, which applies to the population at large and regulates the general distribution of products in short supply, refugees shall be accorded the same treatment as nationals.

Article 21

HOUSING

As regards housing, the Contracting States, in so far as the matter is regulated by laws or regulations or is subject to the control of public authorities, shall accord to refugees lawfully staying in their territory treatment as favourable as possible and, in any event, not less favourable than that accorded to aliens generally in the same circumstances.

Article 22

PUBLIC EDUCATION

1. The Contracting States shall accord to refugees the same treatment as is accorded to nationals with respect to elementary education.

2. The Contracting States shall accord to refugees treatment as favourable as possible, and, in any event, not less favourable than that accorded to aliens generally in the same circumstances, with respect to education other than elementary education and, in particular, as regards access to studies, the recognition of foreign

school certificates, diplomas and degrees, the remission of fees and charges and the award of scholarships.

Article 23

PUBLIC RELIEF

The Contracting States shall accord to refugees lawfully staying in their territory the same treatment with respect to public relief and assistance as is accorded to their nationals.

Article 24

LABOUR LEGISLATION AND SOCIAL SECURITY

1. The Contracting States shall accord to refugees lawfully staying in their territory the same treatment as is accorded to nationals in respect of the following matters:

(a) In so far as such matters are governed by laws or regulations or are subject to the control of administrative authorities: remuneration, including family allowances where these form part of remuneration, hours of work, overtime arrangements, holidays with pay, restrictions on home work, minimum age of employment, apprenticeship and training, women's work and the work of young persons, and the enjoyment of the benefits of collective bargaining;

(b) Social security (legal provisions in respect of employment injury, occupational diseases, maternity, sickness, disability, old age, death, unemployment, family responsibilities and any other contingency which, according to national laws or regulations, is covered by a social security scheme), subject to the following limitations:

(i) there may be appropriate arrangements for the maintenance of acquired rights and rights in course of acquisition;

(ii) National laws or regulations of the country of residence may prescribe special arrangements concerning benefits or portions of benefits which are payable wholly out of public funds, and concerning allowances paid to persons who do not fulfil the contribution conditions prescribed for the award of a normal pension.

2. The right to compensation for the death of a refugee resulting from employment injury or from occupational disease shall

not be affected by the fact that the residence of the beneficiary is outside the territory of the Contracting State.

3. The Contracting States shall extend to refugees the benefits of agreements concluded between them, or which may be concluded between them in the future, concerning the maintenance of acquired rights and rights in the process of acquisition in regard to social security, subject only to the conditions which apply to nationals of the States signatory to the agreements in question.

4. The Contracting States will give sympathetic consideration to extending to refugees so far as possible the benefits of similar agreements which may at any time be in force between such Contracting States and non-contracting States.

CHAPTER V: ADMINISTRATIVE MEASURES

Article 25

ADMINISTRATIVE ASSISTANCE

1. When the exercise of a right by a refugee would normally require the assistance of authorities of a foreign country to whom he cannot have recourse, the Contracting States in whose territory he is residing shall arrange that such assistance be afforded to him by their own authorities or by an international authority.

2. The authority or authorities mentioned in paragraph 1 shall deliver or cause to be delivered under their supervision to refugees such documents or certifications as would normally be delivered to aliens by or through their national authorities.

3. Documents or certifications so delivered shall stand in the stead of the official instruments delivered to aliens by or through their national authorities, and shall be given credence in the absence of proof to the contrary.

4. Subject to such exceptional treatment as may be granted to indigent persons, fees may be charged for the services mentioned herein, but such fees shall be moderate and commensurate with those charged to nationals for similar services.

5. The provisions of this article shall be without prejudice to articles 27 and 28.

Article 26

FREEDOM OF MOVEMENT

Each Contracting State shall accord to refugees lawfully in its territory the right to choose their place of residence and to move freely within its territory, subject to any regulations applicable to aliens generally in the same circumstances.

Article 27

IDENTITY PAPERS

The Contracting States shall issue identity papers to any refugee in their territory who does not possess a valid travel document.

Article 28

TRAVEL DOCUMENTS

1. The Contracting States shall issue to refugees lawfully staying in their territory travel documents for the purpose of travel outside their territory unless compelling reasons of national security or public order otherwise require, and the provisions of the Schedule to this Convention shall apply with respect to such documents. The Contracting States may issue such a travel document to any other refugee in their territory; they shall in particular give sympathetic consideration to the issue of such a travel document to refugees in their territory who are unable to obtain a travel document from the country of their lawful residence.

2. Travel documents issued to refugees under previous international agreements by parties thereto shall be recognized and treated by the Contracting States in the same way as if they had been issued pursuant to this article.

Article 29

FISCAL CHARGES

1. The Contracting States shall not impose upon refugees duties, charges or taxes, of any description whatsoever, other or higher than those which are or may be levied on their nationals in similar situations.

2. Nothing in the above paragraph shall prevent the application to refugees of the laws and regulations concerning charges

in respect of the issue to aliens of administrative documents including identity papers.

Article 30

TRANSFER OF ASSETS

1. A Contracting State shall, in conformity with its laws and regulations, permit refugees to transfer assets which they have brought into its territory, to another country where they have been admitted for the purposes of resettlement.

2. A Contracting State shall give sympathetic consideration to the application of refugees for permission to transfer assets wherever they may be and which are necessary for their resettlement in another country to which they have been admitted.

Article 31

REFUGEES UNLAWFULLY IN THE COUNTRY OF REFUGE

1. The Contracting States shall not impose penalties, on account of their illegal entry or presence, on refugees who, coming directly from a territory where their life or freedom was threatened in the sense of Article 1, enter or are present in their territory without authorization, provided they present themselves without delay to the authorities and show good cause for their illegal entry or presence.

2. The Contracting States shall not apply to the movements of such refugees restrictions other than those which are necessary and such restrictions shall only be applied until their status in the country is regularized or they obtain admission into another country. The Contracting States shall allow such refugees a reasonable period and all the necessary facilities to obtain admission into another country.

Article 32

EXPULSION

1. The Contracting States shall not expel a refugee lawfully in their territory save on grounds of national security or public order.

2. The expulsion of such a refugee shall be only in pursuance of a decision reached in accordance with due process of law. Except where compelling reasons of national security otherwise require, the refugee shall be allowed to submit evidence to clear

himself, and to appeal to and be represented for the purpose before competent authority or a person or persons specially designated by the competent authority.

3. The Contracting States shall allow such a refugee a reasonable period within which to seek legal admission into another
country. The Contracting States reserve the right to apply during
that period such internal measures as they may deem necessary.

Article 33

PROHIBITION OF EXPULSION OR RETURN ("REFOULEMENT")

1. No Contracting State shall expel or return ("refouler") a
refugee in any manner whatsoever to the frontiers of territories
where his life or freedom would be threatened on account of his
race, religion, nationality, membership of a particular social group
or political opinion.

2. The benefit of the present provision may not, however, be
claimed by a refugee whom there are reasonable grounds for regarding as a danger to the security of the country in which he is,
or who, having been convicted by a final judgment of a particularly
serious crime, constitutes a danger to the community of that
country.

Article 34

NATURALIZATION

The Contracting States shall as far as possible facilitate the
assimilation and naturalization of refugees. They shall in particular
make every effort to expedite naturalization proceedings and to
reduce as far as possible the charges and costs of such proceedings.

CHAPTER VI: EXECUTORY AND TRANSITORY PROVISIONS

Article 35

CO-OPERATION OF THE NATIONAL AUTHORITIES WITH
THE UNITED NATIONS

1. The Contracting States undertake to co-operate with the
Office of the United Nations High Commissioner for Refugees, or
any other agency of the United Nations which may succeed it, in

the exercise of its functions, and shall in particular facilitate its duty of supervising the application of the provisions of this Convention.

2. In order to enable the Office of the High Commissioner or any other agency of the United Nations which may succeed it, to make reports to the competent organs of the United Nations, the Contracting States undertake to provide them in the appropriate form with information and statistical data requested concerning:

(a) the condition of refugees,
(b) the implementation of this Convention, and
(c) laws, regulations and decrees which are, or may hereafter be, in force relating to refugees.

Article 36

INFORMATION ON NATIONAL LEGISLATION

The Contracting States shall communicate to the Secretary-General of the United Nations the laws and regulations which they may adopt to ensure the application of this Convention.

Article 37

RELATION TO PREVIOUS CONVENTIONS

Without prejudice to article 28, paragraph 2, of this Convention, this Convention replaces, as between parties to it, the Arrangements of 5 July 1922, 31 May 1924, 12 May 1926, 30 June 1928 and 30 July 1935, the Conventions of 28 October 1933 and 10 February 1938, the Protocol of 14 September 1939 and the Agreement of 15 October 1946.

CHAPTER VII: FINAL CLAUSES

Article 38

SETTLEMENT OF DISPUTES

Any dispute between parties to this Convention relating to its interpretation or application, which cannot be settled by other means, shall be referred to the International Court of Justice at the request of any one of the parties to the dispute.

Article 39

SIGNATURE, RATIFICATION, AND ACCESSION

1. This Convention shall be opened for signature at Geneva on 28 July 1951 and shall thereafter be deposited with the Secretary-General of the United Nations. It shall be open for signature at the European Office of the United Nations from 28 July to 31 August 1951 and shall be reopened for signature at the Headquarters of the United Nations from 17 September 1951 to 31 December 1952.

2. This Convention shall be open for signature on behalf of all States Members of the United Nations, and also on behalf of any other State invited to attend the Conference of Plenipotentiaries on the Status of Refugees and Stateless Persons or to which an invitation to sign will have been addressed by the General Assembly. It shall be ratified and the instruments of ratification shall be deposited with the Secretary-General of the United Nations.

3. This Convention shall be open from 28 July 1951 for accession by the States referred to in paragraph 2 of this Article. Accession shall be effected by the deposit of an instrument of accession with the Secretary-General of the United Nations.

Article 40

TERRITORIAL APPLICATION CLAUSE

1. Any State may, at the time of signature, ratification or accession, declare that this Convention shall extend to all or any of the territories for the international relations of which it is responsible. Such a declaration shall take effect when the Convention enters into force for the State concerned.

2. At any time thereafter any such extension shall be made by notification addressed to the Secretary-General of the United Nations and shall take effect as from the ninetieth day after the day of receipt by the Secretary-General of the United Nations of this notification, or as from the date of entry into force of the Convention for the State concerned, whichever is the later.

3. With respect to those territories to which this Convention is not extended at the time of signature, ratification or accession, each State concerned shall consider the possibility of taking the necessary steps in order to extend the application of this Con-

vention to such territories, subject, where necessary for constitutional reasons, to the consent of the governments of such territories.

Article 41

FEDERAL CLAUSE

In the case of a Federal or non-unitary State, the following provisions shall apply:

(a) With respect to those articles of this Convention that come within the legislative jurisdiction of the federal legislative authority, the obligations of the Federal Government shall to this extent be the same as those of Parties which are not Federal States;

(b) With respect to those articles of this Convention that come within the legislative jurisdiction of constituent States, provinces or cantons which are not, under the constitutional system of the federation, bound to take legislative action, the Federal Government shall bring such articles with a favourable recommendation to the notice of the appropriate authorities of States, provinces or cantons at the earliest possible moment.

(c) A Federal State Party to this Convention shall, at the request of any other Contracting State transmitted through the Secretary-General of the United Nations, supply a statement of the law and practice of the Federation and its constituent units in regard to any particular provision of the Convention showing the extent to which effect has been given to that provision by legislative or other action.

Article 42

RESERVATIONS

1. At the time of signature, ratification or accession, any State may make reservations to articles of the Convention other than to articles 1, 3, 4, 16 (1), 33, 36-46 inclusive.

2. Any State making a reservation in accordance with paragraph 1 of this article may at any time withdraw the reservation by a communication to that effect addressed to the Secretary-General of the United Nations.

Article 43

ENTRY INTO FORCE

1. This Convention shall come into force on the ninetieth day

following the day of deposit of the sixth instrument of ratification or accession.

2. For each State ratifying or acceding to the Convention after the deposit of the sixth instrument of ratification or accession, the Convention shall enter into force on the ninetieth day following the date of deposit by such State of its instrument of ratification or accession.

Article 44

DENUNCIATION

1. Any Contracting State may denounce this Convention at any time by a notification addressed to the Secretary-General of the United Nations.

2. Such denunciation shall take effect for the Contracting State concerned one year from the date upon which it is received by the Secretary-General of the United Nations.

3. Any State which has made a declaration or notification under article 40 may, at any time thereafter, by a notification to the Secretary-General of the United Nations, declare that the Convention shall cease to extend to such territory one year after the date of receipt of the notification by the Secretary-General.

Article 45

REVISION

1. Any Contracting State may request revision of this Convention at any time by a notification addressed to the Secretary-General of the United Nations.

2. The General Assembly of the United Nations shall recommend the steps, if any, to be taken in respect of such request.

Article 46

NOTIFICATION BY THE SECRETARY-GENERAL OF THE UNITED NATIONS

The Secretary-General of the United Nations shall inform all Members of the United Nations and non-member States referred to in article 39:

(a) of declarations and notifications in accordance with Section B of Article 1;

(b) of signatures, ratifications and accessions in accordance with article 39;

(c) of declarations and notifications in accordance with article 40;

(d) of reservations and withdrawals in accordance with article 42;

(e) of the date on which this Convention will come into force in accordance with article 43;

(f) of denunciations and notifications in accordance with article 44;

(g) of requests for revision in accordance with article 45.

In faith whereof the undersigned, duly authorized, have signed this Convention on behalf of their respective Governments,

Done at Geneva, this twenty-eighth day of July, one thousand nine hundred and fifty-one, in a single copy, of which the English and French texts are equally authentic and which shall remain deposited in the archives of the United Nations, and certified true copies of which shall be delivered to all Members of the United Nations and to the non-member States referred to in article 39.

APPENDIX II

PROTOCOL RELATING TO THE
STATUS OF REFUGEES, 1966

The States Parties to the present Protocol,

Considering that the Convention relating to the Status of Refugees done at Geneva on 28 July 1951 (hereinafter referred to as the Convention) covers only those persons who have become refugees as a result of events occurring before 1 January 1951.

Considering that new refugee situations have arisen since the Convention was adopted and that the refugees concerned may therefore not fail within the scope of the Convention,

Considering that it is desirable that equal status should be enjoyed by all refugees covered by the definition in the Convention irrespective of the dateline 1 January 1951,

Have agreed as follows:

Article I

GENERAL PROVISIONS

1. The States Parties to the present Protocol undertake to apply articles 2 to 34 inclusive of the Convention to refugees as hereinafter defined.

2. For the purpose of the present Protocol, the term "refugee" shall, except as regards the application of paragraph 3 of this article, mean any person within the definition of article 1 of the Convention as if the words "as a result of events occurring before 1 January 1951 and . . ." and the words ". . . as a result of such events," in article 1A (2) were omitted.

3. The present Protocol shall be applied by the States Parties hereto without any geographic limitation, save that existing declarations made by States already Parties to the Convention in accordance with article 1 B (1) (a) of the Conventon, shall, unless

extended under article 1 B (2) thereof, apply also under the present Protocol.

Article II

CO-OPERATION OF THE NATIONAL AUTHORITIES WITH THE UNITED NATIONS

1. The States Parties to the present Protocol undertake to co-operate with the Office of the United Nations High Commissioner for Refugees, or any other agency of the United Nations which may succeed it, in the exercise of its functions, and shall in particular facilitate its duty of supervising the application of the provisions of the present Protocol.

2. In order to enable the Office of the High Commissioner, or any other agency of the United Nations which may succeed it, to make reports to the competent organs of the United Nations, the States Parties to the present Protocol undertake to provide them with the information and statistical data requested in the appropriate form, concerning:

(a) The condition of refugees;

(b) the implementation of the present Protocol;

(c) laws, regulations and decrees which are, or may hereafter be, in force relating to refugees.

Article III

INFORMATION ON NATIONAL LEGISLATION

The State Parties to the present Protocol shall communicate to the Secretary-General of the United Nations the laws and regulations which they may adopt to ensure the application of the present Protocol.

Article IV

SETTLEMENT OF DISPUTES

Any dispute between States Parties to the present Protocol which relates to its interpretation or application and which cannot be settled by other means shall be referred to the International Court of Justice at the request of any one of the parties to the dispute.

Article V

ACCESSION

The present Protocol shall be open for accession on behalf of all States Parties to the Convention and of any other State Member of the United Nations or member of any of the specialized agencies or to which an invitation to accede may have been addressed by the General Assembly of the United Nations. Accession shall be effected by the deposit of an instrument of accession with the Secretary-General of the United Nations.

Article VI

FEDERAL CLAUSE

In the case of a Federal or non-unitary State, the following provisions shall apply:

(a) With respect to these articles of the Convention to be applied in accordance with article I, paragraph 1, of the present Protocol that come within the legislative jurisdiction of the federal legislative authority, the obligations of the Federal Government shall to this extent be the same as those of States Parties which are not Federal States;

(b) With respect to those articles of the Convention to be applied in accordance with article I, paragraph 1, of the present Protocol that come within the legislative jurisdiction of constituent States, provinces or cantons which are not, under the constitutional system of the federation, bound to take legislative action, the Federal Government shall bring such articles with a favourable recommendation to the notice of the appropriate authorities of States, provinces or cantons at the earliest possible moment;

(c) A Federal State Party to the present Protocol shall, at the request of any other State Party hereto transmitted through the Secretary-General of the United Nations, supply a statement of the law and practice of the Federation and its constituent units in regard to any particular provision of the Convention to be applied in accordance with article I, paragraph 1, of the present Protocol, showing the extent to which effect has been given to that provision by legislative or other action.

Article VII

RESERVATIONS AND DECLARATIONS

1. At the time of accession, any State may make reservations in respect of article IV of the present Protocol and in respect of the application in accordance with article I of the present Protocol of any provisions of the Convention other than those contained in articles 1, 3, 4, 16 (1) and 33 thereof, provided that in the case of a State Party to the Convention reservations made under this article shall not extend to refugees in respect of whom the Convention applies.

2. Reservations made by States Parties to the Convention in accordance with article 42 thereof shall, unless withdrawn, be applicable in relation to their obligations under the present Protocol.

3. Any State making a reservation in accordance with paragraph 1 of this article may at any time withdraw such reservation by a communication to that effect addressed to the Secretary-General of the United Nations.

4. Declaration made under article 40, paragraphs 1 and 2, of the Convention by a State Party thereto which accedes to the present Protocol shall be deemed to apply in respect of the present Protocol, unless upon accession a notification to the contrary is addressed by the State Party concerned to the Secretary-General of the United Nations. The provisions of article 40, paragraphs 2 and 3, and of article 44, paragraph 3, of the Convention shall be deemed to apply *mutatis mutandis* to the present Protocol.

Article VIII

ENTRY INTO FORCE

1. The present Protocol shall come into force on the day of deposit of the sixth instrument of accession.

2. For each State acceding to the Protocol after the deposit of the sixth instrument of accession, the Protocol shall come into force on the date of deposit by such State of its instrument of accession.

Article IX

DENUNCIATION

1. Any State Party hereto may denounce this Protocol at any

time by a notification addressed to the Secretary-General of the United Nations.

2. Such denunciation shall take effect for the State Party concerned one year from the date on which it is received by the Secretary-General of the United Nations.

Article X

NOTIFICATIONS BY THE SECRETARY-GENERAL OF THE UNITED NATIONS

The Secretary-General of the United Nations shall inform the States referred to in article V above of the date of entry into force, accessions, reservations and withdrawals of reservations to and denunciations of the present Protocol, and of declarations and notifications relating hereto.

Article XI

DEPOSIT IN THE ARCHIVES OF THE SECRETARY OF THE UNITED NATIONS

A copy of the present Protocol, of which the Chinese, English, French, Russian and Spanish texts are equally authentic, signed by the President of the General Assembly and by the Secretary-General of the United Nations, shall be deposited in the archives of the Secretariat of the United Nations. The Secretary-General will transmit certified copies thereof to all States Members of the United Nations and to the other States referred to in article V above.

APPENDIX III

RECOMMENDATIONS: CONFERENCE ON THE LEGAL, ECONOMIC, AND SOCIAL ASPECTS OF AFRICAN REFUGEE PROBLEMS*

The Conference Recommends that, in addition to the definition contained in the 1951 United Nations Convention relating to the Status of Refugees, as extended by the United Nations Protocol of 1967, African States should take into account the specific aspects of African refugee situations with regard in particular to the definition of an African refugee.[1]

THE QUESTION OF ASYLUM[2]

The Conference recommends that African States should be guided in the granting of asylum by the following principles:

1. African States shall use their best endeavours consistent with their laws and constitutions to admit all refugees and to promote the settlement of those refugees who, for well-founded reasons, do not wish to return to their country of origin or nationality.

2. The grant of asylum to refugees is a peaceful and humanitarian act and shall not be regarded as an unfriendly act by any African State.

3. No person shall be subjected by an African State to measures such as rejection at the frontier, return or expulsion, which would compel him to remain in or to return to a territory where his life, physical integrity or liberty would be threatened for the reasons set out in Article 1, paragraph 2 of the above-mentioned Convention.

4. When an African State finds difficulty in continuing to grant

1. See AFR/REF/CONF.1967/No. 2

2. See AFR/REF/CONF.1967/No. 3

*Held at Africa Hall, Addis Ababa, Ethiopia, 9-18 October 1967. Included here are extracts of the document published by the Conference.

asylum to refugees, other African States shall consider, in a spirit of African solidarity and international cooperation, appropriate measures to lighten the burden of the African State granting asylum.

5. If a refugee has not received the right to reside in any country he shall have a claim to temporary residence in the country of asylum in which he first presented himself as a refugee pending arrangements for this resettlement in accordance with paragraph 4 above.

6. Every refugee owes a duty to the country of asylum, which requires in particular that he conforms to its laws and regulations as well as to measures taken for the maintenance of public order. He shall also abstain from any subversive activities against any African country, except for countries under colonial and racist minority domination.

VOLUNTARY REPATRIATION AND SETTLEMENT OF FORMER REFUGEES IN THEIR COUNTRY OF ORIGIN[3]

The Conference recommends that African States continue to be guided by the following principles in regard to repatriation:

1. That the essentially voluntary character of repatriation be respected in all cases and no refugee be repatriated against his will;

2. That the country of asylum, in collaboration with the country of origin, make adequate arrangements for the safe return of the refugees requesting repatriation;

3. That the country of origin, on receiving back refugees facilitate their resettlement and grant them the full rights and privileges of nationals of the country and subject them to the same obligations;

4. That refugees who voluntarily return to their country be in no way penalized for having left it for any of the reasons giving rise to refugee situations. That whenever necessary an appeal should be made through national information media and through the Administrative Secretary General of the OAU inviting refugees to return home and giving assurance that the new circumstances prevailing in their country of origin will enable them to return

3. See AFR/REF/CONF.1967/Nos. 4 and 7.

without risk and to take up a normal and peaceful life without fear of being molested or punished, and that the text of such appeal should be given to refugees and properly explained to them by their country of refuge;

5. That refugees who freely decide to return to their homeland, as a result of such assurances or on their own initiative, should be given every necessary assistance by the country of refuge, the country of origin, and by the voluntary agencies, the international and inter-governmental organizations to facilitate their return;

6. That, in conformity with Article 1.C 5 of the United Nations Convention of 1951, refugee status ceases to apply to any person if the circumstances as a result of which he became a refugee have ceased to exist;

7. That every possible step should be taken to elimintate the causes, whatever they may be, which have forced refugees to leave their country;

8. That the country of origin should help returning nationals to resettle and to take up a normal and peaceful life, with the help of international organizations where necessary, and that all the planning and executive facilities contemplated for the integration of refugees in their country of asylum should, wherever possible, be made equally available to them when they return to their homes.

9. That inter-governmental committees for aid to returning refugees should be set up, consisting of representatives of countries of origin and of countries of asylum and also representatives of refugees and of international organizations, with the approval of the governments concerned.

10. That the United Nations General Assembly should adopt a resolution broadening the terms of reference of the UNHCR to enable it to assist governments in their endeavour to aid former refugees who have returned to their homeland.

11. That an inter-African Committee for African Refugee migration should be set up to deal with the transport of refugees from one country to another.

TRAVEL DOCUMENTS FOR REFUGEES[4]

The Conference recommends that African States issue Travel

4. See AFR/REF/CONF.1967/No. 5

Documents to refugees in accordance with the United Nations Convention relating to the Status of Refugees, and the Schedule annexed to the said Convention, provided that whenever an African country of second asylum accepts a refugee from a country of first asylum, the country of first asylum may be dispensed from issuing a return clause and provided that only genuine refugees shall benefit from this Recommendation.

THE SOCIAL RIGHTS OF REFUGEES[5]

The Conference recommends that African States should make every effort within their possibilities to apply the principles expressed by the provisions referred to above.

EMERGENCY AID[6]

The Conference recommends that, in future, the following considerations be taken into account by the governments, intergovernmental and non-governmental organizations concerned when granting assistance to refugees in emergency situations:

1. A large part of the responsibility in providing emergency aid to refugees rests with the governments of the countries of asylum, particularly with regard to the provision of immediate aid, and to the launching of appeals for assistance to the competent organizations as early as possible;

2. In order that aid may be devoid of any political character, foreign assistance should, as much as possible, be given through the existing international and multilateral machinery;

3. Obstacles of administrative or technical nature which tend to slow down the process of granting aid should be eliminated as much as possible;

4. As regards food aid, particular attention should be paid:
   - (i) to providing the necessary food at short notice,
   - (ii) to the provisions of food items to which the refugee population is traditionally accustomed, with the understanding that whenever traditional or similar types of food items are not available from the aid giving agencies, measures be taken to provide funds for the local pur-

5. See AFR/REF/CONF.1967/No. 6
6. See AFR/REF/CONF.1967/No. 8

chase of suitable food items with due consideration given, as far as possible, to the importance of balanced diet for the refugees.

5. The coordination of emergency aid should be effectively ensured at both national and international level;

6. Adequate measures should be taken with regard to the supervision of emergency aid activities, taking account of the requirements called for by the donor agencies;

7. The relief given must be weighed against the economic and social position of the surrounding local population so as not to create psychological conflicts which might have far-reaching repercussions, particularly if the refugee group is likely to settle in the country of asylum;

8. The relief should not discourage the initiative of the refugees, who should remain aware of the fact that emergency aid is only a temporary measure and that the final solution to their problems depends to a large extent on their own initiative, efforts and cooperation;

9. *The period of emergency aid should be reduced to a minimum and long term solutions should be planned and implemented as soon as feasible, so as to make it possible gradually to discontinue the distribution of relief.*

LAND SETTLEMENT[7]

The Conference recommends that land settlement of the large groups of refugees of rural background be promoted and implemented in Africa, taking into account the following elements:

1. Spontaneous land settlement of refugees should be encouraged whenever it is compatible with the policy of the government of the country of asylum, not only from an economic and social point of view, but also with respect to international relations;

2. Material support of spontaneous land settlement is necessary in view of the fact that in developing countries the physical and social equipment of the settlement area is normally not sufficient to service a sudden increase of population. Therefore, the strengthening of this equipment is required both to provide for the newcomers and to avoid the build-up of tensions between refugees and the local population;

7. See AFR/REF/CONF.1967/No. 8

3. Various circumstances, but more particularly the necessity of settling the refugees away from border areas where their permanence might be a cause of international tension, might justify on behalf of the government of the country of asylum the systematic settlement of refugees on the land in new rural communities,

4. The purposes of material support of spontaneous land settlement as well as of the creation of new settlements in a systematic way, are as follows:

(i) To bring the new communities to a stage of economic viability, enabling the refugees not only to become self-reliant in respect of self-grown food, but also to earn some cash in order to afford elementary day-to-day expenses;

(ii) To bring the new communities to a stage of social viability, providing therefore the settlements with a minimum of health and education facilities which will also serve the local population and provide a means of contact and initial integration;

(iii) To provide the settlement schemes with possibilities of further development, after the stage of initial land settlement has been achieved.

5. A considerable role is incumbent upon the government of the country of asylum, more particularly with regard to the necessary policy decisions, the coordination at national level, and the requests for assistance from the UNHCR, other inter-governmental programmes and agencies, as well as non-governmental agencies which might be of assistance in land settlement;

6. A considerable role is equally incumbent upon the UNHCR, especially with a view to the advice it might give to governments at their request; the making available of funds and other means of assistance, subject to the concurrence of UNHCR in the land settlement schemes in conformity with its terms of reference; and ensuring cooperation with other inter-governmental and non-governmental organizations within the framework of the promotion of international aid;

7. With a view to the later economic and social development of the area where initial land settlement schemes are being carried out, it is desirable to ensure, as early as possible, in the planning

and even in the implementation of the initial land settlement phases, the assistance of those members of the United Nations family which should normally participate in the later development activities, including WFP, UNDP, ECA, UNICEF, FAO, ILO, WHO and UNESCO;

8. Subject to governmental policy of the countries of asylum concerned, but having regard to the general shortage of skilled administrative and technical staff in developing countries, the governments should also consider implementing land settlement schemes through a suitable non-governmental executing agency. In view of the political implications inherent in refugee situations, the executing agency should be of a neutral character or else offer, in a strictly humanitarian purpose, guarantees of a neutral approach to the refugee problem.

ZONAL PLANNING FOR REFUGEE INTEGRATION IN AFRICA[8]

The Conference recommends that zonal integration and development schemes to benefit both refugees and the local population be promoted and implemented in countries of asylum along the following lines:

(a) At an early stage in the settlement effort a comprehensive survey should be undertaken with a view to planning the zonal integration and development scheme.

(b) Any new development proposals should be along the lines of an integrated approach within a defined zone, where the aim will be to establish and strengthen all aspects of rural services required for the total advancement of the human ecology of the region. The overall objective should be an optional exploitation of the resources of the zone. The zonal scheme should, whenever possible, provide an opportunity for the transfer of population from other parts of the country, if this is useful both for demographic and other reasons and with a view to the full exploitation of the zonal resources.

(c) The government of the countries of asylum should make to that effect the necessary requests to the UNDP and other competent agencies and organizations.

8. See AFR/REF/CONF.1967/No. 9

(d) In view of the urgent character of preliminary surveys, the UNHCR should receive authority to promote and finance such surveys within the framework of its financial support of initial land settlements.

(e) The financing of zonal integration and development schemes, particularly within the framework of the United Nations system, should take into account the following factors:

(i) Whereas the urgent implementation of zonal integration and development schemes involving refugee areas might be urgently required for economic, social and very often political considerations, such schemes have normally not been included in long term national development plans,

(ii) It would be contrary to the policy of international solidarity with respect to refugee work, to expect the government of the country of asylum to abandon existing development requirements in order to make room in internationally sponsored programmes for development projects primarily connected with the presence of refugees.

(iii) For similar reasons, it cannot be expected that a government of a developing country make available on the usual terms their share in the financial support of zonal integration and development plans which are in addition to other urgent development requirements.

(f) The considerations concerning the financing of zonal and integration development schemes should also be taken into account in considering the staffing of these schemes in developing countries.

EDUCATION, TRAINING, PLACEMENT, AND MANPOWER REQUIREMENTS OF AFRICAN REFUGEES[9]

The Conference recommends that the African states as well as the inter-governmental and non-governmental organizations interested in the problems of educating refugees whose technical and financial assistance is essential for the success of the work of educating and training African refugees should in carrying out this work, take into account the following considerations:

9. See AFR/REF/CONF.1967/Nos. 6, 11, and 12

In the Field of Education and Training

1. To emphasize that the first concern in the field of refugee education should be the establishment of a sound primary education in refugee communities.

2. To continue to grant essential educational aid to refugees for as long as the refugee status persists.

3. To consider that one of the purposes of educating and training refugees under refugee training programmes should be to prepare them to contribute actively towards the realization of the ideals and aims of African Unity.

4. To take maximum account, when selecting students and drawing up programmes, of the priority manpower requirements of the independent African countries and those under colonial and racist governments.

5. To ensure that whenever possible refugees are trained in Africa at the pre-vocational, vocational and technical levels; also that facilities should be provided in Africa for secondary education and for the first level of university education.

6. To lay greater emphasis on vocational training and technical education to enable the refugees to contribute in as short a time as possible to economic development.

7. To ensure that secondary education programmes for refugees are continued and developed according to the flow of refugee students coming from the primary level during the next few years, on the understanding that extra help must be given to existing secondary schools.

8. To select students as carefully as possible, to give them aptitude tests so that they can be individually guided and advised in the choice of a profession with a view to making them aware of their responsibilities towards their compatriots.

9. To ensure that refugee educational bodies remain in close touch with the proposed Bureau for placement and education of refugees.

10. To ensure that refugee educational bodies endeavour to improve cooperation between themselves and better to coordinate efforts so as to avoid unnecessary duplication. Non-African organizations and governments should undertake to cooperate with the governments of asylum countries, the United Nations and

its agencies, the Organization of African Unity and the relevant African organizations.

11. To encourage all States and organizations concerned with the well-being and education of refugees, in Africa and elsewhere, to realize that educational aid involves responsibilities as regards the employment and well-being of refugees in the long term.

In the Field of Placement and Manpower Requirements

1. To encourage the training of medium-grade skilled manpower and refugees requiring medium-grade vocational training or schooling to be carried out in African establishments.

2. To urge governments, organizations and other bodies concerned with refugee education to allocate part of their funds towards improving and extending educational facilities in Africa for the benefit of refugees, thus permitting the rational use of such facilities in Africa.

3. To reserve vocational training facilities abroad for refugees requiring special know-how essential for the implementation of development programmes in both the public and private sectors in accordance with national priorities.

4. To ensure that qualified refugees have the possibility of carrying out post graduate studies through fellowships for study abroad in the best institutions.

5. To give refugees trained in lower priority fields the chance to pursue appropriate studies so that they can turn to occupations in which there are urgent manpower requirements.

RESETTLEMENT AND PLACEMENT OF INDIVIDUAL REFUGEES[10]

The Conference recommends that in case the Bureau cannot be established immediately for constitutional reasons the members of the proposed Standing Committee should agree between themselves concerning the initiation of such tasks as can in the meantime be undertaken by them in accordance with their present terms of reference; and that the Consultative Board reserve the right to grant to one or more representatives of non-governmental organizations the status of full membership of the Board.

10. See AFR/REF/CONF.1967/No. 10

APPENDIX IV

STATUTE OF THE OFFICE OF THE UNITED NATIONS HIGH COMMISSIONER FOR REFUGEES

INTRODUCTION

In Resolution 319(IV) of 3 December 1949, the United Nations General Assembly decided to establish a High Commissioner's Office for Refugees as of 1 January 1951.

The Statute of the Office of the United Nations High Commissioner for Refugees was adopted by the General Assembly on 14 December 1950 as Annex to Resolution 428(V). In this Resolution, reproduced on page 4, the Assembly also called upon Governments to co-operate with the High Commissioner in the performance of his functions concerning refugees falling under the competence of his Office. In accordance with the Statute, the work of the High Commissioner is humanitarian and social and of an entirely non-political character.

The functions of the High Commissioner are defined in the Statute and in various Resolutions subsequently adopted by the General Assembly. Resolutions concerning the High Commissioner's Office adopted by the General Assembly and the Economic and Social Council are issued by UNHCR as an information document, HCR/INF/48.

The High Commissioner reports annually to the General Assembly through the Economic and Social Council. Pursuant to paragraph 4 of the Statute, an Advisory Committee on Refugees was established by the Economic and Social Council[1] and was later reconstituted as the United Nations Refugee Fund (UNREF) Executive Committee[2]. The latter was replaced in 1958 by the

1. Resolution 393 (XIII) B of 10 September 1951.

2. Economic and Social Council Resolution 565 (XIX) of 31 March 1955 adopted pursuant to General Assembly Resolution 832 (IX) of 21 October 1954.

Executive Committee of the High Commissioner's Programme[3]. Under its terms of reference, the Executive Committee, *inter alia,* approves and supervises material assistance programme of the High Commissioner's office and advises the High Commissioner at his request on the exercise of his functions under the Statute. The Executive Committee was originally composed of 24 States. In 1963[4], its membership was increased to 30 States so as to achieve the widest possible geographical representation.

The Office was originally established for a period of three years (Statute, paragraph 5). By General Assembly Resolutions 727(VIII) of 23 October 1953, 1165 (XII) of 26 November 1957 and 1783(XVII) of 7 December 1962, the Office was extended for successive periods of five years, the present term being until 31 December 1968.

The first United Nations High Commissioner for Refugees was the late Dr. G. J. van Heuven Goedhart, of the Netherlands (1951-1956) who was succeeded by Dr. A. R. Lindt (1957-1960) and Dr. Felix Schnyder (1961-1965), both of Switzerland. The present High Commissioner is Prince Sadruddin Aga Khan (Iran) who assumed office on 1 January 1966.

The Headquarters of the High Commissioner's Office are located at Geneva, Switzerland. The High Commissioner has appointed representatives and correspondents in a number of areas throughout the five continents.

Geneva, December 1966

GENERAL ASSEMBLY RESOLUTION 428 (V)
OF 14 DECEMBER 1950

The General Assembly,

In view of its resolution 319 A (IV) of 3 December 1949,

1. Adopts the annex to the present resolution being the Statute of the Office of the United Nations High Commissioner for Refugees;

2. Calls upon Governments to co-operate with the United Nations High Commissioner for Refugees in the performance of his functions concerning refugees falling under the competence of his Office, especially by:

3. General Assembly Resolution 1166 (XII) of 26 November 1957 and Economic and Social Council Resolution 672 (XXV) of 30 April 1958.

4. General Assembly Resolution 1958 (XVIII) of 12 December 1963.

(a) Becoming parties to international conventions providing for the protection of refugees, and taking the necessary steps of implemention under such conventions;

(b) Entering into special agreements with the High Commissioner for the execution of measures calculated to improve the situation of refugees and to reduce the number requiring protection;

(c) Admitting refugees to their territories, not excluding those in the most destitute categories;

(d) Assisting the High Commissioner in his efforts to promote the voluntary repatriation of refugees;

(e) Promoting the assimilation of refugees, especially by facilitating their naturalization;

(f) Providing refugees with travel and other documents such as would normally be provided to other aliens by their national authorities, especially documents which would facilitate their resettlement.

(g) Permitting refugees to transfer their assets and especially those necessary for their resettlement;

(h) Providing the High Commissioner with information concerning the number and condition of refugees and laws and regulations concerning them;

3. Requests the Secretary-General to transmit the present resolution, together with the annex attached thereto, also to States non-members of the United Nations, with a view to obtaining their co-operation in its implementation.

ANNEX

CHAPTER I: GENERAL PROVISIONS

1. The United Nations High Commissioner for Refugees, acting under the authority of the General Assembly, shall assume the function of providing international protection, under the auspices of the United Nations, to refugees who fall within the scope of the present Statute and of seeking permanent solutions for the problem of refugees by assisting Governments and, subject to the approval of the Governments concerned, private organizations to facilitate the voluntary repatriation of such refugees, or their assimilation within new national communities.

In the exercise of his functions, more particularly when difficulties arise, and for instance with regard to any controversy concerning the international status of these persons, the High Commissioner shall request the opinion of the advisory committee on refugees if it is created.

2. The work of the High Commissioner shall be of an entirely non-political character; it shall be humanitarian and social and shall relate, as a rule, to groups and categories of refugees.

3. The High Commissioner shall follow policy directives given him by the General Assembly or the Economic and Social Council.

4. The Economic and Social Council may decide, after hearing the views of the High Commissioner on the subject, to establish an advisory committee on refugees, which shall consist of representatives of States Members and States non-members of the United Nations, to be selected by the Council on the basis of their demonstrated interest in and devotion to the solution of the refugee problem.

5. The General Assembly shall review, not later than at its eighth regular session, the arrangements for the Offices of the High Commissioner with a view to determining whether the Office should be continued beyond 31 December 1953.

CHAPTER II: FUNCTIONS OF THE HIGH COMMISSIONER

6. The competence of the High Commissioner shall extend to:

A. (i) Any person who has been considered a refugee under the Arrangements of 12 May 1926 and of 30 June 1928 or under the Conventions of 28 October 1933 and 10 February 1938, the Protocol of 14 September 1939 or the Constitution of the International Refugee Organization

(ii) Any person who, as a result of events occurring before 1 January 1951 and owing to well-founded fear of being persecuted for reasons of race, religion, nationality or political opinion, is outside the country of his nationality and is unable or, owing to such fear or for reasons other than personal convenience, is unwilling to avail himself of the protection of that country; or who, not having a nationality and being outside the country of his former habitual residence, is unable or, owing to such fear or for reasons other than personal convenience, is unwilling to return to it.

Decisions as to eligibility taken by the International Refugee Organization during the period of its activities shall not prevent the status of refugee being accorded to persons who fulfil the conditions of the present paragraph;

The competence of the High Commissioner shall cease to apply to any person defined in section A above if:

(a) He has voluntarily reavailed himself of the protection of the country of his nationality; or

(b) Having lost his nationality, he has voluntarily reacquired it; or

(c) He has acquired a new nationality, and enjoys the protection of the country of his new nationality; or

(d) He has voluntarily re-established himself in the country which he left or outside which he remained owing to fear of persecution; or

(e) He can no longer, because the circumstances in connexion with which he has been recognized as a refugee have ceased to exist, claim grounds other than those of personal convenience for continuing to refuse to avail himself of the protection of the country of his nationality. Reasons of a purely economic character may not be invoked; or

(f) Being a person who has no nationality, he can no longer, because the circumstances in connexion with which he has been recognized as a refugee have ceased to exist and he is able to return to the country of his former habitual residence, claim grounds other than those of personal convenience for continuing to refuse to return to that country;

B. Any other person who is outside the country of his nationality, or if he has no nationality, the country of his former habitual residence, because he has or had well-founded fear of persecution by reason of his race, religion, nationality or political opinion and is unable or, because of such fear, is unwilling to avail himself of the protection of the government of the country of his nationality, or, if he has no nationality, to return to the country of his former habitual residence.

7. Provided that the competence of the High Commissioner as defined in paragraph 6 above shall not extend to a person:

(a) Who is a national of more than one country unless he satisfies the provisions of the preceding paragraph in relation to each of the countries of which he is a national; or

(b) Who is recognized by the competent authorities of the country in which he has taken residence as having the rights and obligations which are attached to the possession of the nationality of that country; or

(c) Who continues to receive from other organs or agencies of the United Nations protection or assistance; or

(d) In respect of whom there are serious reasons for considering that he has committed a crime covered by the provisions of treaties of extradition or a crime mentioned in article VI of the London Charter of the International Military Tribunal or by the provisions of article 14, paragraph 2, of the Universal Declaration of Human Rights*.

8. The High Commissioner shall provide for the protection of refugees falling under the competence of his Office by:

(a) Promoting the conclusion and ratification of international conventions for the protection of refugees, supervising their application and proposing amendments thereto;

(b) Promoting through special agreements with Governments the execution of any measure calculated to improve the situation of refugees and to reduce the number requiring protection;

(c) Assisting governmental and private efforts to promote voluntary repatriation or assimilation within new national communities;

(d) Promoting the admission of refugees, not excluding those in the most destitute categories, to the territories of States;

(e) Endeavouring to obtain permission for refugees to transfer

*See resolution 217 A (III)

their assets and especially those necessary for their resettlement;

(f) Obtaining from Governments information concerning the number and conditions of refugees in their territories and the laws and regulations concerning them;

(g) Keeping in close touch with the Governments and intergovernmental organizations concerned;

(h) Establishing contact in such manner as he may think best with private organizations dealing with refugee questions;

(i) Facilitating the co-ordination of the efforts of private organizations concerned with the welfare of refugees.

9. The High Commissioner shall engage in such additional activities, including repatriation and resettlement, as the General Assembly may determine, within the limits of the resources placed at his disposal.

10. The High Commissioner shall administer any funds, public or private, which he receives for assistance to refugees, and shall distribute them among the private and, as appropriate, public agencies which he deems best qualified to administer such assistance.

The High Commissioner may reject any offers which he does not consider appropriate or which cannot be utilized.

The High Commissioner shall not appeal to Governments for funds or make a general appeal, without the prior approval of the General Assembly.

The High Commissioner shall include in his annual report a statement of his activities in this field.

11. The High Commissioner shall be entitled to present his views before the General Assembly, the Economic and Social Council and their subsidiary bodies.

The High Commissioner shall report annually to the General Assembly through Economic and Social Council; his report shall be considered as a separate item on the agenda of the General Assembly.

12. The High Commissioner may invite the co-operation of the various specialized agencies.

CHAPTER III: ORGANIZATION AND FINANCES

13. The High Commissioner shall be elected by the General Assembly on the nomination of the Secretary-General. The terms of appointment of the High Commissioner shall be proposed by the Secretary-General and approved by the General Assembly. The High Commissioner shall be elected for a term of three years, from 1 January 1951.

14. The High Commissioner shall appoint, for the same term, a Deputy High Commissioner of a nationality other than his own.

15. (a) Within the limits of the budgetary appropriations provided, the staff of the Office of the High Commissioner shall be appointed by the High Commissioner and shall be responsible to him in the exercise of their functions.

   (b) Such staff shall be chosen from persons devoted to the purposes of the Office of the High Commissioner.

   (c) Their conditions of employment shall be those provided under the staff regulations adopted by the General Assembly and the rules promulgated thereunder by the Secretary-General.

   (d) Provision may also be made to permit the employment of personnel without compensation.

16. The High Commissioner shall consult the Government of the countries of residence of refugees as to the need for appointing representatives therein. In any country recognizing such need, there may be appointed a representative approved by the Government of that country. Subject to the foregoing, the same representative may serve in more than one country.

17. The High Commissioner and the Secretary-General shall make appropriate arrangements for liaison and consultation on matters of mutual interest.

18. The Secretary-General shall provide the High Commissioner with all necessary facilities within budgetary limitations.

19. The Office of the High Commissioner shall be located in Geneva, Switzerland.

20. The Office of the High Commissioner shall be financed under the budget of the United Nations. Unless the General Assembly subsequently decides otherwise, no expenditure other than administrative expenditures relating to the functioning of the Office of the High Commissioner shall be borne on the budget of the United Nations and all other expenditures relating to the activities of the High Commissioner shall be financed by voluntary contributions.

21. The administration of the Office of the High Commissioner shall be subject to the Financial Regulations of the United Nations and to the financial rules promulgated thereunder by the Secretary-General.

22. Transactions relating to the High Commissioner's funds shall be subject to audit by the United Nations Board of Auditors, provided that the Board may accept audited accounts from the agencies to which funds have been allocated. Administrative arrangements for the custody of such funds and their allocation shall be agreed between the High Commissioner and the Secretary-General in accordance with the Financial Regulations of the United Nations and rules promulgated thereunder by the Secretary-General.

OAU CONVENTION GOVERNING THE SPECIFIC ASPECTS OF THE PROBLEM OF REFUGEES IN AFRICA

PREAMBLE

We, the Heads of State and Government

1. *Noting with concern* the existence of the constantly growing numbers of refugees in Africa and desirous of finding ways and means of alleviating their misery and suffering as well as providing them with a better life and future,

2. *Recognizing* the need for an essentially humanitarian approach towards solving the problems of refugees,

3. *Aware,* however, that refugee problems are a source of friction among several Member States, and desirous of eliminating such discord,

4. *Anxious* to make a distinction between a refugee who seeks a peaceful and normal life and a person fleeing his country for the sole purpose of subverting it from outside,

5. *Determined* that the activities of such subversive elements should be discouraged, in accordance with the Declaration on the Problem of Subversion and Resolution on the Problem of Refugees adopted at Accra in 1965,

6. *Conscious* that the Charter of the United Nations and the Universal Declaration of Human Rights have affirmed the principle that human beings shall enjoy fundamental rights and freedoms without discrimination,

7. *Recalling* Resolution 2312 (XXII) of 14 December 1967 of the United Nations General Assembly, relating to the Declaration on Territorial Asylum,

8. *Convinced* that all the problems of our continent must be solved in the spirit of the Charter of the Organization of African Unity and in the African context,

9. *Recognizing* that the United Nations Convention of 28 July 1951, as modified by the Protocol of 31 January 1967, constitutes the basic and universal instrument relating to the status of refugees and reflects the deep concern of States for refugees and their desire to establish common standards for their treatment,

10. *Recalling* Resolutions 26 and 104 of the OAU Assemblies of Heads of State and Government, calling upon Member States of the Organization who had not already done so to accede to the United Nations Convention of 1951 and to the Protocol of 1967 relating to the Status of Refugees, and meanwhile to apply their provisions to refugees in Africa,

11. *Convinced* that the efficiency of the measures recommended by the present Convention to solve the problem of refugees in Africa necessitates close and continuous collaboration between the Organization of African Unity and the United Nations High Commission for Refugees.

Have Agreed as follows:

Article I

DEFINITION OF THE TERM "REFUGEE"

1. For the purpose of this Convention, the term "refugee" shall mean every person who, owing to well-founded fear of being persecuted for reasons of race, religion, nationality, membership of a particular social group or political opinion, is outside the country of his nationality and is unable or, owing to such fear, is unwilling to avail himself of the protection of that country, or who, not having a nationality and being outside the country of his former habitual residence as a result of such events, is unable or, owing to such fear, is unwilling to return to it.

2. The term "refugee" shall also apply to every person who, owing to external aggression, occupation, foreign domination or events seriously disturbing public order in either part or the whole of his country of origin or nationality, is compelled to leave his place of habitual residence in order to seek refuge in another place outside his country of origin or nationality.

3. In the case of a person who has several nationalities, the term "a country of which he is a national" shall mean each of the

countries of which he is a national, and a person shall not be deemed to be lacking the protection of the country of which he is a national if, without any valid reason based on well-founded fear, he has not availed himself of the protection of one of the countries of which he is a national.

4. This Convention shall cease to apply to any refugee if:

a) he has voluntarily re-availed himself of the protection of the country of his nationality, or,

b) having lost his nationality, he voluntarily re-acquired it, or

c) he has acquired a new nationality, and enjoys the protection of the country of his new nationality, or

d) he has voluntarily re-established himself in the country which he left or outside which he remained owing to fear of persecution;

e) he can no longer, because the circumstances in connection with which he was recognized as a refugee have ceased to exist, continue to refuse to avail himself of the protection of the country of his nationality;

f) he has committed a serious non-political crime outside his country of refugee after his admission to that country as a refugee;

g) he has seriously infringed the purposes and objectives of this Convention.

5. The provisions of this Convention shall not apply to any person with respect to whom the country of asylum has serious reasons for considering that:

a) he has committed a crime against peace, a war crime, or a crime against humanity, as defined in the internation instruments drawn up to make provision in respect of such crimes;

b) he committed a serious non-political crime outside the country of refuge prior to his admission to that country as a refugee;

c) he has been guilty of acts contrary to the purposes and principles of the Organization of African Unity;

d) he had been guilty of acts contrary to the purposes and principles of the United Nations.

6. In the sense of this present Convention, it is the Contracting State of asylum which determines the quality of refugee.

Article II

ASYLUM

1. Member States of the OAU shall use their best endeavours consistent with their respective legislations to receive refugees and to secure the settlement of those refugees who, for well-founded reasons, are unable or unwilling to return to their country of origin or nationality.

2. The grant of asylum to refugees is a peaceful and humanitarian act and shall not be regarded as an unfriendly act by any Member State.

3. No person shall be subjected by a Member State to measures such as rejection at the frontier, return or expulsion, which would compel him to return to or remain in a territory where his life, physical integrity or liberty would be threatened for the reasons set out in Article I, paragraphs 1 and 2.

4. Where a Member State finds difficulty in continuing to grant asylum to refugees, such Member State may appeal directly to other Member States and through the OAU, and such other Member States shall in the spirit of African unity and international co-operation take appropriate measures to lighten the burden of the Member State granting asylum.

5. Where a refugee has not received the right to reside in any country of asylum, he may be granted temporary residence in any country of asylum in which he first presented himself as a refugee pending arrangement for his resettlement in accordance with the preceding paragraph.

6. For reasons of security, countries of asylum shall, as far as possible, settle refugees at a reasonable distance from the frontier of their country of origin.

Article III

PROHIBITION OF SUBVERSIVE ACTIVITIES

1. Every refugee has duties to the country in which he finds himself, which require in particular he conform with its laws and regulations as well as with measures taken for the maintenance of public order. He shall also abstain from any subversive activities against any Member States of the OAU.

2. Signatory States shall undertake to prohibit refugees resi-

ding in their respective territories from attacking any Member State of the OAU through subversive activities, especially through arms, press and radio, which may cause tension between Member States.

Article IV

NON-DISCRIMINATION

Member States shall undertake to apply the provisions of this Convention to all refugees without discrimination as to race, religion, nationality, membership of a particular social group or political opinions.

Article V

VOLUNTARY REPATRIATION

1. The essentially voluntary character of repatriation shall be respected in all cases and no refugee shall be repatriated against his will.

2. The country of asylum, in collaboration with the country of origin, shall make adequate arrangements for the safe return of the refugees requesting repatriation.

3. The country of origin, on receiving back refugees, shall facilitate their resettlement and grant them the full rights and privileges of nationals of the country, and subject them to the same obligations.

4. Refugees who voluntarily return to their country shall in no way be penalized for having left it for any of the reasons giving rise to refugee situations. Whenever necessary, an appeal shall be made through national information media and through the Administrative Secretary-General of the OAU, inviting refugees to return home and giving assurance that the new circumstances prevailing in their country of origin will enable them to return without risk and to take up a normal and peaceful life without fear of being disturbed or punished, and that the text of such appeal should be given to refugees and properly explained to them by their country of asylum.

5. Refugees who freely decide to return to their homeland, as a result of such assurances or on their own initiative, shall be given every necessary assistance by the country of asylum, the country

of origin, voluntary agencies and international and intergovernmental organizations, to facilitate their return.

Article VI

TRAVEL DOCUMENTS

1. Subject to Article III, Member States shall issue to refugees lawfully staying in their territories travel documents in accordance with the United Nations Convention relating to the Status of Refugees and the Schedule and Annex thereto, for the purpose of travel outside their territory, unless compelling reasons of national security or public order otherwise require. Member States may issue such a travel document to any other refugee in their territory.

2. Where an African country of second asylum accepts a refugee from a country of first asylum, the country of first asylum may be dispensed from issuing a document with a return clause.

3. Travel documents issued to refugees under previous international agreements by Parties thereto shall be recognized and treated by Member States in the same way as if they had been issued to refugees pursuant to this Article.

Article VII

CO-OPERATION OF THE NATIONAL AUTHORITIES WITH THE ORGANIZATION OF AFRICAN UNITY

In order to enable the Administrative Secretary-General of the Organization of African Unity to make reports to the competent organs of the Organization of African Unity, Member States undertake to provide the Secretariat in the appropriate form with information and statistical data requested concerning:

a) the condition of refugees;

b) the implementation of this Convention, and

c) laws, regulations and decrees which are, or may hereafter be, in force relating to refugees.

Article VIII

CO-OPERATION WITH THE UNITED NATIONS HIGH COMMISSION FOR REFUGEES

1. Member States shall co-operate with the United Nations High Commission for Refugees.

2. The present Convention shall be the effective regional complement in Africa of the 1951 United Nations Convention on the Status of Refugees.

Article IX

SETTLEMENT OF DISPUTES

Any dispute between Parties to this Convention relating to the interpretation or application, which cannot be settled by other means, shall be referred to the Commission of Mediation, Conciliation and Arbitration of the Organization of African Unity, at the request of any one of the Parties to the dispute.

Article X

SIGNATURE AND RATIFICATION

1. This Convention is open for signature and accession by all Member States of the Organization of African Unity and shall be ratified by signatory States in accordance with their respective constitutional processes. The instruments or ratification shall be deposited with the Administrative Secretary-General of the Organization of African Unity.

2. The original instrument, done if possible in African languages, in English and French, all texts being equally authentic, should be deposited with the Administrative Secretary-General of the Organization of African Unity.

3. Any independent African State, Member of the Organization of African Unity, may at any time notify the Administrative Secretary-General of the Organization of African Unity of its accession to this Convention.

Article XI

ENTRY INTO FORCE

This Convention shall come into force as of the day of deposit of the instrument of ratification by one-third of the Member States of the Organization of African Unity.

Article XII

AMENDMENT

This Convention may be amended or revised if any Member

State makes a written request to the Administrative Secretary-General to that effect, provided that the proposed amendment is not submitted to the Assembly of Heads of State and Government for consideration until all Member States have been duly notified of it and a period of one year has elapsed. Such an amendment shall not be effective unless approved by at least two-thirds of the Member States Parties to the present Convention.

Article XIII

DENUNCIATION

1. Any Member State Party to this Convention may denounce its provisions by a written notification to the Administrative Secretary-General.

2. At the end of one year from the date of such notification, if not withdrawn, the Convention shall cease to apply with respect to the denouncing State.

Article XIV

Upon entry into force of this Convention, the Administrative Secretary-General of the OAU shall register it with the Secretary-General of the United Nations, in accordance with Article 102 of the Charter of the United Nations.

Article XV

NOTIFICATION BY THE ADMINISTRATIVE SECRETARY-GENERAL OF THE ORGANIZATION OF AFRICAN UNITY

The Administrative Secretary-General of the Organization of African Unity shall inform all Members of the Organization:

a) of signatures, ratifications and accessions in accordance with Article X;

b) of entry into force, in accordance with Article XI;

c) of requests for amendments submitted under the terms of Article XII;

d) of denunciations, in accordance with Article XIII.

APPENDIX VI

RESOLUTION 2399 (XXIII) ADOPTED UNANIMOUSLY BY THE GENERAL ASSEMBLY ON THE REPORT OF THE UNITED NATIONS HIGH COMMISSIONER FOR REFUGEES

The General Assembly,

Having considered the report of the United Nations High Commissioner for Refugees[1] and having heard his statement,[2]

Taking note of the progress achieved in the field of international protection of refugees who are the High Commissioner's concern and in the search for permanent solutions of their problems through voluntary repatriation, integration in countries of asylum or resettlement in other countries,

Recognizing the positive effects of the High Commissioner's work on economic and social conditions of the refugees in the countries concerned,

Commending the encouraging results achieved in the field of inter-agency co-operation with the support of the Governments concerned and the other members of the United Nations system and noting with appreciation the untiring activities of the nongovernmental organizations working on behalf of refugees,

Noting that the Executive Committee of the High Commissioner's Programme has approved an increased programme to cover additional needs of refugees, particularly in Africa,

Noting with appreciation the sizable increase in contributions from certain countries, and also the increase in the number of contributing countries,

Expressing concern, however, at the difficulties still facing the High Commissioner in financing his programme,

1. *Requests* the United Nations High Commissioner for Refu-

1. *Official Records of the General Assembly, Twenty-third Session, Supplement No. 11* (A/7211) and *Supplement No. 11 A* (A/7211/Add. 1).

2. See A/C.3/SR.1611 and Corr. 2.

gees to continue to provide international protection and assistance to refugees who are his concern, while giving special attention to groups of refugees, particularly in Africa, in conformity with the relevant General Assembly resolutions and the directives of the Executive Committee of the High Commissioner's Programme;

2. *Urges* States Members of the United Nations and members of the specialized agencies to continue to lend their support to the High Commissioner's humanitarian task by:

(a) Facilitating the voluntary repatriation, local integration or resettlement of refugees who are the High Commissioner's concern;

(b) Improving the legal status of refugees residing in their territory, inter alia, by acceding to the international instruments relating to refugees and by treating new refugee situations in accordance with the principles and spirit of the Declaration on Territorial Asylum and the Universal Declaration of Human Rights;

(c) Providing the High Commissioner with the necessary means of accomplishing the task incumbent upon him and, in particular, by enabling him to reach the financial targets established with the approval of the Executive Committee;

(d) Drawing the attention of the governing bodies of other organs in the United Nations system to the need to support the High Commissioner in his efforts to ensure that the requirements of refugees, including education and training, are taken into full account.

1735th plenary meeting,
6 December 1968.

APPENDIX VII

UNHCR AFRICA PROGRAMS:
SUMMARY ANALYSIS*

BURUNDI

Programs and Administration

The program in Burundi is carried out by the Government, through the International Association for Rural Development Overseas (AIDR). Apart from UNHCR the following agencies are participating in this program, UNDP, FAC, ILO, World Food Program and OXFAM of Great Britain.

Settlements

CONGOLESE

The majority of the Congolese refugees (25,000) in Burundi are living outside settlements.

RWANDESE

Name of Settlement		No. of Refugees
Muramba Kayongozi Kigamba	Settlements established in 1962 by the League of Red Cross Societies and consolidated under the ILO Development Plan (1964/66)	19,000
Mugera	Established in 1965	27,300

The remaining 7,700 Rwandese refugees live outside settlements.

*Prepared by the United States Committee for Refugees.

Financial Assistance from UNHCR
In the years 1962-1967, some $2,300,000 have been allocated for
assistance to refugees in Burundi through UNHCR.

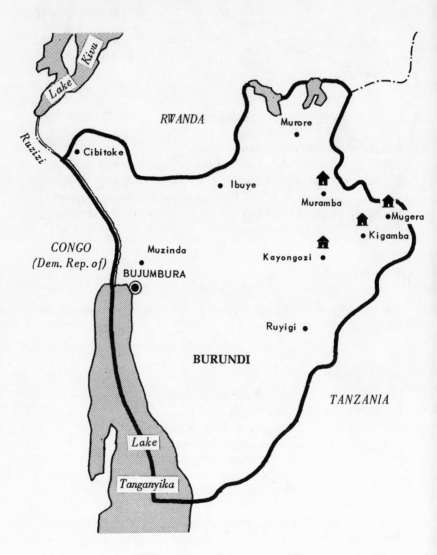

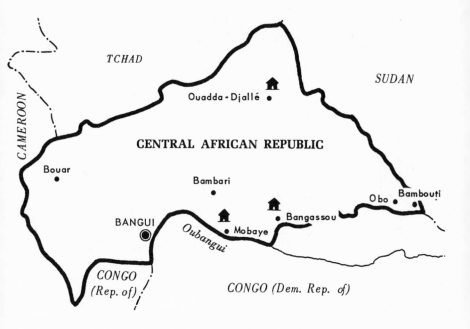

CENTRAL AFRICAN REPUBLIC

Programs and Administration

The Government has undertaken responsibility for the program, and has asked the League of Red Cross Societies to coordinate international aid. Food provided by NCWC/CRS until mid-1967 and thereafter by the World Food Program. Drugs and other assistance C.W.S.

Settlements

CONGOLESE

The 16,000 Congolese refugees are living outside settlements. Approximately 3,000 of them were receiving marginal assistance from the League of Red Cross Societies. It is believed that conditions will soon be favorable for a voluntary repatriation of the Congolese refugees.

Banbouti, established in 1966, has 28,000 refugees. The remaining Sudanese refugees are living outside settlements in Obo, Djema and Ouaida Djalle.

Financial Assistance from UNHCR

In the years 1966 and 1967 a total of $1,050,000 has been allocated for assistance to refugees in the Central African Republic through UNHCR.

THE DEMOCRATIC REPUBLIC OF THE CONGO

Program and Administration

In the Congo, there is no overall administration of the refugee work as a whole.

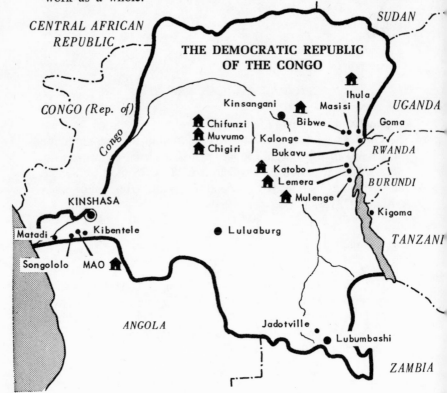

In the Kivu Province of the Congo, the Rwandese refugees (total 25,000) are benefiting from the ILO Integration and Zonal Development Project, in which UNHCR is participating financially. The project covers two refugee villages in the Kalonge area, in Central Kivu, and two settlements in North Kivu.

For refugees from Angola, assistance is being provided by voluntary agencies and religious missions, with marginal financial assistance from UNHCR.

Pending the resettlement of the Sudanese refugees (24,000) in the northeast of the Congo from the border areas to the interior of the country, and the establishment of a land settlement program, the Congo Protestant Relief Agency is implementing a relief program, with the financial assistance of UNHCR and with food provided by Church World Service and NCWC/CRS.

RWANDA

Settlements

ANGOLAN

The Angolans (300,000) are living outside settlements in the west of the country.

RWANDESE

Name of Settlement	No. of Refugees
Bibwe	4,700
Ihula	1,800
Kalonge Area (two villages)	800

SUDANESE

The Sudanese are at present situated near the Sudan Congo/ frontier, in the northeast of the country.

Financial Aid through UNHCR
In the years 1962-67, some $1,200,000 have been allocated for assistance to refugees in the Congo through UNHCR.

SENEGAL

Program and Assistance
The Government of Senegal is administrating the refugee program in its country. The Senegalese Red Cross has been entrusted by the Government with the implementation of the health aspect of

the program. This they are doing with the assistance of the French Red Cross Society, and some further aid may come from the Swiss Red Cross.

NCWC/CRS is responsible for providing food rations to those refugees who are still in need of this type of assistance.

Settlements
The refugees are being settled in a large number of existing villages in the Casamance Province, where they live side by side with the local inhabitants.

Financial Assistance from UNHCR
In the years from 1964 to 1967, $676,000 have been allocated for assistance to refugees in Senegal through UNHCR.

There are 60,000 refugees from Portuguese Guinea in Senegal.

TANZANIA

Program and Administration
Most of the refugee program is carried out under tripartite agreements beteen the Government of Tanzania, the Lutheran World Service/Tanganyika Christian Refugee Service and UNHCR.

Settlements
Of the total of 35,950 refugees, 30,500 live in settlements, and the remainder outside settlements.

RWANDESE

Name of Settlement	*No. of Refugees*
Muyenzi	6,500
Karagwe	2,300
Mwesi	3,100

MOZAMBIQUAN

Name of Settlement	*No. of Refugees*
Rutamba	8,000
Lundo Plain	4,000
Muhukuru	6,000

CONGOLESE AND OTHERS

Name of Settlement	*No. of Refugees*
Pangale	600

Financial Assistance from UNHCR

In the years 1962 to 1967, approximately $1,520,000 have been allocated for assistance to refugees in Tanzania through UNHCR.

UGANDA

Program

The Government of Uganda has taken full responsibility for the settlement of refugees in their country. The responsible Ministry is the Ministry of Culture and Community Development.

Settlements

RWANDESE

Name of Settlement	No. of Refugees
Nakivali	7,000
Oruchinga Valley	11,000
Kahunge	8,000
Ibuga	100
Rwamawanje	2,500
Kyaka	2,200
Kinyara	3,000

CONGOLESE

Name of Settlement	No. of Refugees
Agago	500
Acolpi	931

In addition, 110,000 refugees are living outside settlements in various parts of the country.

SUDANESE

Name of Settlement	No. of Refugees
Nakapiripirit	6,000
Agago	1,800
Onigo	2,700
Kyangwali	800

Additionally there are 110,000 refugees living outside of settlements.

Financial Assistance from UNHCR
In the years from 1962 to 1967, some $1,800,000 have been allocated for assistance to refugees in Uganda through UNHCR.

ZAMBIA

Program
The program is administered by the Government of Zambia, the responsible Ministry being the Ministry of Home Affairs. The Government has now invited the Lutheran World Federation to act as its operational partner.

Settlements

ANGOLAN

Name of Settlement	No. of Refugees
Lwatembo, Established in 1966	3,200
Myukwayukwa, Being established in 1967	500

MOZAMBIQUAN

Name of Settlement	No. of Refugees
Nyimba, Established in 1966	1,300

The remaining 1,285 refugees live outside settlements, including Malawian and Sudanese 120, South African, Rhodesian and South West African 565.

Financial Assistance from UNHCR

In the years 1966 and 1967, some $570,400 were allocated for assistance to refugees in Zambia through UNHCR.

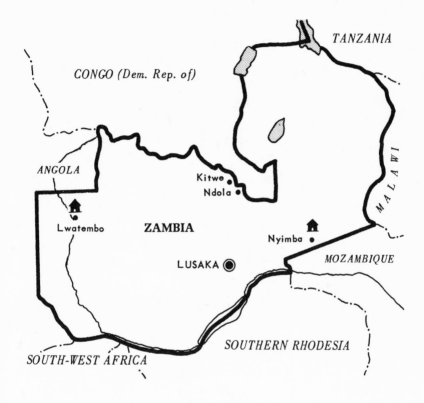

STATISTICAL REPORT ON THE MOVEMENT OF REFUGEES IN AFRICA, 1967-1968*

COUNTRY OF ASYLUM	FROM	1966	1967
North Africa			
Morocco	Algeria	2,700	1,000
United Arab Republic	South Africa, South West Africa, Rhodesia, Mozambique	—	500
United Arab Republic	Europe	—	500
Sudan	Congo	—	9,000
Sudan	Ethiopia	—	25,500
The Horn			
Ethiopia	Sudan	10,000	15,000
Ethiopia	South Africa, South West Africa, Rhodesia	18	30
Ethiopia	Somali	70,000	70,000
Central and East Africa			
Kenya	South Africa, South West Africa, Rhodesia	—	450
Kenya	Sudan	100	200
Kenya	Rwanda	—	50
Tanzania	Congo	2,000	9,500
Tanzania	Rwanda	25,000	13,500
Tanzania	Mozambique	10,000	19,000
Tanzania	Rhodesia	20	30
Tanzania	Malawi	—	150

*Prepared by the United States Committee for Refugees.

COUNTRY OF ASYLUM	FROM	1966	1967
Tanzania	Kenya	2,500	2,500
Tanzania	Southern African Countries	—	500
Malawi	Mozambique	—	20,000
Malawi	South Africa	—	30
Central and East Africa			
Uganda	Rwanda	50,000	68,000
Uganda	Sudan	40,000	40,000
Uganda	Democratic Republic of Congo	38,000	20,000
Zambia	Angola	6,000	3,900
Zambia	Mozambique	5,000	1,800
Zambia	Malawi, Sudan	—	120
Zambia	Southern African States	—	565
Congo, Democratic Republic	Angola	400,000	300,000
Congo, Democratic Republic	Rwanda	60,000	24,000
Congo, Democratic Republic	Sudan	18,000	27,000
Congo, Democratic Republic	Haiti	—	1,500
Burundi	Rwanda	50,000	54,000
Burundi	Democratic Republic of Congo	20,000	25,000
Central African Republic	Sudan	18,000	27,000
Central African Republic	Congo	3,000	16,000
Angola	Zambia	—	3,500
Rwanda	Burundi	—	2,600

COUNTRY OF ASYLUM	FROM	1966	1967
Southern Africa			
Botswana	South Africa, South West Africa, Rhodesia	200	200
Lesotho	South Africa	—	61
Swaziland	South Africa, Mozambique	—	90
West Africa			
Dahomey	Ivory Coast, Senegal, Mali	12,000	12,000
Dahomey	Niger	16,000	16,000
The Gambia	Portuguese Guinea	3,500	3,500
Togo	Ghana	5,700	6,000
Senegal	Portuguese Guinea	55,000	60,000
Various African Countries	South Africa	800	6,000
	TOTAL	923,538	906,276

SOURCES: The United Nations High Commissioner for Refugees (UNHCR); Catholic Relief Services (CRS); The Ecumenical Program for Emergency Action in Africa, The Work Council of Churches; Office of Refugee and Migration Affairs (ORM).

APPENDIX IX

LIST OF NON-GOVERNMENTAL ORGANIZATIONS AND SOCIAL WELFARE AGENCIES PARTICIPATING IN OR CONTRIBUTING TO UNHCR PROGRAMS*

Aid to European Refugees
American Joint Distribution Committee
American Fund for Czechoslovak Refugees
Asociación de Protección al Refugiado, Buenos Aires
Associations des églises libres de Norvège
Association nationale pour la réhabilitation par le travail portégé
Association pour l'éstablissement des réfugiés étrangers/Fonds humanitaire polonais
Australian Care for Refugees
Australian Committee for the Refugee Campaign
Australian Council of Churches
Belgian Committee for the Refugee Campaign
Belgian Red Cross
Brethren Service Commission
Caisse nationale de crédit professionnel
Caritas
Catholic Relief Services/United States Catholic Council
Central Relief Committee (India)
Centre d'initiation pour réfugiés et étrangers
Centre d'orientation sociale des étrangers
Colombian Catholic Committee
Comité d'aide des églises évangéliques de Suisse
Comité d'aide exceptionnelle aux intellectuels réfugiés
Comité franco-arménien d'action sociale
Comité inter-mouvements auprés des évacués
Comité international de la Croix-Rouge
Commission catholique espagnole de migration

* U.N. Document a/7211, Annex III.

Congolese Protestant Council
Conseil international des agences bénévoles
Council of Organisations for Relief Service Overseas
Croix-Rouge congolaise
Cuban Welfare Society in Spain
Danish Refugee Council
Diocèse catholique de Goma
Entr'aide ouvrière internationale
Entr'aide socialiste - Secours international
Evangelisches Hilfswerk - Innere Mission
Evangelisches Siedlungswerk
Evangelisches Verein für innere Mission
Federal Catholic Immigration Committee of Austria
Finnish Refugee Council
Free China Association
Ghanaian Red Cross
German Committee for the Refugee Campaign
German Red Cross
Gulbenkian Foundation
Indian Red Cross Society
Individuell Människojalp (Sweden)
Innere Mission, Austria
International Catholic Migration Commission
International Rescue Committee
International Social Service
Irish Red Cross
Karagheusian Commemorative Corporation, New York
League of Red Cross Societies
Lifeline
Lutheran World Federation
Luxembourg Committee for the Refugee Campaign
Nepalese Red Cross
Netherland Federation for Aid of Refugees
Norwegian Refugee Council
Oesterreichischer Fürsorge- und Wohlfahrtsverband "Volkhilfe",
   Vienna
Oxford Committee for Famine Relief
Pères Dominicains (Bukavu, République démocratique du Congo)
Polish American Immigration and Relief Committee

Pontifica Opera de Assistenza
Provedora da Assistência Pública da Província de Macau
Rädda Barnen (Sweden)
Save the Children Fund, United Kingdom
Secours catholique
Senegalese Red Cross
Service social d'aide aux émigrants
Société de bienfaisance russe du Caire
Société nationale du Croissant Rouge égyptien
Soroptimist Association
St. Raphaels-Verein
Sudanese Red Cross
Swedish Red Cross
Swiss Aid Abroad
Swiss Association for Technical Assistance
Swiss Federation of Friends of the Armenians
Tanganyika Christian Refugee Service
Tolstoy Foundation
United HIAS Service
United Nations Association of Sweden
United Kingdom Committee for the Refugee Campaign
United States Committee for Refugees
United Ukrainian American Relief Committee
Womens Voluntary Service
World Council of Churches
World University Service
World Alliance of Young Men's Christian Association (YMCA)
World Young Women's Christian Association (YWCA)
Zambia Christian Refugee Service
Zambian Red Cross
Zentralbüro des Hilfswerks der Evangelischen Kirchen in
    Deutschland e.V.

INDEX

INDEX